I0477332

THE
BLUE
ECONOMY
3.0

THE BLUE ECONOMY

3.0

THE MARRIAGE OF SCIENCE, INNOVATION AND ENTREPRENEURSHIP CREATES A NEW BUSINESS MODEL THAT TRANSFORMS SOCIETY

GUNTER PAULI

Library of Congress Control Number:		2017913883
ISBN:	Hardcover	978-1-5245-2107-3
	Softcover	978-1-5245-2106-6
	eBook	978-1-5245-2105-9

Print information available on the last page.

Rev. date: 09/07/2017

To order additional copies of this book, contact:
Xlibris
1-800-455-039
www.Xlibris.com.au
Orders@Xlibris.com.au
750453

Contents

Introduction

This is the 10th English edition, and I suppose this will be the last one for a while to come. Ever since The Blue Economy was presented to the Club of Rome as a report in 2009, the book has generated debate. The nearly one thousand presentations and dialogues, interviews and head-on exchanges taught me a lot. While the goal of the book is nothing less than inspiring people to join me and together change the world by using what we have, generating value and responding to people's needs – it is all much easier said than done.

The fortunate reality is that more projects have been undertaken than I had ever imagined possible. The unfortunate reality is that the job generation is far less than I had expected. We barely got over the three million mark, whereas I had imagined reaching the 100 million target. This has motivated me to work on two levels: Firstly, although I am convinced that the message is clear, it is obviously not clear enough yet! Secondly, while I think it is obvious that we should translate idea to action, many people stop to admire the idea – but fall short when it comes to going over to action.

That is why this, *The Blue Economy 3.0,* has been written: firstly to try to communicate better and in more concrete terms what it entails, and then to demonstrate that many scholars and scientists, who are part of our Zero Emissions network (ZERI) and the Blue Economy entrepreneurs, have moved from idea to initiative and from incipient project to investments at scale. I hope that this ultimate version of the book (which is more than 50% different from the first one, and 30% different from the 2.0 version) especially with its strong and totally new opening chapter and the inclusion of "Ethics", offers the reader more ideas, more food for thought – and more inspiration.

This book, in its various stages of metamorphosis, forms only one part of our complete and wide-ranging communication strategy. We have taken a clear step in an exciting new direction: exposing our children to the wisdom and wide reach of a Blue Economy and inspiring them to become part of this worldwide movement towards sustainability and an economy of abundance. Making use of the wonderful technology at out fingertips I, as a father of six, want to contribute by way of an ancient and powerful teaching tool: that of fables.

For this reason this book ends with a list of more than 100 fables, written to present the latest information and transform the sciences, the emotions, the ethics, and the values and virtues taught, into action. In this way we would like to inspire the next generation. Many adults have read previous editions of *The Blue Economy* and while their responses were enthusiastic, many have fall back into their old routines, with explanations for this ranging from "it is too difficult" to "impossible" and even that it is "pure fantasy".

Yet it can be done. The Blue Economy has already taken fantasy to reality – with one million tonnes of stone paper already in production; biochemicals being produced from thistles substituting glyphosate; the speed of the internet improving by a factor of 100 over the best connectivity available today by using light; and more than 5,000 coffee-to-mushroom units operational.

Children have a great advantage: they do not distinguish between fantasy and reality. For them everything is a reality; and if you can dream it, you can do it! This is the reason that this edition, *The Blue Economy 3.0,* is not only an update but also a link to the next generation. You can help make and strengthen the connection by connecting to <www.TheFableShop.com>

Whereas the book has been published in over 40 languages and has found a place in over a million homes, thanks to the support and cooperation of publishers from all around the world (excluding the USA), it is as yet only the Chinese Government that has brought the fables into every classroom in their country and are strongly promoting the study and the application of the principles of a sustainable economy. For us, it is indeed an unparalleled privilege to have contributed to this. Conservative school systems have, however, not yet embraced the use of the fables. We have therefore decided to ensure that anyone who would like access to this book and the fables, can do so through one website.

This is a strategic step forward for my whole network. We are setting out on an exciting journey, with this book being only the first step of many. With the 365 fables we envision as the real backbone of all our work being made available in every classroom and home around the world, we trust that these will serve as an inspiration and a call to action for the next generation, and every generation after that – for the greater good of all sharing our amazing home, our blue planet, with us.

Salzburg,
30th August 2017

Foreword to the Australian Edition of *The Blue Economy 3.0*

It is our pleasure to say a few words before you read through this amazing book. In these pages you will find a wealth of inspiration, backed up by example after example of where these initiatives have been implemented in practice, which provide numerous opportunities for Australian businesses to create new revenue streams, sustainably, long into the future. If you haven't come across the work of Gunter Pauli and his colleagues as yet then you are in for a real treat, and if you have then prepare to be updated, as this Australian Edition is the first to be based on *The Blue Economy 3.0,* which presents a never before seen exposé on the principles used to guide the implementation of this exciting approach. These principles are game changers that have the potential to rewrite the business textbooks and reignite innovation and creativity where many thought it was lost. Crucially, they show that competitiveness is achievable even where costs have traditionally been thought to be 'too high'.

Gunter's vision of a 'Blue Economy' is about creating highly competitive economies that work for everyone on our amazing blue planet. Early in his career Gunter found out that his very successful company, which was receiving awards for its environmental credentials, was reliant on destroying rainforest in Indonesia to provide palm oil. This presented a crossroad: ignore the impact and keep accepting accolades and profits or do something about it. After choosing the latter he dedicated himself to redefining the way business is done so it can deliver real value for decades to come. Gunter's message in this book is simple, yet extremely powerful: '*let's create more value with what we have, much more*'. The book moves us on from a relentless focus on competing on the basis of one or a limited number of products and offers a new approach: a business model that has us uncover new revenue streams and sources of jobs using resources that are widely available locally, and that also creates a multiplier of economic, social and environmental benefits locally.

When we first heard Gunter speak we were, of course, spellbound, but in truth wondered if much of what he was saying was based on 'one-offs' or things that were possible in theory only. While anecdotes inspire us, they do not 'turn the dial'. However, now having visited many of the places where these initiatives have been implemented in practice, we can see that rather than being an academic conversation about what might work, this book lays out a blueprint based on what has worked in practice to form the basis for a refresh of the way we do business around the world.

It has been a pleasure to work with Gunter on this Australian Edition and thanks to the support from participants in The University of Adelaide's 'Sustainability Internship Program' this book provides the 'Australian Sauce', as Gunter calls it, to show how the Blue Economy can be applied here in Australia – and we look forward to working with you all on this endeavour. When you get to the end of the book and are wondering what's next I suggest you contact ZERI and find a Blue Economy initiative that you can go and have a look at. And for those of you who want a detailed understanding to inform your own practice of the Blue Economy or to help you share this amazing work with students, keep an eye out for *The Principles and Practices of the Blue Economy*, a new textbook due to be released in 2018.

Dr Karlson 'Charlie' Hargroves
Adelaide, Australia

Dr Vanessa Tamms
Adelaide, Australia

1

GUIDING PRINCIPLES OF THE BLUE ECONOMY

Nature knows no waste, and everyone has a job.

In honour of Aurelio Peccei, a former FIAT top executive and the founder of the Club of Rome, we created a vision of a "Blue Economy" where Nature returns to its evolutionary path and a positive symbiosis with human systems is achieved; where society is engaged and each person is inspired by the part they play; and by harnessing physics and applying Nature's ingenuity we make better use of what is locally available, so that all needs can be met – starting with the basic needs like water, food, shelter, health care, energy and jobs. This vision is based on a clear understanding that Nature's ecosystems have evolved in the face of nearly every imaginable challenge over the past few hundred million years, and therefore provide a wealth of experience on how we, as a society, can chart a pathway towards the future. When I finished writing the first edition of *The Blue Economy* in 2009 I had a last minute urge to push the 400 pages into a corset of principles. I wondered how I could define and differentiate the approach in order to assist in its uptake. At first, the principles flowed from my pen in no time, and created a sense of originality. However, as time passed and we saw the implementation of the many case studies evolve, I realised that although what I was creating was inspiring, it was not yet practical.

Time has now passed, and I have had the pleasure and privilege of working with teams all over the world, to create projects that aspire to the vision we created in the original book. Learning from this wealth of practical experience, I again pick up my pen with a sense of purpose, as I am now ready to create a framework that clearly defines how we can create a Blue Economy, by being *inspired by Nature, by changing the rules of the game, first growing the local economy, in order to better respond to people's needs through a much greater focus on the use of what is locally available.*

The realisation that much of the world has lost sight of what is now possible, in favour of what has been available everywhere via "business as usual" approaches, has urged me to summarise the Blue Economy approach into a set of guiding principles. Our intention for these principles is to provide a framework to learn, apply and share lessons as we transition the communities, cities, and nations of the world to an economy that works for all, using what we have.

Before presenting the principles we want to point out that the Blue Economy is an open and evolving concept. Thousands of people around the world contributed to it – where nothing is cast in stone, and our philosophy that *we can always do better, much better,* guides our own practice. Therefore the principles will grow and adapt every time they are applied and so are up for continuous improvement. We look forward to sharing this journey with you.

Guiding Principles of the Blue Economy (2017 Edition)

1. Be Continually Inspired by Nature

1.1. Develop non-linear logic

1.2. Optimise the system to the benefit of all

1.3. Build greater resilience through diversification

1.4. Look to physics first

1.5. Go beyond organic and biodegradable – renewable is the new goal

2. Change the Rules of the Game

2.1. Discover interconnected problems as the basis for opportunities

2.2. Shift from standardisation to diversification and abundance

2.3. Strengthen the Commons

2.4. Meet basic needs first

2.5. *Replace something with nothing*
2.6. *Value everything and everyone*
2.7. *Hold out for health and happiness*

3. Focus on What is Locally Available
3.1. *Create portfolios of local opportunities*
3.2. *Design initiatives with multiple cash flows and benefits*
3.3. *Redirect the flow of money back into communities*
3.4. *Look for opportunities for the capitalisation of costs*
3.5. *Revive stranded assets and infrastructure*
3.6. *Let mathematics design your business plan*
3.7. *Always keep ethics at the core*

4. See Change as the Only Constant

1. Be Continually Inspired by Nature

Life on Earth evolved from a few single-cell bacteria to a wealth of biodiversity that thrives in numerous distinctive ecosystems nestled into every corner of our planet. Natural systems inspire us, and while we don't promote a return to life in the forest or in a cave, we marvel at the fact that such a complex balance of co-dependency has been created on this amazing blue planet, where everything plays a part and life can flourish.

Natural systems cascade endlessly, and the term 'waste' has no meaning, as anything that is seemingly of no value for one is a desired item for another, without exception. This creates continuous flows – on which all life on Earth depends. This observation inspired us to reconsider how business is done, and rather than call for closing loops to make material flows circular, or even calling for a stop to waste, we have been inspired by the challenge of imagining value for everything we have, and seeing what sort of businesses we can create together. Considering that in natural systems all contribute to the best of their ability – and the fact that everyone evolves in response to changes to the system – suggest that we could translate this into a clear social objective: full employment. This has inspired us to consider how to design business models that are able to generate jobs way beyond what has been considered possible.

We have also been fascinated by Nature's capacity to pursue autopoiesis: the capacity to self-regulate, to adapt to disturbances, to operate as a network within boundaries, to create networks of networks within ecosystems. Ever since Chilean philosophers Humberto Maturana and Francisco Varela discussed this concept, we have realised that Nature has the power to evolve, create what has not existed before, and to adapt to new realities by adding, out of nothing, what is required to exploit the opportunities or the needs that emerge within its boundaries. Given its magnificence, how can Nature not inspire us to design new business models?

Rather than just being in awe, once we truly embrace Nature as our inspiration, we can transform our perception of the realities around us to see opportunities that were, in fact, right in front of us. We can now revise the logic of past approaches that rely on solutions derived from chemistry (designing new molecules) and biology (even designing new forms of life), to consider how the laws of physics and geometry determine much of life. This then leads us to move away from the linear cause-and- effect model, to a non-linear complex and interdependent reality. This then becomes the search for the optimum for an entire system – rather than just seeking to maximise one parameter for the benefit of a few. Ultimately we see the potential to strengthen the resilience of society and the economy through promoting greater diversity and interconnectivity.

These insights, all inspired by natural systems, offer the first set of Blue Economy principles that seek to guide us to achieve results that traditional 'wisdom' and management cannot even begin to imagine!

1.1. Develop non-linear logic

Modern life is dominated by a linear logic that focuses on seeking to understand cause-and-effect and perform analyses under artificial circumstances, making an abstraction from the context determined by time and place, while ignoring the realities of emotions and social frameworks that affect reality. While we are, for instance, aware of the fact that a patient who *wants* to get better stands a better chance of healing, we continue to study the performance of pharmaceuticals solely using the narrowly defined cause-and-effect approach.

The desire to control the approach to production and consumption based on this tightly controlled linear logic taking us from A to B, has given rise to the management tools that currently dominate our society and the economy. This has forced everyone to translate even basic initiatives into business plans, using Excel spreadsheets to define marketing strategies based on independent data, and to transform these into a rigid form of supply chain management that squeezes all (perceived) inefficiencies out of the system – while creating unintended consequences. This abstraction forces everyone in competitive markets (which are often not functioning as intended) to focus on producing a limited number of products, and to compete on the basis of quality or cost. This puts a strong premium on cutting costs, including through the achievement of greater economies of scale. All core decisions are made on the basis of this simple linear logic.

However, in closely studying Nature as 'Master', we realise that the web of life, both as an ecosystem and a social system, does not follow a linear approach. A caterpillar that transforms into a butterfly undergoes a metamorphosis that cannot be grasped by linear mathematics, as it is a non-linear transformation. In Nature, there are numerous interconnections that have feedback loops and multiplier effects that substantiate many relationships – and these often remain hidden. As we persist in only looking for the shortest and simplest explanation of how "one thing works at a time", we remain unable to grasp the extent of the complex 'web of life' where the whole is always more than the sum of the individual parts.

Non-linear behaviour in Nature expresses itself, for instance, in seemingly erratic growth behaviour, such as bamboo shoots that grow into 'vegetable steel' in a very short time frame or kelp that grows into high nutrient densities at high speed – an efficiency unrivalled by any industrial process. The extraordinary growth and transformation of species are naturally contained by self-imposed limits. A bamboo plant will grow to a height of 25 metres in a few weeks, but due to gravity its unbridled growth will be checked so it does not reach to 100 metres and then 200 metres, even when water and nutrients are available in abundance. Natural systems have clearly defined highly dynamic frameworks within which they operate – where the calculus to restrain growth is as inspiring as the unbridled original growth and transformation that appeal to our imagination. Non-linear approaches to growing a business and responding to societies' needs, help us understand the true impact of our actions and the remarkable opportunities that are within our reach to radically transform the reality around us.

While natural systems always operate within clear boundaries determined by their carrying capacity, with controls in place to limit expansion, our current economy has yet to do so. As a result, much of our growth is based on production and consumption at a rate that not only exhausts our present reserves while generating waste and pollution, but also deprives future generations of access to these resources. The Blue Economy therefore adheres to a non-linear approach, where growth variables are supported to accelerate and transform faster than considered viable under the traditional linear growth models – while at the same time imposing checks and balances. These permit us to operate within the carrying capacity of the territory in which the project is operating and the greater planetary boundaries, building up the quality of the Commons that we all share, strengthening social capital and enhancing resilience.

This is the reason why all Blue Economy project designs are subjected to a systems dynamics methodology based on the modelling approach developed by Professor Jay Forrester at MIT (USA). In the early 1970's, this approach served as the backbone for the research presented to the Club of Rome, in the book *Limits to Growth.* The application of this approach allows us to identify multiple revenue streams, feedback loops and multiplier effects that offer insights that typical linear models like business plans laid out in an Excel spreadsheet, are not capable of providing. This approach is not only a tool for analysis, offering clarity on the long-term impact and potential, it is also a decision-making tool that openly embraces innovations and initiatives while rendering them transparent and reducing risks.

1.2. Optimise the system to the benefit of all

The axiom of business is to maximise profits. This, in turn, requires keeping a close eye on revenues and costs. Revenues can be increased by capturing greater market share, such as building brand following or by making better products. Costs can be reduced by cutting the costs of the factors of production, such as material inputs or labour, or by capturing greater economies of scale, which means that the more you make of something, the cheaper it becomes on a per unit basis.

The logic of striving to get the most profit out of a limited number of offerings, is well entrenched in the prevailing business culture. However powerful the logic is, within an interconnected system that operates like the web of life, it overlooks many opportunities. In practice, the highest possible target for one parameter can only be achieved to the detriment of other interconnected factors. Imagine for a moment that a tree maximises its production of chlorophyll but neglects transpiration, which will result in it overheating. Or, a hen focused solely on laying eggs without paying any attention to raising chicks. It does not take a biologist to realise that a single focus on one outcome cannot only be detrimental to the system, but undermines long-term livelihood.

The tools typically used to calculate how to achieve the greatest possible profit are only capable of maximising one, or at best two, parameters – to the detriment of all others. Such an approach only gets the best out of one parameter and typically is incapable of minimising the associated adverse effects. This is the challenge with a linear approach: it creates blind spots that hide the negative impacts. This leads to unintended damage to the system, as our decision tools did not permit us to see the damage until it was done.

This is why a Blue Economy approach opts for Nature's principle of optimisation of the whole, rather than maximisation of selected parts. An approach of optimisation of the whole involves recognising the delicate balance among all the factors, to cultivate the greatest opportunities for the entire system. This approach ensures that we do not excessively focus on only one target, such as the profit derived from one or a limited number of products, or the amount of resource recycling. This helps us to eliminate blind spots from initiatives that, while they may well generate growth, profit and market share, also may create disguised and unwanted consequences.

In order to do this, a Blue Economy approach maps the inputs and outputs to comprehend the *systems of systems* at play. Such an approach can simulate a range of new results, even ones we could not possibly have imagined at the outset. This may seem like magic, but it is rather a case of discovering and harnessing what there is now, or what was there all along, but not accounted for. This can include stocks and flows of matter, money and energy and connections between phenomena that we previously did not understand. Once these sub-systems are mapped, it is possible to see how several initiatives, projects, businesses and communities are able to co-evolve, continually deriving more advantages and eliminating negative effects.

The power of the Blue Economy approach does not only lie in implementing a project, but rather in creating a fabric of interrelated initiatives that co-evolve, strengthen the capacity to implement, reduce risks and optimise the output – in a way that generates more benefits. The discovery of opportunities within such a fabric of activity generates more benefits (both directly and indirectly) as a result of the non-linearity of the feedback loops and economic multipliers. The case of El Hierro, discussed throughout this book, provides an example of this, where what started as an energy project turned into a fabric of economic activity that saw numerous once lost industries revived, along with solving the energy issue. This strategy, of optimisation and continuous seeking of ever-more value, generates a whole that is more than the sum of the individual parts, whereas a linear model is usually only exactly the sum of its parts, plus unintended or hidden damages.

Such an approach allows us to create a system where all can satisfy their basic needs. This inclusive optimisation model leads to the creation of a much bigger pool of resources and benefits, which makes it easier to engage everyone and obtain a broad commitment to co-evolve along "win-win-win" logic. This approach to optimisation offers transparency and leads to an open dialogue – a participative model. This model permits us to determine what the individual priorities are, how sub-systems determine their optimum, and adjust according to the feedback received, so that more resources are released to enhance other parts of the system and achieve the best possible outcome for all. The ideal level of the overall performance is continuously adjusted, so that it can co-evolve along with the available resources and the desired levels of satisfaction of an ever-increasing and diverse community – one that is fulfilling an increasing number of its basic needs, and continues to discover more of its innate potential.

1.3. Build greater resilience through diversification

The key to profit maximisation in competitive markets where economies of scale exist, is through standardisation of inputs and outputs, global sourcing and worldwide delivery systems in a tightly knit supply chain. The streamlining of everything improves control, provides predictable results, and reduces uncertainties, thereby limiting risks to the business. Brands produce perfect copies of their products and services all around the world: taste and appearance, as well as performance and service are exactly the same, meeting well-defined expectations of customers at a pre-established cost, performance, and quality. McDonald's has got this down to such a fine art, to the extent that *The Economist* calls its index of comparing the prices of a basket of similar goods and services across countries, the "Big Mac" index! This approach to rigid standardisation requires tightly controlled supply chains to ensure the predictability of the product and service. While this reduces the perceived risk to the consumer, the entire set-up is very fragile. The only option is to clamp down on operations, applying a straight-jacket with little or no room to manoeuvre and influence consumer behaviour. Furthermore most, if not all, of the revenue generated, quickly leaves the local economy, missing out on opportunities for local economic development.

Natural systems operate under very different conditions: the basis is diversification, dependence on mainly local flows of matter, nutrients and energy, and ensuring that whatever is needed can be supplied by multiple sources. The system, and not only a single player, is able to supply raw materials, intermediary and finished goods and services and, against great odds, can maintain reserves. In the case of an interruption, the system can redirect basic requirements to ensure that the ecosystem will survive. The Blue Economy approach follows the same logic. Resilience cannot be achieved through the creation of a strictly regulated structure with tight checks and controls on all variables. Resilience is created through embracing diversification – in order to create a fabric of interconnected and mutually reinforcing systems.

In a Blue Economy approach we ensure, by design, that all the kingdoms of Nature are part of the cascade of matter, nutrients and energy around the local economy. While industrial systems based on the Blue Economy do not have to emulate the exact same ecological systems, the same logic applies. According to biological sciences, life on Earth consists of five distinct major families, also known as realms or kingdoms: bacteria (Monera), algae (Protista), Fungi, Plants and Animals. Ecosystems cycle and cascade matter, nutrients and energy through continuous flows and buffers. The more diversity of life in an ecosystem, the more effective the system becomes, and the greater its resilience. If an ecosystem relies on only a limited number of species, then the loss of a single one will affect the entire community. A strike at one plant can stop assembly worldwide. An ecosystem thriving on a broad scope of biodiversity will be stronger in its capacity to withstand stress and will recover from adversity faster. Better still, ecosystems are on a tireless evolutionary and symbiotic path, always searching for new and better ways to survive.

An example of successfully cascading natural realms starts with growing mushrooms (fungi) on the residues produced by brewing coffee (a plant). As we will discuss in the book, the process begins with coffee residues being used as a growing substrate for mushrooms, after it has already been sterilised during the brewing process, thus saving energy. After harvesting the mushrooms, the spent substrate forms an amino acid enriched animal feed. The animal now feeds on fungi and plants and excretes a substance which is an ideal feed for bacteria, both in an aerobic and anaerobic environment. Bacteria extract even more nutrients from the animal waste. The digested material is now mineralised and becomes nutrition for micro-algae feeding on bacteria and animal waste. Continued cascading, that carries on indefinitely, helps us understand ways in which farms, abattoirs and bakeries can be redesigned. It is easy to see how growth, self-sufficiency, and evolution towards resilience result in ever-increasing productivity. The efficiency in terms of energy use and provision of nutrition is a multiple of what any food supply system, even those based on the most advanced GMO technologies, can ever come close to.

This logic does not only apply to biological resources; it can also be applied to inert materials. For instance, consider recycling a glass bottle to create glass foam (using CO_2 as a reactive agent), producing a building material, or a substrate for hydroponics, or an abrasive for stripping paint from wood. Using foam glass ensures continuous creation of value, as it replaces mined material that has to be shipped around the globe. This recycled form of glass is able to eliminate the need for fire-retardants or even paint, and creates a more efficient network of production and consumption (one with the added advantage of eliminating toxic components people are exposed to during daily use). Both these production cases, inert or biological, release the power of diversity, and leave the logic of core business far behind.

Instead of focusing on one output only, and forcing all to cut costs and streamline supply, this offers opportunities to diversify and create much more value with locally available resources, decrease the need to maintain stock or build logistics centres, lowers risk and increases resilience. The logic of resilience through diversification relies on the capacity to embrace multiple flows of raw materials, multiple products and services, as well as multiple residues in the local economy, which are quickly reclaimed as sources of value by multiple players in the system.

These new connections build a network that is created by the continually increasing number of players and participants. This offers a chance to respond to many basic needs, with resources available locally, and all within the carrying capacity, substituting what is not needed (and toxic) and creating more value from what is available. This reduces risks and creates resilience — and this is what ecosystems demonstrate in their remarkable ability to create 'something' from what appears to be 'nothing'.

1.4. Look to physics first

Modern industry has all too often relied heavily on chemistry alone, creating hundreds of thousands of different molecules from mostly petrochemical sources. Chemistry has certainly made extraordinary contributions to modern society but it has also left us with an unintended legacy, namely the rising number of toxic additives recognised as carcinogens, the development of super-powerful greenhouse gases, and growing mountains of waste and even continually expanding 'islands' of plastic debris in our oceans, where salt preserves the molecules and seawater prevents decomposition by ultraviolet light. This inventory of unintended consequences requires an urgent response.

Current scientific thinking with regard to responding to the basic needs of society, is shifting towards rather manipulating biology instead of designing more complex chemistry, adapted to fundamentally different conditions: soil, light, air, fresh and salt water. The biological approach includes changing genes, embracing genetic modifications, and unravelling genomes. It is alarming that genetic modification is presented as a pathway to resolving the critical problems of modern society. How could the injection of a carrot gene, producing beta carotene, into a rice kernel ever provide sufficient nutrition to several billion people on Earth? While the introduction of golden rice has been heralded as one of the proven benefits of genetic modification, it is astounding that the scientific community remains ignorant of the fact that rice paddies produce micro-algae that are rich in trace minerals, and in concentrations that are multiples of what could ever be achieved by genetic modification.

Life is subject first and foremost to the laws of physics, a fact that is often ignored by the scientific community and political leadership. These natural laws are the true guiding principles of all ecosystems. There are no exceptions to these laws: everything always performs according to expectation. Hot air rises, apples fall from the tree at the same speed, and coconuts fill with water according to the lunar cycle. It is unfortunate that we are no longer in tune with these cycles of life, these flows of energy, and these natural powers of the universe, and that the wisdom of ancient cultures regarding these cycles, flows and powers is being lost.

For some reason we have come to believe that we hold the power to direct life as we see fit, and that we know better than Nature. Observations on how ecosystems operate, allow us to design production and consumption systems, and the built environment, that make best use of the laws of physics, ones that offer predictable results and in the process reduce risks. Application of the laws of physics also reduces the burden of unintended consequences.

The Blue Economy approach suggests that business embraces natural powers that are guaranteed to work. When exposed to heat air and solids expand, and this allows us to design heating and cooling systems that will function without the need for pumps. This is how Anders Nyquist designs houses that are energy-efficient and healthy to live in, cycling air. Insights into the laws of physics allow us to utilise differences in temperature, pressure, alkalinity/acidity (pH) and salinity, to generate abundant flows of energy, predictable in size and magnitude, and locally available. Once we understand that these differences, that are always present, create natural forces, then we can design production and consumption systems that 'go with the flow', instead of trying to create the flow at high cost. Reflecting on this, I can see that this logic applies to both the natural world and its inhabitants. As long as I have tried to be the change agent, I expended too much energy on attempting to create a flow or current in the direction I saw best for society. Once I realised that there are under-currents and waves that are created in society, irrespective of what I do, I became able to effortlessly surf the waves. It was only then that I really started to see things being accomplished.

The laws of physics are beckoning, offering us forces that will allow us to achieve targets and goals previously considered costly or too energy-intensive. We should therefore, in seeking a portfolio of solutions, first explore the opportunities offered by physics. In the case of Las Gaviotas (discussed in Chapter 4), we saw the regeneration of the rainforest in the Vichada of Colombia being made possible by the discovery of the laws of physics, specifically related to temperature and evaporation, which enabled trees to survive on denuded land. In planting the first pine trees, the goal was not to populate the area with pines and certainly not to introduce a monoculture, but rather for the pine trees to create a biological cover to protect the soil from further denudation via exposure to ultraviolet rays. Seeds, once they protected from the destructive powers of ultraviolet light, could now germinate and biodiversity re-emerged. Scientists who had advised against the project had rightfully argued that no tree would ever survive the harsh environment. We welcomed their input as it led us to finding out how Nature goes about creating conditions that promote and even restore life.

The pine tree was selected primarily for its survival capability, and also for providing shade, a factor that triggered another major change in the local ecosystem. The tree cover protected the soil and a symbiosis with a nourishing mycorrhizal fungi led to a change in temperature. As long as the soil was hotter than the rain, the rain landing on warmer soil would splash, re-evaporate and not penetrate the soil, depriving emerging plant and animal life of water for the nine dry months of the year. With tree cover, the soil was now cooler and the rain quickly filtered into the soil. Water now percolated through the delicate layers of a thin 'skin' of earth, enriching the (mineral free) rain water. In doing so, it now provided high-quality drinking water to the local population, improving and ensuring healthy living conditions. And there was more: this extended green island in a vast area comprising of 20 million hectares of savannah, formed a cool spot where any cloud floating over it, was more likely to shed its excess humidity, resulting in more rain, replenishing the groundwater. This process of regeneration of the source of drinking water through the replanting of a monoculture that evolves into a biodiverse rainforest, is inherently a process based on physics.

In applying our knowledge of physics to our advantage, our actions and methods have led to the soil being enriched by water and nutrients, thereby allowing chemical and biological processes to unfold unhindered and convert a once desolate place into a thriving nature reserve — one that will continue to evolve into an increasingly diverse biome for centuries to come. It has also created a community of healthier and happier individuals, a fact we discuss later in the book. Unless we understand physics, we will not be able to grasp the opportunities before us to steer society towards sustainability.

1.5. Go beyond organic and biodegradable

The "Green" movement gained momentum in the 70's and 80's and highlighted the fact that dependency on petroleum and petrochemicals presented numerous problems, with ecologists urging societies and industry to search for a pathway beyond petroleum. One of the outcomes of this is that products have been increasingly scrutinised as to their toxicity and biodegradability. Chemicals like those used in Teflon (non-stick surfaces used in cookware, for cooking without oil or butter) and brominated compounds (fire and flame-retardants) are functional. The widespread use of these molecules do, however, have many unintended consequences. The combination of all these engineered chemicals leads to a cocktail with implications we have not yet fully grasped.

Plastics, having a half-life of thousands of years, were rightly identified as incompatible with our consumption patterns and throw-away society, filling landfills all over the world and creating huge islands of plastic debris in the oceans. How is it possible that a water bottle, one that consists of a container made from poly-ethylene and a cap of poly-propylene, both of which have half lives of hundreds of years, has become a standard on the market, when the functional use of the bottle is only a few weeks long? The drive towards the elimination of toxic compounds and the imposition of biodegradability was logical and widely supported.

The awareness that we needed to go beyond only the absence of toxic compounds, and that we needed to create conditions for sustainable consumption, required becoming conscious of the fact that even when the materials are 'green', their sources should not deplete existing stock or go beyond its rate of replacement, causing over-consumption. While both production and consumption should avoid unintended consequences and operate within the means of Nature and society, we now need to go beyond these basic and commonly accepted principles.

When manufacturing soap made from palm oil, I at first argued that these products were biodegradable and from a renewable source. Furthermore, these products were manufactured in an ecological factory, constructed from wood, with the (then) largest green roof of any industrial facility. Driven by marketing success, the popular demand for these products increased. However, as I have mentioned previously, an unintended consequence was the increased demand for the natural raw materials used in the manufacturing process. This required establishing millions of hectares of oil palm plantations, resulting in the destruction of vast tracts of rainforest and the elimination of the habitat of the pygmy elephant and the orangutang. Being faced with this hard reality motivated me to seek new business models, ones that are based on much more than only producing what is biodegradable and renewable, organic or free of child labour.

Compared to the old standard of petrochemical surfactants, these biodegradable and renewable products were an improvement. Soap removes dirt by reducing the surface tension of water, but a prolonged decrease in water surface tension has a negative effect on aquatic life. The biodegradable and renewable products could claim to be four or five times less harmful to frogs and fish. However, this was clearly not good enough, especially if the increase in demand from consumers considering the product to be better than others, is taken into account. Because of the increase in demand, the total overall impact would then be much greater than before. How can I save aquatic life in Europe while destroying the rainforest in Indonesia? I concluded that sustainable business models have to go beyond the obvious standards set before.

Based on this personal experience, and as a lifelong proponent of organic farming, I started questioning the certification of organic products. Terms like *organic* and *bio* implied the elimination of synthetic fertilisers, pesticides and herbicides. Certification was a step forward, but only being made aware of the chemicals that are *not* included in a product, unfortunately does not offer any information or insights into what the product does contain, or what it has to offer the consumer. This insight is compounded by the fact that it is hard to defend shipping organic produce around the world, creating a substantial carbon footprint. How can one do so and then claim to be doing things that are "less bad" for the environment? My slogan of "stop doing less bad, start doing more good" was born.

I studied the case in great detail and concluded that we need to embrace the principles of autopoiesis and diversification in order to go beyond organics. This approach has been tested numerous times and has gone to scale through a series of initiatives around an organic tea plantation in

Assam, India. With its original decision to go organic, the tea plantation successfully stopped the run-off of chemicals into the large adjacent rhinoceros park and UNESCO World Heritage Site, but productivity decreased due to the resulting poor state of the soil. The application of the Blue Economy approach led to the implementation of a portfolio of initiatives that will continue to unfold for decades to come. These initiatives, built on the bold decision to create the largest organic tea farm in India, now proceeds with the development of the largest economic development initiative in the area, while also protecting the rhinoceros from poachers through the creation of jobs and by increasing the revenues of the local communities.

To begin this process we asked the obvious, but seldom asked, question: "What is in the product and the production process that makes this product sustainable?" This then led us to look to culture, tradition, health, and all that we associate with the wealth of social and environmental diversity around us. Does this food item, that has been organically produced, also regenerate top soil? Does this certified organic food item promote biodiversity? Or is it merely another product mass-produced, the same as those grown all over the world, as a result of standardisation of production?

The important standards set in the 1960s for green and organic products were a great target. If we, however, want to be truly sustainable, and capable of responding to the basic needs of all, then we need to go way beyond this. The hard bottom line question is: "Are our production methods consistent with Nature's approach, and do they contribute to resilience, social capital and promotion of The Commons locally?" Only once we are able to answer with a resounding "yes!" to both parts of this question, will we have gone beyond *organic* and *biodegradable*. This attitude and culture of always going beyond what we know, doing better than we have done before and achieving more than we imagined possible, form the core of the Blue Economy approach.

This is why the core inspiration for the Blue Economy is Nature.

2. Change the Rules of the Game

The Blue Economy takes a radical approach that not only embraces change but actually designs for continuous change. The business models that emerge are open to change and ready for improvement. A Blue

Economy approach advocates a portfolio-based approach to competition: multiple, interconnected revenue streams are established, such that the basis of competition is at the system level, rather than at the level of the individual product or service (on a stand-alone basis).

The clustering of innovations allows for the creation of so much value that some products can be offered at much reduced rates, or even free at the point of use to consumers, thereby creating new Commons, as well as broad popular interest in receiving what is considered necessary for life for free. For example, the supplying of free pure drinking water to the local population of Las Gaviotas in Colombia, where water is produced and filtered as a result of the regeneration of the rainforest; and the supplying of free nappies in Berlin (Germany) to families with babies, as a result of the creation of high quality top soil for the planting of fruit trees.

Ideas like these that change the rules of the game are not something inherently radical or revolutionary, it is rather a choice of how to identify opportunities, and how to produce, deliver and consume, in order to both increase competitiveness and improve the capacity to respond to the basic needs of all.

2.1. See interconnected problems as opportunities

The principle that "Problems are opportunities", is an age-old proverb created in ancient Chinese times. Peter Drucker, the management guru, popularised this concept in the seventies. The Blue Economy takes it a step further. As mentioned previously, when we attempt to solve a problem we often inadvertently create new problems, known as 'unintended consequences'. While we never intended to cause any damage, our focus on solving one problem – without the ability to understand the ramifications of intervening in the complex system that surrounds it – creates other problems. Therefore, when confronted with a problem, the Blue Economy approach looks to identify and recognise any other problems that exist in the same system. Unless we impose the discipline of discovering such connections, they can remain unnoticed and as a result may be hard to unravel and correct. We therefore map the problems and take stock of their ramifications.

As I have shared, I learned the hard way that even when products are biodegradable and renewable, they are not necessarily sustainable. As soon as I became aware of the destruction caused by the demand for palm oil, I could have pretended that over time the negative impacts would decline, but the unintended consequences would have turned into collateral damage – and this is unethical! It was when faced with this problem that I dedicated myself to the creation of alternatives, like the production of detergents from the extracts of citrus fruit peel (a residue from juice production) and the regeneration of the rainforest, demonstrating clearly that the damage done can be undone if we are prepared to dedicate time and resources, and if we are committed to going beyond the established science.

Whenever we discover these unintended consequences we need to turn our attention to the opportunities arising from pursuing an alternative path, using all of the Blue Economy principles. The key is to realise that interconnected problems can unveil portfolios of opportunities, as is done as part of a Blue Economy "scan and screen" approach discussed elsewhere in this book. Hence, instead of trying to find a solution to one problem, following the cause-and-effect approach, which often only addresses the symptoms and not the root causes, a Blue Economy approach redirects existing flows of energy, materials and funding towards the implementation of what matters most: ensuring that everyone has their basic needs met and can flourish within their community.

2.2. Shift from standardisation to diversification and abundance

The emulation of natural systems, where interconnected problems create the basis for portfolios of opportunities, provides us with new ways of imagining how society might be transformed. It also offers fresh insights into ways in which we can better ensure that Nature continues on its evolutionary path. As people become increasingly aware of the environmental damage already done (and the damage that continues to be done), we hear a lot of talk about polluting less, and of commitments being made to reduce the impact of industry on the environment. As most people are seemingly unaware of the scale and intensity of the havoc being wreaked, they are not able to comprehend the magnitude of the actual damage being done. The 'solution' we are currently adopting is to take measures to reduce the negative impact. This is simply not good enough. We need to *replace* current practices, products and industries with those that not only eliminate such negative impacts but create compounding positive outcomes. A key reason why what has been practiced to date, namely 'doing less bad' – as polluting less is still polluting – is not enough, is that overall demand is increasing. While some can take positive steps to reduce impact, the world population is increasing, many with aspirations to the same sorts of consumption patterns as the ones who created the problems in the first place. Instead of setting targets around causing less environmental damage, our first priority should be to ensure that, in the first place, no damage is done at all. Instead of merely doing less of what is harmful, we should not be causing any harm at all. A criminal is not rewarded for stealing less, so how can it make any sense to reward a company for polluting less? Stealing less is still stealing — polluting less is still polluting. How can we then be satisfied with merely cutting down on emissions and reducing waste when we know that this is not sustainable?

We need to understand ways in which our actions, which often have unintended and unforeseen negative effects, can now have a series of positive effects. We need to study ways in which new business models are able to go beyond minimising damage to neutrality (zero emissions) – and then go beyond neutrality to positive effects – from which all will benefit. If we were truly students of Nature we would ensure that our industrial processes and our consumption habits evolve from standardisation and monocultures to a rich and diverse tapestry. The power of natural systems lie in their drive towards ever-more diversity. More diversity increases the number of relationships, and this strengthens resilience, and raises the productivity of the system by improving the flow of matter, nutrients and energy.

When pine trees were planted as the first step of the Las Gaviotas project, Nature quickly made use of the new physical conditions. Within a decade biodiversity had increased from 17 plant species (including 11 non-native species) to 256 plant species. Non-native species were eliminated naturally through a process driven by indigenous grasses, bushes and trees better suited to the area. The resulting thick undergrowth ensured retention of moisture and nutrients; thriving ant and termite colonies replenished the deep soil with nutrients, which contributed to improved filtration and mineralisation of water. While fauna and flora flourished, pure drinking water was made available to the local community free of charge – improving the health of all to the point where the hospital was closed – due to a lack of patients.

2.3. Strengthen the Commons

Once we realise that we have the ability to transform interconnected problems into portfolios of opportunities – just as it happens in Nature – we will be able to respond to the basic needs of all, with products and services that are strategic for life, and that can be made available locally at much lower cost – for the common good of all. There is a compelling logic for this. Nature does not only deliver air, food, water, chemicals and minerals, but also genetics, medicine and beauty. It regulates climate, decontaminates and mineralises water, and converts residues into food. Nature prevents erosion, maintains soil fertility, pollinates, and balances pests and populations. It maintains life cycles and genetic diversity. These enhance life and enable us to all share in what we have. It is unfortunate that the Natural Commons are at best neglected, at worst exploited; pasture is overgrazed and air polluted. What is even worse is that some believe they are entitled to take from Nature all they can, without offering it any respite to strengthen its capacity to cope. Even more disconcerting is when services provided by Natural Commons is privatised and monetised, like the supply of drinking water.

The Commons, such as spring water aquifers, are exploited beyond replenishment capacity, often turning water — the essence of life that belongs to all — into a commercial product that is bottled (mostly in plastic bottles) and shipped all around the world. Genetics is up for grabs (with many 'inventions' being nothing more than a discovery of what Nature invented millions of years ago), with the sole purpose of exploiting it for commercial interests, thereby reserving access to it for only those who are able to pay a fee. It is alarming to see how bees and other insect pollinators are affected by the ill-considered and unregulated use of toxins. While the unintended consequences are viewed as collateral damage and written off, such companies retain their licences to operate, and continue to damage the Commons in the name of so-called progress and productivity. When will people realise that without a free pollination service there would not be any fruit, vegetables, wine or nuts on our dinner tables? Or, should pollination be turned into a private and commercial service only?

Soil, and the continuous generation, carbonisation and mineralisation of top soil is another part of our Natural Commons that is critical for our long term survival, and yet it is mostly neglected. It seems that a blind belief exists that genetic modification, hydroponics, computer systems and satellite surveillance of changing weather patterns will help create all the food required to feed nine billion people. The hard reality is that without soil rich in carbon, or 'black earth', there will be no sustainable farming for future generations. Soil is now exploited with the simplistic view that one only needs to add nitrogen, phosphorous and potassium to enhance productivity, ignoring the fact that a wealth of micro-organisms, each with a very specific role in Nature, thrive in topsoil, which we call the 'thin skin' of the Earth.

Land and sea are not only over-utilised by current farming and fishing methods, nutrients are consumed without replenishing them. This leads to unbalanced climate conditions, as a result of dramatic temperature increases and the acidification of air, water and soil. It is with this understanding that a Blue Economy approach ensures that any new initiatives empower Nature to maintain its capacity to offer free and abundant products and services, that range from soil, food and water, to beauty.

2.4. Meet basic needs first

Once we clearly understand the concepts of a portfolio of opportunities and the Commons, we need to set clear priorities. Are we supporting a society where people are only considered to be consumers with buying power, or are we imagining a society where human dignity is respected by ensuring that all have access to the bounty offered by Nature, and that the basic needs of all are met, without endangering future generations from enjoying the same? The Blue Economy first and foremost steers innovation and entrepreneurship towards initiatives that respond to the basic needs of all with whom we share life on this planet. As far as water, food, shelter, employment and health care are concerned, approximately 25% of the world's population is not reached by the globalised economy. Even more disconcerting is the fact that 50% of the world's youth is excluded from it. Only one out of every two young people has a chance of ever earning a decent wage. Under the current business model, we run the risk that half of the world's young people will remain unemployed, searching for opportunities elsewhere, causing massive waves of emigration. A major portion of those who do have jobs, do not earn enough to buy a house, even with mortgage rates at all time lows.

Many great initiatives already exist with the aim of improving resource efficiency, reducing the impact of climate change, cutting pollution levels, or eliminating toxins. What sets the Blue Economy apart is that every project designed, supported, implemented or participated in, has a direct and traceable reach to the currently unreached. Being circular is not enough, as it does not respond to the basic needs of all. We know, through experience, that applying systems design and using portfolios of opportunities, all can be reached and all will benefit.

The power of systems design lies in the fact that one initiative has the potential to respond to many needs at the same time. When we embarked on the production of earthquake resistant housing in the Andean highlands using a variety of local species of bamboo, we responded to the urgent need for shelter. Creating 50 prefabricated one-family houses per day (which sold at approximately US$ 1,000 per unit), required planting 2,000 hectares of bamboo to guarantee the supply of building materials. Once the bamboo had grown to 25 metres, which takes about three years, it was harvested. While this was happening the area started producing filtered water, as contaminated effluent from the informal settlements situated higher up in the highlands was purified. Here one initiative responded to the need for housing, water and jobs.

In investigating the production of paper from crushed stone, a residue product of mining, our aim was not only to offer a locally produced alternative to internationally traded paper manufactured from tree cellulose, but also to reduce the carbon footprint of paper manufacture. As the manufacture of stone paper requires no trees and very little water, this initiative relieves the pressure on sources of potable water and releases massive land resources. These land resources can now be used for restoring indigenous forests or expanding farm land that produces food for the local population. As a result of this systemic approach, supported by computer modelling, this initiative succeeded in producing paper that is competitive in price and quality, while saving 20 trees and 60 tonnes of water per tonne of paper produced, and consuming 60% less energy. Now that we no longer require trees for making paper, ecosystems can be liberated from monocultures such as pine and eucalyptus plantations that are known as 'empty forests' and which have led to the depletion of top soil, without any measures having been put in place to replenish the nutrients for generations to come.

While paper is not considered a basic need, its current production model impacts adversely on the ability to provide water and food for local people. The manufacture of stone paper on the other hand, improves living conditions as it contributes to minimising the adverse effects of the mining process, by eliminating tailing dams that subject the local population to dust and to acid leaching into waterways. The latest innovation permits crushed rocks to be blended with synthetic or renewable polymers and air, reducing the average weight of stone paper to that of cellulose paper. The stone paper project therefore is not only an opportunity to generate value from waste. In addition, it offers opportunities to improve water supply and purity, make land available for food production and enhance living conditions – while generating a thousand jobs for every 100,000 tonnes of rock converted into stone paper, a product that is 100% recyclable indefinitely, without requiring water.

2.5. Replace something with nothing

The dominant model of production and consumption around the world creates that which sustains and nourishes life, but it also creates numerous products and services that we could do quite well without. Human beings are the only form of life on Earth that has created such a model of production and consumption, which unnecessarily consumes valuable resources and creates massive volumes of waste, and is ultimately unsustainable. A Blue Economy approach however, considers how we can replace many of the artefacts of modern life we consider indispensable, with alternative systems that meet the needs and provide the services of value. Even though traditional engineers, supply chain managers and designers are trained to replicate the well-known, our experience suggests that embarking on something that is unknown, is one of the key thought processes that allows us to be innovative.

When we observe how Nature deals with a wide variety of challenges, we find that the solutions are kept simple, and the chemistry benign. This insight offers great inspiration for the design of new technologies and the implementation of new business models that allow us to go beyond 'business as usual'. For instance, dolphins fish without nets. Fishing nets, especially dragnets, clear the ocean of all fish and damage the ecosystem while catching many unwanted forms of sea life that we do not eat. On top of that is the unintended consequence that this fishing technique destroys the sea floor in order to catch our food. Dolphins, on the other hand, fish by creating air bubbles in the ocean that lift smaller fish to the surface and allow larger fish to escape to reproduce. This is clearly practical and sustainable, given dolphins have succeeded in feeding themselves using this technique for around one million years. Humans have been fishing for 6,000 years, initially relying on spears, hooks, cages, and hand nets, and then graduating to enormous nets, electronic devices for finding fish, and even dynamite and acids. These forms of fishing have resulted in overfishing, leading to the collapse of fisheries around the world. The substitution of nets with the use of air bubbles opens up a new world that includes the ability to recover depleted fish stocks by saving female fish with eggs, as they are heavier and are not caught up in the upward flow of bubbles. So the challenge is to design fishing boats that catch fish with air bubbles, substituting "nets" with "nothing".

The substitution of "something with nothing" is a powerful principle that allows us to simplify a process, to avoid consumption of materials and resources, to reduce reliance on energy, and to eliminate causes of social and environmental distress. This is perhaps one of the most fundamental shifts away from the traditional practice of "inventing better" and improving what is there already. It is not in defiance of what has been achieved, it is rather a profound question that we can ask every time, and reach fresh insights into the possible, instead of merely trying to reduce the damage. The key is the determination to ask "the *not* question": what can I not achieve when we do *not* use what has been traditionally used. The absence of a battery (using water storage and flywheels), chemicals (using the awesome power of a water vortex) and the fishing net (using bubbles like dolphins do) opens our minds to imagine new possibilities and, with inspiration from Nature, the possibilities are endless.

2.6. Value everything and everyone

As I have stated, the linear process of production and consumption, focusing on a few isolated priorities, creates a lot of waste. The narrow focus on global supply chains, outsourcing, and distribution centres handling the final product for sale considers everything else as of secondary importance. There is nothing wrong with the generation of residue, which is part of every natural process. The key is that the residue should not be wasted, and whatever is a leftover of one process is converted to an input for another process. This principle can be extended to all flows of matter, nutrients and energy. When we believe that everything has value, we can go beyond the mere recycling of residues, beyond putting waste in a cycle, and give it real value, even with things like weeds and stranded assets. If we agree that everything has value, but not everything has to have financial value, then we change our perception of many resources. This approach creates the opportunity to convert whatever is around us, even wastes that contaminate our air, water and soil, into something that generates value.

The present model of streamlined production and standardised consumption creates a lot of redundancies – where even human resources are often considered without value. It is within this context that a Blue Economy approach not only assumes that "everything has value," but also that "everyone can create value." This insight permits us to design production and consumption systems that are not only capable of responding to basic needs, but also make use of basic resources widely available at low cost, with someone getting paid for accepting the waste and the liabilities associated with it. This generates jobs, which permit people to be part of society while deploying their creative minds and contributing to the best of their ability. This allows everyone to evolve beyond their best.

Residue is not only limited to biological waste and the poor mobilisation of human resources. To address the lack of basic goods and services, a Blue Economy also needs to find ways to create ongoing value from stranded assets. Capital investments in facilities accumulated over the years lose their value when markets shift, say in response to the dangers of certain products, like asbestos, PCBs, and fossil fuels. These defunct installations are all too often left behind through planned bankruptcies, leaving the clean-up to society, at high cost. A Blue Economy approach searches for ways and means to generate new uses for these assets that go beyond, for instance, the recycling of the scrap metals or recovery of leftover materials. Hence a Blue Economy approach offers new insights into how to offer new life to abandoned facilities, enabling workers who have lost their jobs to retrain and contribute to rebuilding their community. This approach also promises a full clean-up of the site over the years to come, so that it stops being a threat to public and environmental health, and finally puts a local area back on track.

As will be discussed in Chapter 11, an early leader is Novamont, the Italian leader in bio-polymers, who has spearheaded such an approach by converting abandoned petrochemical plants into platforms for the creation of value from readily available local resources, such as the humble cardoon, an artichoke thistle. These stranded assets now provide the core infrastructure on which to build new facilities for the production of polymers, elastomers, lubricants and herbicides, using a renewable local biomass. Once considered to be a weed, the thistle used now creates multiple revenue streams and has turned the local economy around, while creating a competitive force in the chemistry market. By 2016, Novamont had converted four stranded assets across Italy, establishing a new biochemical industry that has now become integral to the re-industrialisation of the European economy.

2.7. Hold out for health and happiness

While the Blue Economy approach starts with a clear focus on the basic needs of humans and Nature, it maintains clarity about the ultimate goal, which is to have a healthy and happy society. This is achieved by designing portfolios of projects in communities where money circulates locally, and strong social cohesion and cooperation develops as a result. Such an approach is transformational, as has been shown in the case of Las Gaviotas in Colombia as well as at the Songhai Centre in Benin (see Chapter 4). These two case studies have shown that even under the most adverse initial conditions, it is possible to create jobs, provide products and services, and even compete on price and performance against the global players, while striving towards health and happiness for the community.

The key is to have clarity from the beginning that, rather than continuing with past development models, a Blue Economy approach be adopted that seeks to chart a pathway towards the future, where we cannot pretend to know the outcome with certainty, nor have guaranteed results. Here we rely on creating a system with autopoiesis: meaning that the system has the ability to self-regulate, to adapt to disturbances, and to thrive within clear boundaries. Hence the Blue Economy approach searches for a healthy balance between the creation of value and the strengthening of community with local resources, and appropriate integration into national, regional and even global economies. The goal is not to create local economies that are economically self-sufficient, nor do we want to develop local economies that are wholly dependent on serving international markets, the goal is to create a balance among the options available, one that serves the local community and economy.

For instance, in Las Gaviotas the project sells colophon, the processed resin from pine trees, to the local paint industry, outcompeting Chinese and Venezuelan imports. It also sells excess naturally filtered water on the national market, working with restaurant chains like WOK that are keen on offering an alternative, one that is local and of high quality. These water sales, minute in global terms, compete locally with giants like Coca Cola and Nestlé, but unlike sourcing water from the international market the local offering generates welcome additional local cash flow that permits Gaviotas to maintain drinking water as a Commons in the local community where the water is captured. On top of that, the turpentine is purified and transformed into a fuel that operates both diesel and gasoline engines, eliminating the need for the import of petroleum. Apart from this, the planting of oil palms in-between the pine trees and the emerging local biodiverse forest, and processed in a local plant, offers the region its own cooking oil. These two substitutions of imports at lower cost, which also generate income through wages, substantially increase the cash available in the local economy, which circulates faster and thus contributes to the creation of more local wealth and social capital.

The Songhai Centre produces and consumes along the same principles. Local fruit, vegetables, fish and meat set the stage for a productive farm in a peri-urban region of Porto Novo, the capital city of Benin. However, it is not only food that is locally produced: all equipment is maintained on site, and missing parts are not ordered with waiting times that would silence engines for months on end, but are rather manufactured locally, even if this requires the maintenance of a foundry and a metal workshop. The quail eggs produced, with birds fed predominantly on maggots farmed in offal from the slaughterhouse on site, are of high quality and much desired in France, enabling the Songhai Centre to regularly export its excess at prices that would never be viable on the local market. This offers an extra stimulus to business operations and permits the building up of social capital at an accelerated pace, providing the healthy and happy environment we all seek. The Blue Economy approach is not against globalisation, but rather in favour of a much better version of it.

3. Focus on What is Locally Available

In the first set of Blue Economy principles we focused on the need for a fresh mindset, one that is inspired by Nature, to develop non-linear approaches that optimise the greater system, and build resilience, by looking to physics first – and by creating diversity. In the second set of principles we focused on ways to change the rules of the game by using portfolios of problems as the basis for new opportunities, shifting from standardisation to diversification, and meeting basic needs by using what is locally available while strengthening the Commons. We now present the third set of principles, and this is where the fun really begins! Here we focus on the core of the Blue Economy approach, which is to focus on what is available locally to design initiatives that can deliver multiple benefits. This is done by designing interventions where money is redirected back into communities, innovative approaches are taken to renew and create industries, and ethics is always at the core. In order to do so we need to change how we perceive economic opportunities, how we manage their scaling up, and how we maintain control of their performance.

As pointed out previously, the traditional business model focuses on profit maximisation which, in markets where there is effective competition, means a strong focus on increasing output, in order to increase revenues and capture economies of scale (thereby reducing per unit costs). In practice, this tends to mean producing more of the same limited number of goods and services, at lower marginal cost, and a production system enforced through supply chain management that tends to reduce the number of suppliers and eliminate inventory, relying on just-in-time delivery, supported by tight control of logistics. The net effect of this is that the relative proportion of labour and raw materials in the total value of the product typically decreases, meaning that the amounts received for raw materials or by workers in terms of pay and benefits typically decreases. Automation permits manufacturing largely "without labour"; robotisation in warehouses eliminates the need for staff for delivery. Drones and driverless cars even eliminate labour from the 'last mile'. At the same time, raw materials are managed through a complex system of futures, options and hedging, where the terms are negotiated via brokers who use automated trading systems. This entire system is designed for one goal, to maximise profit, and it has a staggering legacy both in social and environmental terms. There is, however, another way to generate value while strengthening social structures and regenerating environmental system, and we begin by revisiting economies of scale.

3.1. Create portfolios of local opportunities

A Blue Economy approach allows the creation of portfolios of opportunities that harness existing infrastructure in multiple ways and increase labour input. The approach weaves together local materials and energy flows to transform local social, economic and environmental outcomes. Whenever problems emerge, there is typically a knee-jerk reaction to getting solutions, materials, or products from elsewhere. While this may be justified in an emergency, like a tsunami or a cyclone, in the Blue Economy approach it is kept as the last option. Communities that are not able to respond to their most basic needs cannot be dependent on others, since aid and imports create dependency and this will never allow diversification to occur. This is not the only reason: the import of external solutions renders the local communities blind to the wealth that they have locally. While many are not aware of the resources that are within reach, it is the discovery of these opportunities that will help to alleviate the harsh realities of life.

The Blue Economy approach is focused on the discovery of all local resources, known and unknown. However, as we have learned over the years, it is not only the presence of a mineral, an ocean or a mountain that makes the difference, it is the opportunity to recognise the dynamic interrelations that are always offering matter, nutrients and energy that could be deployed in a sustainable manner. This process of identifying what is local and useful, builds self-confidence among the community, strengthening the belief that they have the ability to progress. If a critical mass of citizens believe that they can advance, then the society will indeed advance. In addition, we cannot ignore the fact that whenever there is a dependency on imports, there is a need to export. Otherwise you have to pay cash from the reserves you have, or borrow money which needs to be repaid. Furthermore, a high reliance on exports often requires the satisfaction of local needs to be subordinated to the needs of overseas customers.

It is for these reasons that we propose a strong focus on locally available resources. Even when we are told that there is "nothing", we pursue the search and enjoy the discovery. That is why a key exercise required of my students before they can graduate, is the design of a refugee camp where food, water, health care and housing need to be provided on a daily basis. The students initially complain that this is pushing everyone to the edge, since everyone knows that there are no resources available in such a camp. The end results have always been impressive: the discovery of the flows of nutrients, matter and energy, and soon a process unfolds whereby the students identify opportunities and the interrelations amongst all, to create a self-sufficient refugee camp, over time.

I once took a group of students to Namibia, and spent time along the Atlantic coast between Swakopmund and Henties Bay. We travelled the 120 kilometres, observing Nature, walking the salt pans, enjoying seeing the seals on the coast, the kelp washed up by the cold Benguela Current, and the abundance of lichens in the dry strip of land adjacent to the seashore. Sandwiched between the cold ocean water and the oldest desert on earth, estimated to have been created 70 million years ago, students had to imagine ways to produce food. The challenge is to realise that even with an untrained eye, we can quickly discover that there are many opportunities that are not at first obvious or self-evident.

The production of bread illustrates how such an approach locally can outperform a global business model. Consider that in an international distribution model, a fully automated factory can produce millions of loaves per day with only around one hundred staff. Labour and raw materials represent less than 20% of the cost of the bread; other costs include marketing and distribution costs, as well as the cost of finance. The supply chain is supported by the purchase of futures, option agreements, hedging schemes, just-in-time deliveries from suppliers (which change all the time), logistic centres, and supply chain management. Global cash management supports these operations, facilitating the ongoing trade in options and futures, with flows of funds through cyberspace to facilitate deliveries, while a network of (outsourced) warehouses and logistics ensures on-time delivery.

Applying a Blue Economy approach, however, leads to a very different production model that first does all that can be done locally, with available resources. The size of the bakery shifts from one that produces millions of loaves per day to ones that produce dozens of loaves, or at most a few hundred, for local consumption. This immediately implies a different model with regard to ovens. The radius of delivery is within a few kilometre instead of thousands of kilometres between cities. The primary market consists of the local schools, clinics and social centres, all within walking distance. This simplifies the packaging, and eliminates plastic bags and cardboard boxes, as well as the preservation agents required to prevent moulds. The logistics systems and warehouses are not necessary, and trucks will not get stuck in traffic, as no trucks are needed.

The baking oven operates on solar power, heating an oil that preserves high temperatures for days. The new power panels provide heat and electricity, enabling the bread buyers to charge their phones, and providing enough electricity to power street lights. The bread is not based on a pre-mix, but rather includes vitamins and minerals derived from the seeds and peels of locally produced sliced-and-diced fruits. Instead of a spongy bread with poor nutritional value and containing sugar-producing excessive CO_2, this bread is turned into a staple food with a daily supply of vitamins and trace minerals. The value of labour and raw materials increases to nearly 50% of the value of the bread, even though the sale price is the same, and the capital costs of the bakery can be amortised within two years. The oven can operate 24 hours a day. The excess capacity is available to dry mushrooms, to purify water, to bake pizzas or to provide warmth during a cold winter day. This portfolio of opportunities creates a sense of community, where some products and services are paid for, and some are offered for free. This is a competitive model based on diversifying output and capturing economies of scope.

3.2. Design initiatives with multiple cash flows and benefits

One of the key differences between the current dominant business model and the Blue Economy approach is that at the core of the approach is that our projects always ensure that whatever we do, there will always be multiple cash flows and multiple benefits. Just like ecosystems that never pursue just one or two benefits, the Blue Economy approach is designed to generate numerous financial and non-financial advantages. This approach is inspired by Nature's brilliance, where a leaf on a tree is not only there to capture solar energy, but also to offer shade and manage trans-evaporation, prevent water loss, transport nutrients, allow gas exchanges, and protect the plant, and when it catches the wind the movement facilitates flows through its capillaries. The Blue Economy approach emulates these multiple actions, exchanges and advantages through the implementation of a portfolio of initiatives. As each initiative has multiple cash flows, the immediate result is an increase in revenue streams and a lowering of risk. It also permits the generation of much more than just income – it creates the basis for communities to regain an economic and social dynamism that is in harmony with their environment. This is a key consideration, given that the prime motivation for the creation of the Blue Economy approach was to provide a business model that firstly ensures that basic needs are met and then spurs economic growth that can compete with international competition where it best serves the community.

For example, when mushrooms are farmed on coffee residue, the used substrate left over after harvesting the mushrooms is an ideal organic feed for chickens, that then produce eggs. So, from one waste stream we can generate at least four extra direct cash flows, namely the revenue from 1) handling the waste from the coffee shop; 2) using it to farm mushrooms; 3) using the waste from this process as animal feed; 4) the local production of eggs; and 5) the generation of manure that can be used in biodigesters to make fuels. All this, while reducing the need to transport coffee waste away and bring chicken products and eggs in! Not to mention the fact that the process will avoid the methane produced by decomposing coffee waste by replacing it with CO_2 generation from growing mushrooms. All of this make the production of food cheaper and keep it not only located in the local community but sees the revenues circulate through that community. The beauty of the Blue Economy approach is that while securing the required financial returns, we witness the unfolding of multiple benefits. As the case of mushroom growing demonstrates, along with many other applications of the Blue Economy approach, there can indeed be a range of benefits beyond the financial. Each initiative seeks to also strengthen the Commons, regenerate biodiversity, and increase the resilience of the community, which may not have direct financial outcomes but which do underpin the entire economy.

The Blue Economy approach moves beyond thinking of waste as something to be "taken care of" in a responsible manner. Furthermore, the approach does not see the merit in continuing 'production as usual' and then setting aside a proportion of profits to try to undo some of the damage caused, in order to demonstrate corporate social responsibility. The value of the Blue Economy approach is that it always cultivates multiple cash flows and multiple benefits from all initiatives, while building economic, social, and natural capital form a core part of the approach. The approach looks anew at what is locally available, from that which was once thought of as a waste product or a weed, to infrastructure or assets that have been phased out and are left unproductive. In a Blue Economy, business does not relentlessly pursue short-term profit and only take responsibility for the impacts once it is forced to do so, but is capable of ensuring more income both in the short and long term, while providing multiple benefits to the community and ecosystems.

3.3. Redirect the flow of money back into communities

The traditional business model has embraced supply chain management, which advocates firm control over every aspect, from the raw materials (sourced wherever is cheapest globally), all the way through to delivery to the consumer. This has been successfully achieved through outsourcing and delegating responsibilities to a select group of suppliers and logistics companies. This has resulted in the creation of global markets for each input or activity: for ores from mines, planted trees or grain harvests, which are traded around the world, with prices set through commodity exchanges. This system means that when a business accesses these commodities the money quickly leaves the community and disappears into the global economy.

Commodities are traded with no concern as to where they finally end up. Once these raw materials are traded and processed, then there is a secondary global market for purified metals, pulp for paper, and flour for bread and biscuits. Next the gold ingots or the steel sheets, the paper rolls and the industrially blended bread are traded on a different set of world markets. Next the metal sheets are pressed into car bodies, and the paper rolls into books or packaging, and the biscuits are branded and traded yet another time across the globe. We are trading everything all the time, all around the world, to the extent that distribution has become one of the most important sectors of the world economy, steadily increasing the use of polluting fuels and contributing to horrendous traffic jams in our megacities.

The creation of at least three and often even four or five 'horizontal' markets means that at each horizontal level, residue is generated, goods are traded, options are created and hedging takes place to reduce exchange risks. The result is that by the time gold dust particles are integrated into medical or electronic equipment, or notebooks are delivered to schools, or biscuits are bought in the supermarket, all ingredients have travelled around the world several times. Even though the implications of this in terms of cost of transport and carbon dioxide emissions are absurd, the current business model does not see any harm in it!

Following the Blue Economy approach, however, means that the focus is on local economic development, using locally available resources first (even some that have not been considered resources before), and responding to local needs and markets first. This approach rests on linking the supply chain locally from raw material to finished product wherever possible, across the local economy – from farming, fishing, forestry and mining to industrial production. This leads to genuine local economic growth that sees the value added by local businesses retained in the local economy. The approach also eliminates significant expenses related to global sourcing, such as excess packaging, the need for preservatives, and the logistics of lengthy transporting that not only impact the cost of product (requiring costs to be cut elsewhere) but also generate unnecessary waste and emissions.

In basic terms the question is: "Why pay for something to be brought into the community that we can create ourselves?" At first this seems like a pointless question but as one steps into a Blue Economy approach new opportunities arise. A now famous example is that of the Island of El Hierro (introduced in Chapter 4). Led by the then Deputy Mayor, Javier Morales, El Hierro redirected part of a €9 million annual diesel bill to invest in wind power, with freshwater pumped by hydropower. Combined with the creation of cooperatives dedicated to fishing, farming and manufacturing, this has reinvigorated the island's agriculture and created 1,250 jobs, where such jobs were considered lost and where the dependence on imported diesel was likely to place even greater pressure on the local economy in the future.

Prioritising the growth of the local economy and strengthening the networks of local businesses, is why Lung Meng can produce stone paper at low cost in Taiwan, and why Novamont is competitive in biopolymers, since it can source directly from farmers. These cases show that the integration of local resources such as rocks and weeds, with final products in the form of a notebook or a capsule for coffee, ensures that all the unnecessary costs are eliminated, while the value added through design, addition of labour, and conversion of residue to value, increases the local circulation of money. This approach triggers the multiplier effect where money circulates through the economy rather than leaving it as soon as the first transaction is completed – for instance: the person who was paid to take the coffee waste from the café then buys a meal (one that includes the mushrooms or chicken products), at the local restaurant and then the mushroom and chicken farmers head to the café for a coffee.

Let's look at the case of the local production of spirulina. Saumil Shah of the company EnerGaia in Thailand has demonstrated this approach through rooftop spirulina farms with the Novotel Hotel chain in Bangkok. There is a global market for spirulina, with large centralised producers in Mexico and Hawai'i selling to a wholesale market at premium prices. This highly nutritious additive is rich in essential amino acids and trace minerals and is usually dried and then traded. When looking locally first, the cost of drying, packaging, transporting (spirulina is often transported by plane) and trading, is substituted by a cluster of farming, processing and consumption.

The fresh spirulina, rather than the re-hydrated globally traded alternative, is processed on site into smoothies as a breakfast power drink for hotel guests. The rest is mixed with fresh noodles produced in the restaurant. This is generating local value, compared with the globalised business model that focuses on trade. It is not difficult to calculate the difference in local value generation when the 150 kilograms of spirulina is converted into food without drying or transporting, versus the model of specialisation, a focus on core business and global trading. Professor Jorge Alberto Vieira Costa, department head of biosciences at the Federal University of Rio Grande in Brazil, has dedicated two decades of research into how these photo-biorefineries of spirulina and other blue-green bacteria generate jobs, nutrition, material for textiles, and even methane gas and biofuels for power generation, within a local economic context.

3.4. Look for opportunities for the capitalisation of costs

Although a Blue Economy approach prioritises non-linear system dynamic models, it can still translate progress into annual or quarterly results using traditional accounting tools. This is an important part of linking the wide range of newly created opportunities to the specification of how these initiatives and proposals can be incorporated into the traditional tools for measuring the health and performance of a company, or a cluster of enterprises.

A few examples will illustrate this. The business model design sometimes allows costs to be capitalised, as is the case with stone paper. This type of paper is recyclable indefinitely, unlike regular tree-based paper that can only be recycled four to five times before the fibres are too short and become ill-suited for reuse. Therefore using stone paper means that now the cost of the paper in books can be treated like a deposit, as it is easily and endlessly able to be recycled: just like drink companies are able to list the aluminium from cans as an asset on the balance sheet. By charging a deposit that also strengthens revenues, the recycling of paper will reduce costs on P&L (profit and loss statement) as paper is now an asset, with the majority of the cost paid upfront and then reused to generate ongoing revenue. Publishing companies can offer a reduction in subscription rates if the old magazines are returned, creating a closed-loop for stone paper at low recovery cost, in cooperation with customers that are committed to returning the paper. The reduction of subscription costs will increase circulation, improve higher advertising revenues and put more stone paper on the balance sheet. This approach also works in the case of farming mushrooms on coffee waste, where the large amounts of spent grounds in a café shifts from being a liability to be dealt with, to a product.

3.5. Revive stranded assets and infrastructure

Negative and stranded assets, which are covered through provisions, can be converted into investments and even cash generating instruments. Tailings from mine waste dumps, for which provisions were made and ongoing costs are borne by the mining company, can now be converted into raw materials for paper, thus turning waste disposal into a cash flow. Over the years, this liability will begin to provide positive cash flow, turning tailing dams from an expense of US$ 25/tonne to something generating revenues of US$ 200/tonne. Considering that mining companies have millions of tonnes of tailings, this could become a major capital gain, if the company so desires. Companies which have been over-leveraged can now strengthen their balance sheet, not through asset stripping, fire sales, closures or divestments, but through putting value on something that, according to the traditional business model (and accountants), has no value.

Stranded assets could also have a fresh start, even those fully depreciated. As we know, any old industrial site runs the risk of requiring a massive clean-up, which can be expensive. If sites with well-maintained, infrastructure could be cleaned-up over time through new activities that generate cash flows, like the case of the petrochemical refinery in Sardinia (discussed in Chapter 11), that was converted to a biorefinery to process a local weed. This then offers the opportunity of major capital gains over decades, eliminating the need for a full provision on the day of the announcement of closure. Such opportunities can be quantified case by case, through the basic tools of accounting. The secondary benefits include increasing the buying power of the local population, speeding up the circulation of money in the local area, while converting an operation from something that damaged Nature to something that is in harmony with Nature and which allows it to return to its evolutionary path.

Say a major instant coffee producer believes that the best way of dealing with the millions of tonnes of spent biomass after the extraction of the soluble part of coffee, is to burn it for energy, then at best one can calculate an investment of X against a savings in energy costs of Y, where payback periods of 8 to 10 years are considered a good result. This is better than sending it to a landfill, and is indeed to be applauded, but it can, however, do better – much better. If the same company were instead to use 100,000 tonnes of spent coffee grounds, recently processed under the most stringent hygiene conditions, to cultivate 100,000 tonnes of mushrooms, it would more than double the profits of its coffee operations. The residue of the coffee would also represent an additional 50,000 tonnes of chicken feed, providing a wide range of nutrients and significantly helping with food security. Job generation would run to as many as 10,000 to 20,000 jobs, injecting money into local economies in a way that the adherents to the incineration approach could not even begin to imagine. The same capital investment in burning the residue could instead be deployed to generate food. While shareholders of a company making instant coffee may not see the value of entering the food and farming business, they will surely not object to increased revenue, not to mention the multiple benefits for the community operating the factories.

As is often the case when taking a Blue Economy approach, the results are regularly beyond expectations. As discussed before, the Las Gaviotas case demonstrates that this integrated approach leads to another accounting success: the increase of biodiversity. The original savannah in the Vichada of Colombia had 17 plant species, of which 11 were non-native grasses. The latest count indicates the presence of 256 plant species, and the return of dozens of animal species that were driven to near extinction in the region. Then, there are the statistics on health, with gastro-intestinal diseases dropping to next to nil. The introduction of free drinking water for the local population, and bicycles as the preferred means of transportation, rendered the local communities so healthy that the local hospital needed to be closed, due to the lack of patients. At the same time, the land that was acquired for next to nothing in a land program, is now valued, according to an expert team from JP Morgan, at more than a thousand times its purchase price. This puts the local community amongst the members of the middle class – within one generation.

3.6. Let mathematics design your business plan

Since the Blue Economy approach opts for transformative and radical change of the existing business models, the initiatives must lead to real action on the ground. The approach is based on multi-disciplinary teams learning, by doing, the translation of an idea, backed up by good science, into businesses that not only outcompete, but generate significant economic development opportunities in the local community. In emerging economies this can be a real mechanism for lifting a whole community out of poverty. However, if such an approach was to be assessed using traditional business planning tools such as market analyses, financial spreadsheets and technology audits, the value that has been demonstrated time and again, would likely be incomprehensible. This is mainly due to the fact that such as assessment would focus only on a competitive analysis based on strengths and weaknesses, centred around core business activities built on core competences that are protected by patents.

This does not mean that the Blue Economy approach requires no planning! On the contrary, the approach relies on the *Participatory System Dynamics Model* as a tool to design, support and implement innovative business models. The mathematical modelling built into this tool informs acceleration and broadening of the implementation of opportunities, while determining the interactions with natural systems, taking into account their limitations. The power of the tool is that it can quantify tangible feedback loops and economic multipliers, enabling a clear understanding of the synergies that stand to be created by various Blue Economy-style initiatives.

In 1964 Professor Jay Forrester created the origins of this tool as an urban development model at MIT (Massachusetts Institute of Technology). Inspired by the description of the world's problems given to him by Aurelio Peccei, a former top executive of FIAT and Olivetti, it was later converted into a global model that served as the basis for a report presented to the Club of Rome, in the famous book *Limits to Growth*. A simplified version of this model is available open source, permitting its use even by beginners in mathematics, who are committed to understanding and modelling the dynamics of a Blue Economy. Hence, mathematics and modelling are at the heart of the Blue Economy approach and this stops us from using a linear approach that overlooks the potential portfolios of opportunities to be created.

3.7. Always keep ethics at the core

The Blue Economy approach presents its business models in an uncompromising way. It has a clear objective and acts according to transparent principles. While some consider the approach revolutionary, we consider it to be one of the ways to ensure that we succeed in responding to the urgent social and environmental needs of our time, using the best tools that we have. The philosophy, concepts, methodologies, and tools outlined above are not axioms or laws, but rather emerge from our observation of the initiatives that have been successfully implemented. We learned lessons from initiatives that had not succeeded (as yet) or were much delayed because we had to learn how to execute better. These reflections on how the Blue Economy vision has been translated into reality, offer us the understanding of why and how we progressed the way we did, and can serve as inspiration and mentoring for others. We adhere to the German principle that *Schaffen ist Wissenschaft* (Doing is science).

We have the privilege of receiving continuous input from thousands of scientists, and when one or two confirm new insights and we discover fresh opportunities to improve the systems before us, we are prepared to adapt and transform again. We have a clear pathway forward and nothing will divert us. We only desire to improve, accelerate and spread the options we are discovering. Our approach is not dogmatic, we reach rather than teach, and seek to expose rather than impose. This strategy of continuously exposing people to opportunities, and the successful implementation and continuous improvement, creates conditions to keep ethics at the core.

In simple terms, it is unethical to settle for doing less bad. Stealing less is still stealing; polluting less is still polluting. Mere talk about minimising the negative impact on the environment is not good enough. We cannot celebrate those who reduce pollution, nor can we accept that players in the market knowingly inflict social, economic and environmental damage. Concretely, ethics at the core means that we will not tolerate "more efficient batteries": we will continue to strive to have no metal batteries at all, since batteries rely on mining, and a dramatic increase in demand for batteries will lead to more mining, and thus put more scars on the face of the Earth. This does not mean that we are against storage of energy and power: we just search for methods that free the world of an increased reliance on mineral resources.

Ethics at the core also implies that we make our business models open source. Since we benefit from the free contributions of thousands on the design of Blue Economy approaches, we cannot and will not use this for our personal gain. If our goal is to have a fast and profound acceleration of transformative change, then the open source policy must be creatively pursued, without using the traditional shackles that restrict access (such as patents or intellectual property rights). After all, the key is not the technologies themselves, but rather the new business models the Blue Economy approach creates, which are always ready for adaptation to time and place. With respect for the originators of the ideas and the technologies, these models will allow us to steer society away from a fixation on products and processes, towards the design of approaches that are ethical at the core, use what is available, and direct us towards health and happiness.

Finally, ethics at the core implies that we cannot solely focus on the here and now, working only with the wisdom that we have accumulated to date. We have a responsibility to inspire children, and to accept that all our diplomas and degrees have an expiry date. Children have the power to consider fantasy a reality. Children believe that everything is possible. Adults, at home or in the office, continuously try to weed out all creative ideas, classifying something new as something impossible. Others may label a new proposal a vision, one that may be possible, but that will never materialise in the short term. Keeping ethics at the core includes the ability to awaken the child within each one of us, to see what may seem like a fantasy, can quickly become a reality. This is why I personally ensure that successful projects are translated into fables that I do enjoy sharing personally with children all over the world.

The power of keeping ethics at the core lies in deciding on a path, and while we may not know exactly where it leads, we faithfully include the best of all, and know that the results will be better than ever before, and certainly better than what we could imagine today.

4. See Change as the Only Constant

The principles presented herein are just the beginning, and as our experience evolves we are ready to prioritise and shift the principles against which we are continuously testing ourselves. The Blue Economy approach differs from those that have prescriptive (even dogmatic) axioms, or copyrighted and trademarked concepts, by resolutely focusing on making a difference on the ground, in communities. This book does not pretend to have all the answers. The practitioners of the Blue Economy approach rather embrace change as the only constant in life, recognising that us humans are late arrivals on Earth, and that we have to be prepared to unlearn what we have learned. We do have the curiosity to know and understand what we did not know and understand before.

2

EVOLVING THE BUSINESS MODEL

Doing less bad – is still bad!

The onslaught of bad news about the environment, poverty, unemployment, human rights abuses and the ineffectiveness of policy makers, combined with the short-term profit-driven approach by corporations, leave many concerned citizens baffled and dismayed. The data before us is clear: climate change is advancing and is having real impacts on people, ecosystems, and the world's economies; inequality is rising with hundreds of millions of unemployed youth. Clearly a response focused on consumption-driven growth only, which leads to ever accumulating debt, is not likely to lead us out of this situation.

There is a lot of time and effort spent on the analysis of information. While many desperately search for alternative solutions, there is no silver bullet in sight that seems capable of reversing the negative trends. There is a blind belief in one solution: growth – no matter how it is attained – typically including the liquidation of non-renewable natural assets or reducing investment on healthcare and education. The challenge is that experts can approach information from their perspective, framed in a disciplinary ivory tower. This can make it hard to see the entire system and to develop the knowledge that is required to create a vision, indispensable to designing a fresh and effective pathway forward.

This chapter has been added to the original version of the book to attempt to open our minds to such an opportunity. I myself had my eyes opened through a bad experience and, as is often the case, it led me to figure out what was not working. At the time I had one of the most prominent biodegradable soap factories in the world, and I was very proud of cleaning up the rivers in Europe – until I visited Indonesia and realised that my actions led to the destruction of the habitat of the orangutang. I realised that I could not reconcile being 'Green' in Europe with being destructive in Indonesia. Out of this frustration was born a desire to reimagine business.

The lack of comprehensive knowledge of how economic and social systems interact, leaves no space for the wisdom urgently needed to mobilise the best minds and the committed individuals to evolve from analyses of the unfolding dramas to a pragmatic portfolio of initiatives. Too much effort is reserved to analyse the problems, to theorise solutions and fiercely debate these options as if the prevailing theory is considered a dogma. Hardly anyone focuses on the demonstration on the ground and sees that it is possible to outcompete the present growth model by performing better – even according to his or her parameters of success.

Through continuous exchanges with Professor Anders Wijkman, co-president of the Club of Rome, one of the thought leaders in policy design towards sustainability, and a member of the Royal Swedish Academy of sciences, it became clear that few people have realised that analysis and theory, concept development and case studies, cannot make a dent in the present negative trends – unless there is a fundamental shift in the business model.

> *We should evolve from the logic of economies of scale and cost-cutting, towards a society that uses what it has, responds first to basic needs of all, circulates the newly gained purchasing power in the local communities and generates capital, especially social capital and strengthens the Commons.*

Blind Belief in Growth as the End not the Means

While we can imagine many shifts and models, there is one factor that determines the corporate world's culture and modus vivendi: the focus on the core business and achieving growth, however derived. Whatever is imagined, from tax policies, to international conventions, and new innovations to recycling programs, it will all fail to steer society towards an environmentally and socially competitive model unless we overhaul the business model itself. While I very much appreciate the efforts by many thought leaders like Walter Stahel, Michael Braungart and Ellen MacArthur, and I believe in the best of their intentions and those of many others, their valuable proposals all remain trapped in the logic of the Master of Business Administration (MBA): which is to focus on the core competency and reduce costs to make more money.

The millions of students aspiring to a better financial reward, thanks to their investment in an MBA degree, hardly realise that they are all learning the same business models that were once conceived at the world famous Harvard Business School. The MBA is as much a product of economies of scale and standardisation as the industries they are supposed to manage in the future. Everything is translated into financial results, market share, economies of scale and ranking. This dominating model prescribes that you sell what you produce and that growth combined with market dominance will not only offer the best return on investment to the shareholders, it will even align performance through the management of rewards and bonuses. And if the company were faced with pollution scandals or social problems, then the system will do its best to cut pollution and reduce the social injustice. We know that doing less bad, simply, is no good. Business needs to embrace the opportunities to do much better.

This prevailing business model that has guided the corporate world is framed by a simple logic: focus on a limited number of products and compete on the basis of price and quality. This core model has been translated into the theory and the practice of the economies of scale, with an unrelenting search for ever lower marginal costs through standardisation, leading to a dramatic concentration of production, with *only a few corporate leaders determining the standards of the market*. The obsession to cut costs, especially the reduction of labour input, has led to a logic that when companies merge, and subsequently lay-off thousands of workers, the listed enterprises are immediately rewarded by the stock exchange with a higher share valuation.

The sheer size of these mega-mergers leads companies to focus on their core business by building on their core competence and eliminating outside activity through outsourcing, and a strict discipline known as supply chain management. Let there be no doubt: companies are on a permanent search for lower costs and are continuously sacrificing quality in order to ensure growth through multiple consecutive sales. And if this strategy needs to be pursued through the design of service models, whereby the product is not sold but leased, then the suppliers succeed in locking in the customer long-term to their technology. Thus the new service strategy generates more profit and a secure cash flow over the years.

The logic of free trade enhanced the rapid globalisation of fewer players through the adoption of this business model, driven by this quest for ever lower costs. Amazingly, people are forced to buy three refrigerators with similar performance over 25 years, saving 30% on the first one and 50% on the third one, without realising that over a quarter of a century, double the amount of disposable income has been spent on imported cheaper goods than on the 'good old local manufacturer' who produced white goods that once lasted 25 years. This not only implied the loss of the local industry, it is a loss of on-going maintenance services, a deterioration of resource efficiency consuming three times more material, forcing on society the cost of dismantling and disposing, which in turn leads to a permanent loss of cash flowing through local industries and communities.

The sales and marketing strategies have successfully blinded the customer with a lower price and the promise of the latest innovation, even better energy efficiency – not realising that at ultimately this strategy leads to the predictable collapse of local industries. Worse, the monies that used to circulate in the local economy are now channelled outside the community, leading to a deceleration of local development, a loss of competitiveness and an increase in unemployment. This cycle drains more purchasing power out of the community and even an entire nation.

The Urgent Shift

The core shift in the business model that is needed, is to go beyond this relentless cost-cutting drive, and to embrace a business strategy that aims to generate more value with what is locally available. This fundamental shift requires companies to get out of the straight jacket of focusing on one product and move towards an integrated portfolio-based approach. The acceptance of this novel – yet easily understood – strategy, is a major challenge, since it is fundamentally different from what MBAs have been trained to pursue as the pathway to success. The upside is that this new business model offers opportunities to generate multiple revenue streams, with resources that are within the immediate reach of enterprise and entrepreneur. The surprise is that when one generates several income streams from available resources, then one can extract business from the hard game of world market prices for one or two products only! Imagine, farmers and miners can look at the flashing numbers on their Bloomberg screen and relax: it is only an indication of one of their revenue streams and does not decide on life and death anymore. This new local production and consumption system must be organised locally and must be connected through networks spanning the globe.

How often are farmers or small scale manufacturers booted out of the market by huge overseas competitors who can beat prices, including transport from the other side of the globe, and who find a ready partnership with large distributors who are indifferent about the generation of local purchasing power? What would the remedy be? Is the liberation of the labour market an option? It is quite obvious that if the workers' remuneration is reduced to a fraction of what it is today, then the European social security system would put every nation into default. Is the reduction of social security an option? While economists and industrialists join in to call for a much more flexible labour market, there is a firm limitation imposed on immigration in Europe, North America and Japan.

The call for "flexible labour markets" is a covert slogan that in reality demands to cut labour costs and social security across the board in order to become more competitive. The elaborate assessment and the ranking of competitiveness of nations and industries are determined on the basis of this core business logic, where the overall cost/quality balance decides the position of a country and their industries. While this competitive game is successfully played by less than one percent of the largest corporations in the world, the remaining 99% have hardly any chance of survival. As a result consumers are increasingly purchasing globally sourced materials, food and energy provided by a few players who control capital. Europe seems to have accepted the inevitable demise of its social system and imagines solutions that are based on more of the same – like the free trade agreement with the United States, claiming to create a level playing field for 800 million consumers, while imposing strict austerity measures on the nation state. The contraction of the economy forces people to look for cheaper products, accept lower quality and low costs and the vicious circle has started.

Use Local First

This book presents a new business model that forms the basis of the Blue Economy and has been implemented in over 100 sectors of the economy. It generates not only more value locally, it also secures that more money will circulate locally. Better: it creates corridors of double-digit growth in areas of high unemployment and poverty, and out-competes the present globalised model in return on investment, cash flow, poverty alleviation, and the capacity to respond to basic needs, including jobs without the need for subsidies. Governments can now dedicate time and effort to ensure that there is a level playing field.

It is of course very difficult to pursue a smart and inclusive growth strategy in any region or nation, when cash is permanently drained out of the economy. When the primary and the secondary sectors are not capable of competing with the prices dictated by the international market, then the hard- earned income leaves the local economy, engendering unemployment and economic contraction that has become characteristic of many nations today. The only way to reverse the trend of high unemployment and the downward spiral of economic development, is to ensure that more value is created by using available resources to create more money that is designed to flow through local businesses and stay in the local community. While this logic goes against the prevailing dogma of free trade at the macro-economic level, and the typical MBA approach that one must search for ever lower costs at the micro-level, the results of implementing such a new approach clearly demonstrate how societies can be extracted out of the poverty and unemployment.

Traditional economics, however, promotes another way, that is to dramatically reduce the cost of labour and even embrace social dumping and saddle the government with health care, unemployment compensation and pension costs. This leads to an untenable increase of government debt, which is followed up by a long period of austerity in order to keep the tax burden, that is already too high for a dwindling working population, within limits. Let us not forget that global corporations do not pay taxes, and therefore the burden is squarely on the shoulders of the citizens. Now if we accept that an increase in government expenditure, as well as the widening of the government deficit are not options to embrace, then there is an urgent need to change the rules of the game because otherwise the next option is a focus on austerity.

Thus the first and foremost rule of the game that needs to be changed is the shift from *"ever lower costs"* to *"ever higher generation of value"* with what is locally available. That is to shift from assuming scarcity to generating abundance. The ZERI Foundation, which is in reality a network of organisations throughout the world, has demonstrated through study and practice that this shift is not only viable, it can be implemented in the short term. We have seen the mobilisation of US$ 4.3 billion in capital and the implementation of +200 projects that generated 3 million jobs and embrace this logic with such ease. The pursuit of value – and not the urge to cut costs – very quickly brings additional products and services to the local market, which can quite easily outcompete the internationally traded merchandise too. This puts the local economy into a growth spiral that goes beyond overconsumption of scarce resources. This is counter-intuitive, yet easy to explain.

The Cascading of Benefits

China is the leading supplier of photovoltaic (PV) panels to the world. The cost per unit has dropped so low that it is within cents of competing with traditional sources of fossil fuels. However, an innovative technology from Sweden permits the combination of energy from the PV panels, with hot and cold water generated by the capillary tubes inside a sandwich of PV panels. This is a thicker panel, one that is strong enough to be the roof (provided that the base is heat resistant), instead of being placed onto a roof. The basic structure is ideally made from recycled heat resistant plastics, again offering more jobs since this partly substitutes aluminium that was globally mined, processed and sourced. The cascading of benefits continues since water is now stored at high temperature, not only killing bacteria, but also storing energy, replacing the batteries that all too often make renewables uncompetitive. The break-even of local assembly is reached with only 250 units per month sold. The combination of all these benefits translates into a cost per kilowatt per hour that is a fraction of PV solar panels. This is not a game of beating the Chinese PV panel makers on cost; it is winning the competitive game by generating so much more value! It comes as no surprise then that, in 2014, Solarus won the innovation prize for process industries in China!

A focus on coffee has been at the core of our work for the past 20 years. The recent developments amply demonstrate that this internationally traded commodity has a tremendous growth potential, which makes a cup of coffee look like a by-product rather than the primary value generator. The key link to make is that both on the farm and in the city, coffee waste can be converted to a substrate for mushrooms. For example in Australia some 75,000 tonnes of spent coffee grounds is produced each year with the majority sent to landfill, while Australians consume some 95,000 tonnes of mushrooms. A typical café uses some 5 kg of coffee beans a day and pays approximately US$ 900 a year in waste collection costs to send their spent grounds to the landfill. Inspired by this opportunity, Ryan Creed and Julien Mitchell left their 'fly-in-fly-out' jobs in mining to set up the first urban mushroom facility based on coffee waste in Australia in Fremantle, Western Australia in late 2015, and have since also set up operations in Margaret River, Melbourne and Noosa.

The spent coffee substrate used to grow the mushrooms, with the leftover after harvesting the mushrooms, can be converted to animal feed, generating three revenues instead of one. Now the cost of protein (mushroom and animal feed) is lower than the cost of imported food and feed. Better yet, this generates local jobs and local income. Given that the worldwide volume of coffee waste surpasses 10 million tonnes, at least 10 million tonnes of mushrooms and 4 million tonnes of animal feed can be locally produced. Now add the potential for new biochemical industries to emerge, using coffee waste to generate products with UV protection and odour control, and we have a cascading of value. Given these cascading opportunities, imagine if the trade in coffee could rival that of, for instance, soy feed stock or sunflower seeds, then the multiple income streams could add billions of dollars to the coffee economy, cash that not only comes in, but circulates within local communities! Now the same can be done for tea.

Any Change is Hard

Large corporations have great difficulty in embracing this multiple revenue stream model, as they are incapable of explaining their shift from a core business to a multiple cash flow model to the financial analysts on the stock exchange. This situation is exemplified by Nestlé's response to the opportunity of mushroom farming on sterile coffee grounds from instant coffee factories. Indeed, the largest coffee processing company in the world, with a guesstimated one million tonnes of waste, decided to instead recover energy from coffee waste, reducing its reliance on fossil fuel. Whereas the generation of power from waste figures prominently in sustainability reports outlining the performance of this food group in cutting its carbon emissions, it subscribes to the traditional logic of cutting costs. This case would be celebrated under the traditional business logic and repeated at international forums as a successful case of the green economy. And it is a major step forward. Waste that needed to be discarded at a cost, now generates power and adds to the bottom line. This fits perfectly with the prevailing business model where the company demonstrates its social and environmental responsibility by "doing less bad". Would it be possible to convert this strategy from "doing less bad" to one that is "doing more good"?

Imagine if Nestlé had instead shifted from the "cost cutting" to the "value generation" model. The financial, social and ecological benefits from burning a few million tonnes of coffee waste will pale compared to the total value harnessed by the generation of healthy food at low cost (nutritious mushrooms) and the provision of animal feed (that normally rely on imported soy from Brazil or the conversion of slaughterhouse waste). One does not need to be an experienced economist to quickly calculate the impact of mushrooms and feed on the local economy. The internal opposition to the proposal, held first that mushrooms are not one of Nestlé's businesses. Secondly, we often hear it said that mushrooms are not part of our daily diet. Our response is that hamburgers and corn flakes were not part of the daily food intake either. However, the greatest obstacle to the pervasive logic of the food and feed proposal is that Nestlé has determined it is neither in the mushroom nor in the animal feed business, and therefore will not pursue this chance to add a few billion dollars in turnover. It is interesting to wonder what the shareholders would think of this refusal to reject additional turnover on existing resources, offering returns above average in food production today.

We realise that companies are not prepared to embrace this new business model, and the millions of MBAs who leave the thousands of business schools around the world, are all indoctrinated within the same logic, streamlining competition with the search for cost cutting as the safe way to improve cash flow. This imposes a tight discipline on the supply chain, enforcing strict adherence to the financial objectives outlined in budgets, reducing the number of suppliers, and putting the screws on downward price negotiations. The successful implementation of these numbers cast in budgets and forecasts, determines the management's bonuses. This ensures that everyone performs as is expected.

Whatever insensitivity there is to the hard social and environmental realities that may emerge as unintended consequences perceived by society, it is then quickly overcome through corporate social responsibility programs. These programs present such companies as if they were responsible ones, even when they have just reneged on the opportunity to generate thousands of jobs and provide millions of tonnes of quality food and feed at low cost. The local economy could have been stimulated by using readily available resources, and can help to stamp hunger out of this world – not through genetic modification that puts the seeds and the profits in the hands of a few producers in the world.

We need to shift from the present model to a Blue Economy model with double-digit growth that alleviates unemployment, hunger and poverty. That can never be achieved through massive additional taxation on citizens nor by a forceful austerity program throwing thousands out of a job, cutting pension plans and reducing health care programs. Time has come to accept that the only way forward is to change the way we do business. This requires a minimum critical mass that demonstrates to the market that a new model can out-compete whatever has dominated the logic until today. After all, we are not against anyone or anything; we are in favour of doing better, much better indeed.

3

LEARNING FROM NATURE'S BRILLIANCE

Nature uses the longest threads to weave her patterns. Each small piece of her fabric reveals the organisation of the entire tapestry.
—Richard Feynman

As Janine Benyus so eloquently describes in her book *Biomimicry*, we can learn from the elegantly simple methods perfected by species as varied as the way termites and zebra deal with climate control, the way the Namibian desert beetle captures moisture, the way mussels stick to rocks to withstand pounding waves, and geckos are able to walk on any surface, even the ceiling, without suction or an adhesive. According to Janine, biomimicry encourages us to "*create conditions conducive for life, rather than simply minimising our impact*". Such inspiration suggests that if we follow such an approach, we can achieve much more using much less energy and fewer materials – while ensuring better health conditions. We can even eliminate components and products that are considered indispensable in modern construction. How is this possible?

For example, let's consider how climate control is currently achieved in buildings. Buildings are typically designed to be entirely closed and fully insulated to reduce energy consumption. This leaves them with little chance to self-regulate. Air pumps are required to push controlled air volumes through the building to maintain comfort levels for occupants.

Unfortunately, closed buildings accumulate humidity; especially in the basement (as moist air is heavier and moves downward). Bedrooms are heated with dry air that burdens our respiratory systems, while dust particles accumulate from the ample use of electronic equipment. Many of these particles are electrostatic. Mites proliferate in the carpets because triple-glazed windows with an ultraviolet filter provide them with an ideal breeding ground.

Dust mites are microscopic relatives of the spider. These tiny creatures live by feeding on the detritus of a building's occupants. The dust mite is a common culprit in dermatological and respiratory allergies such as eczema and asthma. Removing mites requires harsh chemistry, which may lead to chemicals circulating for months in a closed building, along with the volatile organic chemicals contained in most furniture and carpet glues. This is not how one may imagine an energy-efficient "ecological" building to be! Though we may have a 30% energy saving, or even a 100% passive house (in fact, all power could have been generated by solar cells), the costly use of chemicals and the stress to our immune systems are unintended side-effects. On the other hand, if energy-efficient building design included solutions with a proven track record, benchmarked for millions of years by species living in a similar habitat, then we would notice a radical difference in the way healthy buildings look, and how their systems function. Healthy buildings can indeed be doubly efficient by reducing both energy costs and adverse health impacts, requiring less risk capital to build and securing a better return on investment. But how?

Termites, the Masters of Flow

The first farmers on Earth were termites and ants. Perhaps as early as 100 million years ago, termites successfully responded to the need to survive changing weather conditions. Their adaptation involved a greenhouse-like farming system. They perfected a method whereby the nest's internal temperature and humidity can be controlled, allowing their larvae to hatch, and permitting efficient harvesting of fungi, the termites' primary food source. They successfully achieved food security and evolved from hunter-gatherers to a domiciled species – well before *Homo sapiens* evolved.

These admirable masters of temperature, humidity, and atmospheric pressure follow the laws of physics as well as the application of complex mathematics to engineer construction and farming. Termites have perfected the design of chimneys, where air warms and predictably rises, creating a pressure differential within the nest below. Since the nest is connected to its ambient surroundings by tiny underground tunnels, the outside air then flows into the nest to equalise the air pressure. This precisely illustrates Newton's Third Law of Motion, namely, "For every action there is an equal and opposite reaction". However, since the air that flows through underground tunnels is within a narrow temperature range, one that is kept stable by the temperature of the deeper soil, the humidity and temperature of the exterior determines how much moisture remains in the air that enters the greenhouse nest. Termites everywhere in the world know how to calculate and construct their nests, in any climate, securing ideal growth conditions for the rich, white mycelium that is their principal source of nourishment.

Swedish architect Bengt Warne observed termites in Zimbabwe in the late 1950s. His original drawings of termite mound airflows, published in *On the Conditions of the Acacia: to build and live in harmony with Nature* (1993), look simple but are challenging to adapt for modern architectural purposes. It took another brilliant Swedish architect, Anders Nyquist, to develop mathematical formulae that codified Warne's insights into a model that makes present automated climate control systems obsolete. Based on studies of termite architecture, Nyquist discovered that it is possible to design energy-saving buildings that are warming or cooling as needed, providing comfort, without locking inhabitants into an airtight and heavily insulated space. Where air cannot flow, harmful bacteria and microbes readily proliferate. In such a space, when one person sneezes, everyone catches a cold. Surely we cannot allow this to be the unintended consequence of saving energy!

The Laggarberg School in Timrå, just outside Sundsvall, Sweden, was Nyquist's design adaptation of the genius that both termites in Nature and ancient civilisations, throughout history, have used to keep warm or stay cool – without guzzling energy or using elaborate chemical insulation to keep heat out or freshness in. A system of vents and channels achieves air conduction that moderates temperatures and maintains freshness. The air is fresh all year round and when one child sneezes, no one else is affected. Fresh air circulating offers an exit for dust and charged particles. The students are the healthiest in the nation, as measured by days lost due to illness, and perform amongst the best academically.

What happens when parents learn that children who attend this public school are healthy and achieve well? Families want to move into the neighbourhood, as it is the only way to secure entry into the school. And what happens to real estate prices when people move in like that, in droves? Land value increases as a result of the strategy to emulate Nature's design. The skills used by termites are of great instructive value, even though these insects are subjected to eradication around the world for their voracious appetite for wood. Were we to consider that termites are traditionally responsible for the long-term fertilisation of the soil, we may have less animosity and a greater appreciation of them. In fact, typically 15% of the Earth's vegetation becomes the nutrient source for the fungi that termites consume. The decomposing debris produces heat that warms them in the winter while enriching the deep soil for decades and centuries to come.

From the termite we can learn how to continuously refresh the air in a building without artificial heating or cooling. If the air is refreshed, there will be less risk of "sick building syndrome", where stagnant, microbe-laden, stifled air is trapped inside and leads to illness as a result of fungal and microbial contamination. In the termite's world, the airflow system controls humidity, which determines the productivity of the fungi on which termites rely for nutrients. The termites' airflow system precisely and permanently secures 86 °F (30 °C) and 61% humidity. The only variable that the termites do not control is water. In case of heavy rain, the nest may be flooded. This stressful environment is the signal for the *Termitomyces* mushroom – a gourmet delicacy, even for humans – to ensure survival by reproducing. In addition to this the termite queen knows how to store spores and carry them to safety in her mouth, to start farming at a new nest.

It is fitting that the first multi-story building emulating the ingenious work of termites, was erected in Harare, the capital city of Zimbabwe. The award-winning Eastgate Shopping and Office Centre, a 10-floor edifice designed in the late 1980s by Mike Pearce, a local architect, uses just 10% of the typical energy demand and is cooled solely by natural airflows. As in the termite hill, air is drawn through the very structure of the building through pipes that run through its floor slabs, to be released through ducts that run all the way to the roof. The building is also designed to act like a desert cactus in the way that it effectively releases heat overnight, to reduce the heat building up inside the building.

The economics of this innovative system is convincing. Eliminating the space between floors used traditionally for central cooling ducts drops the break-even point from 55% to 46% (even with some stand-alone air conditioners, which are rarely used, installed to meet international occupant expectations). This essentially adds an extra floor in the same elevation while reducing investment costs (in this case, a savings of US$ 3.5 million) and operational expenses by 10 to 15%. Banks fund construction projects that can demonstrate lower risk and better returns, while requiring less capital and offering better rental rates to occupants. Sustainable features leading to low cost, maintenance-free passive air conduction instead of expensive mechanical air conditioning also attract financing options.

Why Do Zebras Have Black and White Stripes?

The zebra offers an additional insight into technologies that would reduce or, in some cases, even eliminate the need for insulation of buildings in many parts of the world, through control of surface temperature. The zebra is capable of reducing its surface temperature by 17.5 °F (around 10 °C) with air currents generated by the interplay of its black and white stripes. Here is another ingenious distillation of the laws of physics that are taught at school but perhaps not well understood in practical application. Although architectural design looks for moderating of temperature through the heat-reflective properties of white, the case of the zebra would argue that buildings should rather be painted with alternating black and white stripes. We know that the colour white reflects the sun, and thereby reduces heat. The colour black absorbs the sun, thus increasing surface temperature. The air above the white stripes is therefor cooler than the air above the black stripes. The heated air above the black stripes rises, creating a pressure differential with the higher air pressure above the white stripes. This generates micro-sized air currents that cool the surface without mechanical ventilation. Does this make a notable difference? Can this be commercially developed?

A Daiwa House office building in Sendai, Japan, designed once again by Anders Nyquist, also capitalises on this interplay of black and white while utilising the wisdom of the termites. While controlling the surface temperature on the exterior of the building, the interplay between the oppositely coloured surfaces decreases the building's indoor temperature in summer by 8.5 °F (4°C). By extrapolation, we can see that the mere physical effects of black and white striped surfaces reduce interior temperatures, saving an estimated 20% in energy usage.

Us humans, with our 8.5 °F heat reduction that is nowhere near as impressive as the zebra's 17.5 °F, have only been at it for a few decades though, whereas the zebra has mastered the technique over hundreds of thousands of years. On the zebra's skin the low and high pressures are levelled due to micro-gusts of wind. When it comes to buildings, instead of insulating the interior of a building, the interplay of physics removes heat from the exterior, reducing the need for polyurethane (with fire-retardants) or glass fibre in the interior. The zebra, in fact, has an insulating layer of fat only under its black stripes, since the tissue below the white stripes does not need it. It makes sense – it saves materials; it is very simple. It never stops working as long as there is interplay of black and white, which is guaranteed as long as the sun shines and the laws of physics apply. The zebra has an added advantage: no mosquitos will land on its skin, since the turbulence in the air deprives them of a safe approach. Ever considered black and white stripes to keep mosquitos away?

Aiming to save energy, architects today recommend insulation on the inside of a building and placing it beneath the roof to block the transfer of heat or cold. Builders typically use polyurethane chemicals, or glass fibres produced with mined materials and processed at high energy cost, to insulate the indoors from the outdoors. The zebra shows how taking advantage of the predictable laws of physics, to first reduce heat or cold at the exterior, can translate to less need for chemical products or expensive heating and cooling installations. This interplay based on pressure and temperature requires no additional expense and works all the time. Indeed, the laws of physics have no exceptions.

A Desert of Plenty

The dark colouration and extraordinary life span of *Welwitschia mirabilis*, a desert plant species, give us further cause to consider that using white alone may offer only short term comfort when it comes to beating the heat. The Namib Desert has been arid for at least 55 million years and is believed to be the oldest desert in the world. A grasshopper leaping from a rock onto the hot desert sand would be scorched and die in only a few minutes. In this water-starved environment, with rainfall only once every seven years, the Welwitschia not only survives but, with an estimated life span of 2,000 years or more, seems to hold the record as the oldest living plant on Earth. The Welwitschia, with its two long leaves, has mastered, with near perfection, the capture of dew, a mechanism previously poorly understood. It shares this skill with the Namibian desert bug. The Welwitschia also has the ability to source moisture from two metres below the surface. The plant and the insect make use of the darkest part of their surface to capture the first sun rays in the morning, creating a better temperature differential, resulting in a higher water condensation due to a lower dew point.

The *Onymacris plana*, a beetle also indigenous to the Namib Desert, is not simply dark, but intensely black. Lighter colours reflect sunlight and reduce heat absorption at the surface. While humans value cooler colours, these have a disadvantage in a desert setting. In the desert the main target is not coolness, but rather decreasing the dew point so that a minute quantity of moisture can be predictably captured. A cooler surface increases the dew point and thus reduces the quantity of moisture available for harvest each morning. Darker colours induce a lower dew point in the early morning with a warmer surface and a cooler air. This means greater heat absorption during the day, and desert plants and beetles can conduct that heat away. Members of this desert ecosystem survive through heat reduction achieved through ventilation and conduction, another demonstration of the ecological use of physical principles.

It achieves better dew point management results than plants in the same habitat by using heat conductivity with the addition of another physical effect: extreme hydrophobia. At first, a desert beetle's capacity to repel water may seem as irrelevant as windshield wipers on a submarine. However, the careful analysis undertaken by UK scientist Andrew Parker reveals that small drops of dew form microscopically each morning as soon as the sun appears over the horizon. These droplets are rapidly rejected from the hydrophobic (water-repelling) wing surface of the beetle or leaf surface of the plant, before they evaporate. The minute droplets of rejected water are collected on extremely hydrophilic (water-attracting) patches around the beetle's wings. This interplay of hydrophobic and hydrophilic surfaces assures the Namibian desert beetle an ample daily water supply; enough, in fact, to drink and shower! Curiously, this system of water and temperature control is counter-intuitive: black creates the ability to survive in the hottest climate and water-repellent surfaces secure drinking water.

The Namibian Desert is also home to a large array of lichens. These are, in fact, not a plant species, but rather a symbiosis or composite of two organisms, namely a fungus and an alga. The fungus functions as the body and harvests water for the lichen from morning and evening fog. By photosynthesis the alga produces the nutrients required for the survival of both. Though their mycelium may be barely two cells thick, these lichen are perhaps the best miners in the world, able to penetrate seemingly solid stone.

"However is that possible?" we may ask. Our logic when it comes to penetrating rock has been shaped by Alfred Nobel, who invented the chemical reaction known as "dynamite," our only current means of extracting mineral ores from deep within the earth. Humans takes recourse in chemistry, while natural systems first employ physics. Lichens do not use dynamite; there is in fact nothing in Nature that would use such an excessive and destructive force. The microscopic size of the lichen's mycelium allows it to easily navigate the spaces between rock crystals. When a magnesium atom is found, it is moved to the surface for plant, bird, or animal life to partake of. As a result of the lichen's precise mining technique, Namibian fauna and flora gain access to the trace minerals needed to function in this delicate environment. The contribution of each species ensures survival for all those living within this framework of temperature, moisture, and light.

Sophisticated Sticking

Geckos do not mind a storm. They cannot be moved by any force, as they effortlessly adhere to surfaces wet or dry, rough or smooth. The gecko has hair on its feet, one-tenth the size of a human hair, that branch out at the ends into billions of tiny spatula-shaped fibres that hug the surface and aggregate the weak intermolecular-electrostatic forces of attraction (called van der Waals forces) between objects, to create a powerful force of attraction. Amazing, isn't it, that things stick together because of the underlying physics! One day innovative products inspired by the intermolecular manipulations of the gecko could compete with VelcroTM, itself inspired by the hooks on cocklebur seeds, that have, over the ages, applied a "sticking without glue" solution. We may even suggest that the geckos and cockleburs have greater sophistication when it comes to "sticking" than, say, mussels. Geckos and cockleburs use physics first, guiding their biology to grow cells that achieve the desired performance. Mussels rely on chemistry. This does not mean that mussels do poorly by relying on a chemical solution. In fact, they are a remarkable inspiration for how we can replace the toxic compounds that have been developed for any number of commercial adhesives.

Mussels are constantly battered by waves. As a consequence they have perfected a glue to attach themselves to rocks. They have learned how to build such great elasticity into their water-resistant glue that even the strongest surf will not detach them. Kaichang Li from Oregon State University (USA) studied the resin that mussels produce in order to develop a commercial glue, one that Columbia Forest Products uses to replace formaldehyde-based epoxies, the standard glue for particle fibreboard. Indoor air quality is markedly better when formaldehyde is not a component of the building materials.

When market leaders use green chemistry to replace toxic chemistry in using nature-inspired innovations for their products, they achieve both profitability and sustainability. Therefore, while we admire the gecko and the cocklebur for elegant use of only physical forces without the need for chemistry, all respect is due to the mussel for teaching us how to eliminate toxins from our homes, schools, and offices.

Vortices as Bactericides

Natural systems don't solve problems with a shower of harsh chemicals. There are a few well-publicised biological exceptions, such as aggressive snakes, toxic frogs, venomous spiders, and deadly mushrooms. However, their toxicity is nearly always directed against another species, hardly ever members of the same family, though the black widow spider is a notorious exception to the rule, as is often found in biology. Prior to reverting to any form of deadly chemistry, and certainly chemistry that could be mutagenic or carcinogenic to members of the same family, natural species apply the forces of physics. Where living species, especially fauna and flora, are an inspiration for humans – from poetry to technologies, the inanimate part of Nature also has lessons to share.

Have you ever wondered how rivers purify themselves? They use physics and the nutrient needs of two diverse families of bacteria. The pervasive movement of a river allows the continuous creation of vortices in the water. A vortex increases pressure at the core of its swirl, to the point that nanoscale pressure and friction rupture bacterial membranes. Bacteria are thus rendered into nutrients for other species further downstream to enjoy. These finely distributed nutrients, combined with spaces enriched with dissolved oxygen and areas where air is eliminated from the water, allow bacteria and micro-algae to mineralise any excess biomass quickly and efficiently. At the same time, this shift, from spaces rich with dissolved air to spaces vacant of air, makes it impossible for detrimental aerobic bacteria to flourish.

The power of the vortex, induced merely by flowing water abiding the laws of gravity, is among the most impressive demonstrations we have studied. Have you ever seen a river flow in a straight line? What might be the logic of a river's meanderings? Curiously, modern industrial engineers design everything in straight lines with 90° turns. Even though the famed 20th century Viennese artist-designer-architect Friedensreich Hundertwasser once declared that, "The rigid straight line is fundamentally alien to humanity, life, and the whole of creation".

Viktor Schauberger, a brilliant Austrian inventor and the founder of the contested implosion technology, spent much of his career as a forester. He observed that the dual vertical and horizontal swirl of river vortices caused solids to deposit in the centre of the river bed, while eroding the rock and soil along the banks. One of his early design breakthroughs was a log transport system that curved as a river does, allowing logs to pass without jamming or blocking. Remarkable! Straight transportation systems block while meandering ones flow. Straightened rivers accumulate sediment and meandering rivers provide fresh, clean water, while replenishing underground water tables.

Swedish innovators Curt Hallberg and Morten Oveson developed a non-linear mathematical model that made the power of any vortex predictable. With developing vortex technology, we can now replace polluting chemical solutions with physical solutions. The potential energy savings from vortex technology, and an increased understanding of the natural geometry of a vortex, makes possible a plethora of opportunities for businesses and societies. If we combine these insights with hydrophobic and hydrophilic checkered rooftops borrowed from the Namibian beetle, we reduce energy and material consumption, and can generate water on the top of any building – only using fog and dew. From there it can follow the law of gravity and flow into the premises. With vortex technology, the same grey water that washes clothes on the tenth floor can be reused just one or two floors below, thus reducing the water wasted by a factor of five to ten.

The Swedish startup company, Watreco, offers a device that uses their patented Vortex Process Technology® to eliminate air from water. This is an attractive proposal for anyone needing to produce or maintain large amounts of ice. When you produce ice, you freeze both water and air. Air is an insulator. The energy needed to freeze and maintain the ice in hockey rinks and ice skating arenas, for example, is thus dependent on the amount of air the water contains. Because the vortex technology eliminates the air, the energy savings (up to 43% according to Ohio State University trials) is a positive contribution. It reduces costs and decreases the input to climate change by eliminating the greenhouse gases from ice-making that are produced by 100,000 kWh per year of electrical generation.

What clinches it from a business standpoint, however, is that the ice produced from the vortex water is crystal clear, permitting advertising displays placed beneath the ice to be highly visible. Ice normally cracks under the weight of the hockey players, since the air bubbles cause imperfect ice crystal formation. With air removed, the ice remains clear, even under the weight of the crisscrossing players. Surely advertisers with diminished budgets would comprehend the added advantage of their logo easily viewable on sports broadcasts. Then again, perhaps advertisers could even be motivated to foot the bill. This could be a strategic new business tactic: advertisers paying for energy-saving devices!

The income generated by additional advertising revenues is a multiple of the energy savings and can be measured by multiple means. While substantial sums might be contracted with large hockey league sponsors around the world, at thousands of smaller ice rinks the use of vortex technology to clarify the ice could generate additional revenue and reduce the pressure on local government budgets. Interestingly, the town-owned ice rink in Telluride, Colorado is second only to their water treatment plant as the biggest energy consumer in town. The town then purchased a vortex system for their ice rink. They enjoyed greatly reduced energy costs starting in 2010, once the system was fully installed. Elsewhere, the city of Malmö, Sweden, quickly realised this savings/earnings potential and installed a full system of ice-making using vortex technology. David Henderson, head coach of France's men's national ice hockey team, reports on his team's evaluation of the vortex-produced crystal-clear ice, "Elite players have been unanimous in their praise of the improvement of ice quality in regards to hardness and durability. The ice has also become more transparent, which leads to a second major improvement: the visibility of on-ice publicity for the sponsors."

Value created by such extrapolations of physics is enormous, and far outpaces investment costs. It does make the energy savings seem like an added benefit! A simple technology created a new competitive edge in advertising, one that at first glance had nothing to do with air, energy, or ice. There are an estimated 16,000 indoor ice rinks around the world. The total savings in electrical expenditures could reach approximately US$ 200 million per year, if all were to adopt this technology. Better yet, the costs would be well below the first year's savings. And, by the way, we cut carbon emissions.

Electricity from Sea Currents, Inspired by Kelp

An estimated US$ 190 billion of investments in new energy supplies over the next two decades has been earmarked for tidal, current and wave-based technologies. The International Energy Agency estimates that tidal power could generate 200 terawatt (TW) per year, while wave power could produce 8,000 TW.

Water is a liquid and therefore wave and current energy contains roughly one thousand times more kinetic energy than wind. This permits smaller devices to produce more power. In addition, sea waves are produced around the clock. However, there are challenges with the design of tidal generators, including mechanical design (as generation of electricity requires high speed – and waves and currents consist of high forces at slow speeds), maintenance, environmental impact and the harsh weather conditions, which can pound submerged devices during storms and tsunamis.

Prof. Tim Finnigan, an adjunct professor at the University of Sydney with a degree in environmental fluid dynamics, observed how giant kelp moves with the rhythm of the currents and the waves. When a storm or a tsunami hits, these huge underwater forests simply lie flat on the bottom of the ocean. Prof. Finnigan studied the fluid dynamics of kelp movements and converted these into mathematical models, which served as the design parameters for an electric generator. His approach overcomes both speed and tethering challenges. His design is based on a geometry borrowed from proven systems in Nature.

Prof. Finnigan's bioWave generators move in the ocean's ecosystem as if they were kelp. His devices have no rotary movements that resemble fans or mills, nor creates barrages that stop the flow of nutrients which causes siltation, thus not posing any known danger to aquatic life. Perhaps the most important feature is that bioWave moves with the flow of the currents and the waves. Instead of bracing the mechanics against the excessive forces created by the unavoidable storms, Prof. Finnigan succeeded in adopting the ultimate safety system: when a storm hits the area, the bioWave will lie flat on the ocean floor, just like kelp does.

The bioWave technology has left the development phase and in 2015 the company, BioPower Systems (BPS), deployed a 250 kW bioWave pilot unit near Port Fairy, Victoria. The project received funding from the Australian Renewable Energy Agency (ARENA) and the Government of Victoria. The bioWave oscillating structure is 26 metres tall, and feeds the generated electricity, and connects to the grid, via an undersea cable.

Natural Ways to Avoid Fire and Flame

Asbestos was once appreciated as a naturally occurring mineral fibre that provides roofing and insulation that did not burn. It has since been conclusively identified as a carcinogen. Yet, decades after incontrovertible scientific and medical studies have proven this beyond any doubt, asbestos remains available on the market in some countries. Even more ironically, countries like Canada, that pride themselves on a progressive approach to sustainability, permitted open-pit asbestos mining up until 2011.

Both Europe and the USA have sharply restricted the use of asbestos. A number of billion-dollar out-of-court settlements suppressed industry's appetite to pursue its use. However, there is another side to the coin. Legislation around the world mandates the use of fire and flame-retardants in children's clothing, car seats, interior textiles, airplanes, and office furniture. The quest for a family of chemicals that lowers the possibility of fires started by cigarette butts or candles, has stimulated the development of bromine and halogen-based chemicals. These fire and flame-retardants work. The only inconvenience is that they too seem to cause cancer. Worse, mammals in the Arctic accumulate these fire-retardants in their fatty tissues and reproductive organs, when these chemicals find their way to the Arctic. However, since no one can explain the pathway by which they arrive, there is no verifiable link to bromine and halogen-based products. Thus, no legal responsibility can be assigned. Industry will continue to manufacture and sell these products.

Will consumers continue to ignore the havoc caused by the dumping and incineration of halogens and bromines? Scientists wonder if polar bears will become extinct more quickly from chemically induced infertility or from habitat disruption through climate change. A few substitutes like phosphorus-based retardants have been introduced to the market; however, industry claims that there is no substitute for the effectiveness of bromine. Mats Nilsson, a scientist and the founder of the Swedish firm Trulstech, has developed a portfolio of gels and powders made from abundantly available food-grade ingredients that he calls "Molecular Heat Eaters (MHE)". The product is successfully manufactured and commercialised through Deflamo AB, based in Malmö, Sweden. It is a product that makes sense. Our bodies have a unique capability to manage heat and oxygen. If heat is channelled away from a fuel source, and if oxygen is converted to carbon dioxide, there is no risk of fire. Most chemistry students learn this as the Krebs Cycle. Here is a worthwhile substitution: replace carcinogenic chemicals that have a negative impact on our health with food-grade materials that are available in abundance at comparable prices. Imagine the competitive advantage of Nilsson's fire and flame-retardants. It is no longer necessary to choose between immediate death by fire or slow death by cancer! We can replace products that destroy life with products that promote life.

The biochemicals needed for Nilsson's inventions could be derived from grape pomace, a by-product of wine making, or citrus peel that is waste from juice production.

These products succinctly illustrate the advantages of learning from Nature. The crowning beauty of Nilsson's technology is that it has the potential to solve massive ecological challenges. When wildfires devastate California or Colorado, the US Forest Service rushes to spray chemicals by plane. Now, we can blanket the area with food-grade chemicals, instead of phosphorous, and secure fast relief from fire without detriment to the ecosystem.

In future, the same technology could be used to eliminate the risk of explosions in mines. Excessive concentrations of naturally occurring methane fill mining tunnels and lead to underground disasters when mining equipment create sparks while gouging out rock. At present, mining equipment is manufactured from expensive nickel and cobalt metal alloys to reduce the risk of sparks. Using the air channels already in place to mist the mining space with food-grade fire-retardants could suppress sparks and prevent explosions. This would additionally reduce the demand for cobalt and nickel mining, and the subsequent expensive processing into high-performance metals.

These advances in applied physics, physical chemistry, chemistry, and biology give us reason to believe that innovations inspired by Nature are shaping a new economy. In an interview, Achim Steiner, Executive Director of the United Nations Environment Programme, and since 2017 the administrator of the United Nations Development Programme declared, "*Many technologies are in commercial use. We're not talking about theory anymore; these are real results occurring in the real world and in the real market*".

Unlocking Solutions

The vital relationship between the laws of physics and the basic conditions of how we produce, consume, and survive, is not given much attention in physics classrooms at present. Yet, as I pointed out in the first chapter, it is in observing the basics of physics that we realise how minute shifts in pressure, temperature, and moisture content create outstanding products and processes that, with their artfulness, precision, and effectiveness, far outshine the results of genetic modification. Instead of manipulating the biology of life, we can find inspiration in the ways that Nature employs physics.

Quick, once-off solutions do not appear to be resolving the complex problems we are confronting, both in our individual homes and places of work and our greater common home, our Earth. Successful businesses and industries will be the ones that are re-examining the basics of science and seeking inspiration for innovative solutions that apply physics first and chemistry second. If we consider the underlying forces and the systemic conditions that predict the results prescribed by physics, then we will understand why chemistry in Nature differs markedly from the chemistry that dominates our lives today. Retaining molecules in natural products and production processes reflect the best possible use of physics. The gecko and the mussel demonstrate two sticking systems, each of which performs within clear physical parameters. While green chemistry and even sustainable biology are important goals, if we look more deeply, we will grasp the forces that determine both. When looking to apply a Blue Economy approach, we always look first to territory in which the solutions are needed, and then to how physics can be harnessed to deliver them. Such a completely different approach is unmatched by market leaders – and is delivering staggering results, as this book will detail.

This may well be the logic that we need to pursue in an era of economic slow-down. Instead of using chemistry – traditional or green – Nature shows us ways to eliminate the need for any harsh chemistry. We need to go beyond the closed loop, recycling everything. We need to eliminate many components from the loop, and physics allows us to achieve that goal. Green chemistry and sustainable biology face the challenges of finding funding and navigating the lengthy approval processes required by the government authorities of developed nations. Such drawbacks hamper the rapid business reconfigurations required by economic crises. The market's competitive framework needs encouragement to help fast-track procedural regulatory requirements as new insights unfold from our observation and implementation of what Nature achieves.

Imagine the impact such innovations can have on building design. There is a great number of breakthroughs that could be utilised in homes, offices, and factories. Buildings that use these technologies are, first and foremost, healthier for their occupants, and an additional benefit, as demonstrated by Renzo Piano's Centre Pompidou in Paris, France (together with Richard Rogers and Gianfranco Franchini), is that everyone who has the chance to explore such a building sees the elegant application of the laws of physics. As we adopt a Blue Economy approach our use of non-renewable resources can dwindle to just a fraction of what it is at present, requiring less investment and less cost. Now imagine we apply these innovations and creative business models to cities. Then real smart cities and real eco-cities would emerge – where we go beyond the monitoring and steering of energy and water consumption and embrace building and city design that truly transforms our way of living.

In a Blue Economy we would go well beyond only efficiency and better return on investment. Much of what we believe we need is entirely unnecessary, and can be replaced by products and methods that are better and simpler than those most widely used today. Perhaps something, made from chemistry can be replaced by something made from 'nothing', an effect created by physics. Rather than diminishing our economy, these alternatives can make it stronger, freeing up material resources and currency, empowering us to respond to the needs of all. Thus, with a bundled portfolio of innovations based on pragmatic solutions to critical issues across an entire territory, where they have already been faced and solved by many species on Earth, we can redefine the competitive model. Such insights can help solve many of the sustainability challenges we face while giving power and precedence to entrepreneurs. When we create pathways for strengthening our capacity to respond to the basic needs of all – water, food, health care, housing, and energy – with what is readily available, we are building an openly sourced Blue Economy from the ground up.

The few insights shared here, from dew point management through the interplay of colour, heat conductivity and hydrophilia, put us on track for new thought patterns. Please read the work of my dear friend, Janine Benyus, for a plethora of inspirational stories of learning from Nature. The design of a building or home need no longer be only about saving energy. Instead it can be about replacing old ideas, like the use of polyurethane, with new ideas that go beyond insulation. This is a refreshing approach. The growth economy was always driven by consuming and investing more, which is not sustainable and certainly not wise. By applying the insights shared here, a reduction in consumption provides a stimulus to the economy, whereby a material or a process that uses a harsh chemical solution is replaced by a solution that merely utilises the properties of physics, to great effect.

Something … is replaced by … nothing. This sets the tone for our emerging model of the Blue Economy.

4

REAL CASES OF EMULATING ECOSYSTEMS

***Motanai* Waste not, want not.**
—Japanese proverb

A vibrant economy is essential to sustainability. The reverse is also true. Without true sustainability no economy can continue to function. With that in mind, perhaps it will not surprise you to learn, as you will while reading this book, that a solution to our current economic troubles lies in understanding and applying the logic of an 'ecosystem'. Nature demonstrates true effectiveness – and true sustainability – all the time. If we were to develop our economies following Nature, we could use energy and resources efficiently and without waste, and create hundreds of millions of jobs. Has it ever occurred to you that in Nature everyone contributes to the best of their ability and no one is unemployed or relegated to a kindergarten or a retirement home?

Ecosystem models offer the keys to abundance, and the means to share with all. An economic system inspired by ecosystems would work with what is locally available, such as naturally occurring energy resources that express the laws of physics, first and foremost. Physics describes the underlying forces that are dynamically utilised by every species on Earth. This insight is the pathway to sustainability. Transforming the current economic model by emulating the logic modelled in ecosystems will not only allow us to meet basic needs but create an economy of abundance – a

Blue Economy. Emulating the function and effectiveness of ecosystems and natural habitats is a pragmatic way to achieve sustainability and high resource productivity while remaining competitive and generating additional value.

Cascading nutrients and energy is another ecosystem elegance that we would do well to emulate. It is Nature's method of transforming apparent scarcity into sufficiency and ultimately abundance. We can picture a cascade as a waterfall, as a flow of nutrients that requires no power source other than the force of gravity. It offers a visual metaphor to help us comprehend how nutrients are transported from the species of one biological kingdom to that of another, for the benefit of all. Absorbed minerals feed micro-organisms, micro-organisms feed plants, plants feed other species, with the waste of one becoming nourishment for another. It is the cascading of energy and nutrients that leads to sustainability. It does so by reducing or eliminating external inputs such as energy, and also by eliminating waste and its cost, not just waste as pollution but also as inefficient use of materials.

Around the world there are successful and well-established examples of entrepreneurship – ones that illustrate how a Blue Economy is able to not only benefit the land but also its inhabitants, with the result that food security, livelihood security, and contributory occupations are available to all. In this chapter, we visit six projects on four continents where we clearly demonstrate that this is not merely an idea, but that it has been translated into reality:

Forest in Colombia

The remarkable revival of a tract of the Vichada savannah at Las Gaviotas in the Orinoco Basin of Colombia, accomplished by Paolo Lugari, that caught the attention of JP Morgan.

Tomatoes in Australia

The inspiration of Charlie Paton leading to the astounding case of growing tomatoes in an arid climate, simply using the forces of physics and seawater to generate a surplus of fresh water.

Livelihoods in Benin

A project in Benin, West Africa, where food and livelihood security were established through a symbiotic approach to waste management by Father Godfrey Nzamujo.

Carrots in Sweden

The vision of Håkan Ahlsten, for the island of Gotland to harness an iconic local agricultural produce, the humble carrot, to spur the development of an integrated, competitive local industry.

Native Americans in the USA

The efforts of Picuris Pueblo in reframing forest fire prevention into the possibility of creating an integrated biosystem, one that sustainably generates jobs, as well as provide highly nutritious food, an animal feed industry, and high quality construction materials.

Energy and Water in Spain

The pioneering efforts of Javier Morales and the citizens of the island El Hierro (part of the Canary Islands), who used a renewable energy project to not only create clean energy but also fresh water, which stimulated the local economy and revived lost industries, and in the process drew back young people that had left in search of work.

What all of these cases have in common, is the fact that they emulate Nature's nutrient cascade, and the utilisation of energy sources that function mainly according to the laws of physics. In addition, each case achieves food and energy security while generating multiple benefits, including positive cash flow, reduction of material intensity, and energy savings. These are all competitive communities; ones that are not against globalisation but which have simply designed a production and consumption model that works much better for them.

Regenerating Rainforest in Colombia

When Paolo Lugari first proposed regenerating a worthless tract of land along the Orinoco River in the Colombian Vichada savannah back into a lush rainforest, it was thought to be impossible. The land was considered worthless, the soil pH was low, the water was not potable, and there was no easy access to it via land, water, or by air. Who would purchase even an acre? Paolo Lugari, however, could envision a lush rainforest and saw to it that land was obtained through land grants, which cost approximately US$ 2.50 per acre. Lugari persevered, and with neither experience nor funding, he started planting, using a creative approach to regenerate the dry savannah, and transforming it into a haven of lush tropical biodiversity. Now, a quarter-century later, Lugari welcomes visitors to the 20,000 acres of restored rainforest. The innovation came when he and his team discovered that the symbiosis between mycorrhizal fungi and the Caribbean pine tree not only secured the survival of 92% of the seedlings planted in the waste land, but also changed the physical attributes of the region. But how?

When inoculated with the fungus *Pisolithus tinctorius*, the small Caribbean pine tree, *Pinus caribaea*, creates a discrete shaded space protecting the soil, seeds and shoots from the sun's ultraviolet rays. Although the heat stress remains high, contributing to a thick carpet of dropped pine needles, the pine tree grows to maturity because it is well-nourished by the fungus. This carpet improves the moisture content of the soil, simultaneously trapping producers of humus that would otherwise wash away in the torrential rains that are a characteristic of that climate for at least three months per year.

Importantly, this debris cover also moderates the temperature of the soil. When rain falls on hot soil, it does not penetrate easily, even if the surface is porous, and thus washes away more readily, never permitting the build up of new soil. When rain falls on cooler soil, it is more likely to be absorbed into the ground. Thus the increase in soil permeability, caused by cooling of the soil, creates an environment for new seeds to gain hold. As the emerging forest grows, diversity flourishes and rain becomes more abundant. The dry savannah with poor quality drinking water and overly acidic soil now becomes not just a forest, but a rainforest abundant in fresh water, with a richer soil ideal for flourishing plant life.

A Japanese film crew, arriving in Las Gaviotas to record what few could believe possible, observed clouds approach and float above the savannah. The moment these clouds drifted over the forest's cooler sphere, the crew was amazed to experience the refreshing rain that began to fall. The green forest is indeed fresher than the heat-absorbing plains. When over the cool surface, the clouds drop their moisture as a result of the lower dew point.

> *Leaving behind 450 years of slash-and-burn agriculture and the cultivation of invasive grasses used as cattle fodder, Las Gaviotas entwined fungi and trees in an elegant symbiosis, creating the conditions that revived an entire rainforest.*

Despite these stunning meteorological and soil shifts, perhaps the most highly touted result of all has been an equally stunning increase in land value. Land that produces is land that has value. Over a 21-year period, the value of each acre of savannah converted to rainforest, measured solely on the values of fresh water, harvestable food, industrial output, renewable energy, fuel for mobility and available livelihood, increased as much as three-thousand fold. Before restoration, people in the region around Las Gaviotas had no chance of employment. They suffered from gastrointestinal diseases, could not obtain safe drinking water, and lacked reasonably available medical care. Just one generation later, water is a Commons distributed practically for free. The sale of surplus water to the rich in Bogotá, who are prepared to pay the same price they pay for a bottle of imported branded water, such as San Pellegrino or Evian water, provides Las Gaviotas with an important cash flow.

Inspired by its healthy cash flow, its portfolio of technologies licensed worldwide, its generous wages, and its contributions to the local community of 2,000 inhabitants, William B. Harrison Jr, the Chairman of JP Morgan, championed the expansion of Las Gaviotas from 20,000 to 250,000 acres. Based on JP Morgan's Emerging Markets analysis, he offered Pres. Alvaro Uribe, the President of Colombia, a US$ 300 million investment package. Such an expanded initiative could generate an estimated 100,000 jobs over the next decade, while offsetting the carbon emissions of countries like Belgium and the Netherlands.

Where government services and traditional business didn't provide direct benefits to the local population, one man's vision and his seminal work saw to it that the people could meet their own needs – and more – with what was locally available to them. This accomplishment of social and environmental caretaking, by embracing the ideals of entrepreneurship, achieved success by emulating the natural processes of ecosystems. The success of Las Gaviotas illustrates that it is the interplay of physical factors such as pressure, temperature, surface tension, conductivity, magnetism, and so much more, that makes the wind blow and the trees grow. Once we understand the dynamic connections and interactions of Nature's interwoven tapestries, whole new approaches will unfold. Attempts to improve agricultural productivity through techniques such as genetic manipulation and even drip irrigation will soon seem antiquated.

The Las Gaviotas project serves as an example that suggests that these once-rich rain forests can be recovered to generate not only thriving environments but a range of viable industries that can create jobs and strengthen struggling communities all around the nation. Another example of this comes from the South Australian town of Port Lincoln, where an innovator saw what no one else had seen: the potential to use arid conditions to grow tomatoes, not by pumping in vast quantities of water, but by harnessing the laws of physics to create perfect conditions for growing tomatoes – while, in fact, at the same time generating fresh water!

Growing Tomatoes in Seawater Greenhouses with no Water!

Following the mining downturn and closure of Port Lincoln's two major power stations, the local economy then looked to tourism as Port Lincoln, with the magnificent Flinders' Ranges as its saviour, is the gateway to the Australian Outback. No one would, however, have guessed that inspiration would come from a Brit, Charlie Paton, who had designed a seawater greenhouse. In the process, greenhouse crops can be cost-effectively grown in arid conditions using the basic laws of thermodynamics – and rather than requiring water as traditional greenhouses do, it in fact generates fresh water. The system is based on seawater which creates conditions that see condensation form in the greenhouse in two ways. Firstly, seawater is drawn from the ocean to cool the ground under the greenhouse to around 15 °C. Secondly, seawater is dripped through the porous cardboard walls, with outside air at somewhere between 30 °C and 45 °C being drawn through the walls, using large fans to cool the air and increase the humidity.

After setting up small scale seawater greenhouses in Oman, Abu Dhabi, and the Canary Islands, Charlie co-founded the company, Sundrop Farms. It had set up a seawater greenhouse in the saltbush plains surrounding South Australia's coastal town of Port Augusta in 2012, as it has the perfect conditions for such a process. A significant opportunity existed here for Australia to harness the low-cost concept of seawater glasshouses, one that could be used in cities and towns all along the 5,000 km stretch of coast – to create jobs, avoid the need to transport produce long distances, and create a range of additional economic opportunities.

Once it was proven that tomatoes could be cultivated in Port Augusta's arid climate, demand for produce grew rapidly and the facility evolved. Under the leadership of German entrepreneur, Philipp Saumweber, a AUD$ 200 million investment was made to upscale the plant and shift from the use of wind and temperature to generate water, to harnessing the sun through a state-of-the-art solar thermal plant to desalinate seawater, still using the evaporative properties of the cooling baffles. Securing a 10-year forward commitment from supermarket giant Coles, some 15,000 tonnes of tomatoes were produced on the farm in 2016.

Charlie Paton and Philipp Saumweber have shown that there is enormous potential to harness the simple mechanisms of Nature to farm crops using seawater, and that these can be expanded, using state-of-the-art technology, to large scale operations, even in arid areas. This represents a revolution in the way countries with arid land consider agriculture – with the potential to affect millions of people worldwide. There is a window of opportunity here, to turn this into a mainstream production system anywhere in the world since the hydrological cycles can be emulated at all altitudes without restriction, and assuming a 15 °C differential can be created between land and air temperatures, the magic of thermodynamics will generate water.

Using Maggots to Provide Food Security in Africa

The Songhai Centre located in Porto Novo, the capital city of Benin in West Africa, was created by Father Godfrey Nzamujo, a Dominican priest, in 1984. It was in the same year that Paolo Lugari launched his Las Gaviotas reforestation scheme that Father Nzamujo undertook a programme to provide food for the people, eradicating hunger and malnutrition. It began on a few acres of swampland granted to them by a former President, Matthieu Kérékou. A quarter-century later, it has come full circle – from environmental degradation to an impressive endorsement of the possibilities for African food and livelihood security.

Under Father Nzamujo's guidance, Songhai developed a logical system for cascading nutrients and energy to achieve remarkable outcomes. Waste water (both grey and black) from toilets, washing, as well as all animal and human waste, is collected in a three-chamber digester. Chopped water hyacinth, an invasive aquatic plant, is added. In the digester the combined biomass produces methane, providing energy for local use. After mineralisation, the remaining material becomes feed for zooplankton, phytoplankton, and benthos, which in turn feed fish in their aquaculture project. The digester design provides a high level of curing and gas production, imitating the acid-alkaline switch our body uses to restrain the growth of detrimental bacteria. The pH evolves from being acidic in the digester, to being highly alkaline in the neighbouring algae ponds. Anaerobic bacteria, complemented by sunlight, aid the powerful transformation of CO_2 into oxygen by micro-algae, and complete the natural systems design that eliminates pathogens. Songhai faced another major hygienic challenge: flies. Although chemical spraying was considered, this could not be recommended in a food-producing environment that aspired to the organic label. The strategy pursued by Father Nzamujo was extraordinary. He turned to maggots, the larvae of flies, to solve the problem.

All slaughterhouse waste at Songhai is collected in a special area where hundreds of small, barely hand-width-deep cement squares are completely surrounded by canals patrolled by carp. The open area is covered with a huge net so that birds cannot enter. The mesh is just large enough for hungry flies to pass through. Flies thrive on the castoffs of the slaughtering process – everything that cannot be turned into edible product. This feast for flies turns the area into a massive maggot farm, with a production capacity of nearly one tonne of maggots per month. And there is not one fly to be spotted anywhere else at the centre! All the flies converge on what is, to them, a delectable soup of nutrients, gorging themselves and laying eggs to produce larvae in abundance. Water is then sprinkled over the half-digested waste, so that the maggots float to the surface, to be easily harvested. What can you do with maggots? The primary local economic use is as an inexpensive feed for fish and quail. Both quail eggs and fish contribute to good nutrition and food security. However, it is the maggot enzymes that offer an even greater potential for economic value. They have medicinal properties that are proven to heal wounds, by stimulating the growth of fibroblast cells. How do you extract the enzymes while reserving the live maggots as feed for fish and quail? A brilliantly simple solution: in the same way that we use salt water to induce vomiting, maggots will regurgitate when they are immersed in salt water.

Here is another case of elegant ecosystems design. Father Nzamujo's initial goal was to provide food security, and here he is now also committed to reducing fly-borne disease by finding a natural means of controlling flies. His solution, in turn, provided bird and fish feed as well as the enzymes that effectively accomplish natural healing. While the biology and biochemistry of maggots clearly demonstrate medicinal properties, a new hypothesis proposes that these enzymes generate a barely measurable electrical pulse, to date undetected as there is no appropriate instrumentation with which to do so. This pulse stimulates cell regeneration and promotes healing. An innate ability to apply the laws of physics (electricity and magnetism) as a stimulus for healing, exists in maggots.

Maggot treatment is approved by governments worldwide, especially for patients suffering from diabetes. The "purified" version – without the maggots – gained fast-tracked regulatory approval with the support of the British National Health Services (NHS). This is most welcome, since the main cause of amputations in Africa is untreated wounds.

David and Jason Drew were inspired by this example and raised millions of dollars to recreate this business model at the Elsenburg agricultural research centre, which is owned by the University of Stellenbosch and is situated north-east of Cape Town, South Africa. Their company, AgriProtein, which aims to replace fish protein used in animal feed with maggots, thereby reducing the stress on the oceans, had by 2014 surpassed the production capacity of Songhai. The brothers had raised sufficient funds to scale production to 50 tonnes per day by 2017.

For South African farmers, maggots represent a valuable source of protein for feeding chickens, pigs, and fish. It is a feed that is produced locally, so there is no longer any need to clear rainforests for soy production. It also decreases the demand for marine fish meal. AgriProtein believes that what makes maggot farming highly lucrative, is the fact that the prices of both protein sources (soy and fishmeal) have soared in recent years – as a result of an increase in global food demand, environmental issues and over-fishing depleting the supply of fish meal. Jason Drew points out that insect larvae are a natural food source for chickens in the wild and fish in streams, and that, “their nutritional composition is nearly as good as that of fishmeal, and better than that of soya”.

The interest is spreading around the world. The National University of Colombia based in Bogotá, is pursuing this health and business opportunity, under the leadership of Dr Hilderman Pedraza Vargas, a medical doctor who uses the saliva of maggots to treat the wounds of victims of land mines.

Carrots and Beer Keeping an Island Dream Afloat

Nearly a millennium ago the greatest merchants of Florence and Russia built churches and warehouses on Gotland, a small but remarkable island in the centre of the Baltic Sea between Sweden and Latvia. Arriving in Visby, the capital city, leaves a lasting impression on visitors. The large stone wall that surrounds the city encompasses not only the historic buildings and cathedrals, but generations of tradition. As the 21st century arrived, the island’s inhabitants struggled to find ways to prosper in a globalised world economy. It seemed that tourism was the only option. With just under a million visitors annually, tourism is indeed the largest contributor to Gotland’s economy. During the summer holidays the population numbers grow ten times in size, only to implode for the rest of the year.

The citizens of Gotland had a fervent wish to create a future for their island, and particularly for succeeding generations, who would otherwise leave the island as soon as possible. Their vision was to design a sustainable community, in harmony with the resources of the land, juxtaposed against the background of its great historic accomplishments, and the recognition by UNESCO of Visby as a World Heritage City. At the invitation of Prof. Dr Carl-Göran Hedén, a member of the Swedish Royal Academy of Sciences, the community undertook an envisioning exercise, one that gathered together students, bankers, policy makers, researchers, and businessmen, to seek solutions.

Any observer looking for development opportunities other than tourism, will immediately focus on the countryside. Dotted with picturesque churches and domiciles, the agricultural landscape has been lovingly shaped throughout the centuries. When sugar beets were introduced a hundred years ago, it was produced successfully enough to create a new industry. Lacking appropriate economies of scale, the sugar mill closed down eighty years later, as globalisation consolidated the industry. There was little incentive to pursue any form of agriculture, except growing carrots. Carrots from Gotland, famous for their "sandy" look, have a superior taste due to the island's alkaline soil. Although producing carrots was not a problem, selling them from the middle of the Baltic Sea was a challenge. Furthermore, it was common for grocery store purveyors to reject a substantial portion of the harvest that did not meet their rigorous shape conformation standards.

The citizens evolved an innovative approach that took advantage of the natural cascading of nutrients while generating value and jobs. Håkan Ahlsten, the local banker, liked the idea of manufacturing a simple product: oven-fresh carrot cake. With such ready access to a fresh and abundant raw material, the idea of a carrot cake enterprise was impossible to ignore. Agreement was reached, and a delicious carrot cake recipe was quickly developed. Baked, then frozen, the Gotland cakes became much in demand throughout Sweden and as far abroad as Singapore and Hong Kong. In five years, employment at the local bakery jumped from a mere five to thirty employees.

The next major initiative was precipitated by the desire to achieve better market value by utilising the entire harvest. Mr Yngve Andersson, another of Gotland's upstanding citizens, invested in a carrot-sorting centre where nearly the entire island's harvest could be stored, sorted, and processed throughout the year, using sophisticated machinery. The massive harvest was machine-sorted into specific categories. Every variety was individually packaged, from baby carrots, long carrots, thin carrots, stronger and shorter carrots, to odd-shaped roots. Surprisingly, cleaned and packaged baby carrots, which were formerly considered too small to have any market value, could be sold for four times more than standard carrots. The largest carrots are not packaged but become carrot juice, a very profitable niche market. Interestingly, the largest carrots produce the most juice – as much as 40% more by volume. The shredded carrot pulp, rather than becoming waste, is an ideal pig feed.

Carrot sorting to generate higher value from the existing harvest posed major challenges. The optimal operation of the machinery called for the harvest to be processed as a large batch, but this presented a problem as the yield of carrots was spread out over time. In order to keep the carrots crisp and fresh until a sufficient batch was accumulated, the warehouse would need to be kept at a constant temperature of 0 °C, creating a substantial energy demand. When the economic persuasion of a better price supported the feasibility of this undertaking, the next challenge was meeting the operation's now increased energy requirements.

With the figures before him, Mr Yngve Andersson decided to take the risk of powering the facility exclusively with wind energy. The entire operation: warehousing, sorting, processing, packaging, selling into market segments – including deep-frozen carrot cakes – is entirely powered by wind energy. The capital investment in wind energy was recovered from international sales in just five years. The total estimated direct and indirect employment adds up to 250 jobs. Rethinking the farming of carrots generated jobs, cut costs, and successfully pointed the Gotlanders to a progressive path of job generation and livelihood security.

This is yet another case where finding value by integrating what is locally available creates sustainable and competitive industries that can influence economies, even when they are located on an isolated island in the Baltic Sea. To the Gotlander's credit, this is not their only initiative. Other breakthroughs demonstrate Gotland's pioneering spirit. Carrots are the most impressive case, but the combination of beer and bread production is just as commendable. The Gotland Brewery supplies excellent beer to the local population. The spent grain, left over from the brewing process, is shipped to the local bakery, Eskelunds Hembageri AB, where it is made into bread – another fine example of turning waste from one process into raw material for another. By using what is locally available, cascading nutrients, and encouraging entrepreneurs to implement competitive ideas, the citizens of Gotland have secured a core industry to underpin their livelihoods for years to come.

Fighting Fires and Raising Bison - A Progressive Pueblo

Raging forest fires often make the news, with wild fires regularly devastating vast ecosystems in the western United States. In an attempt to reduce this risk, the New Mexico Bureau of Land Management obtained a grant from the federal government to pay for the removal of small-diameter (up to seven inches) wood from the lands of Picuris Pueblo. Whether burned or dumped in a landfill, this cleared debris would contribute to the atmospheric carbon load. Lynda Taylor and Robert Haspel proposed an alternative, and worked with the Picuris Pueblo elders to design a solution that cascades nutrients and energy in harmony with Pueblo customs.

The reduction of forest fire risk by removal of the small diameter wood was quickly accomplished. The bulk of the cut wood was then processed for use as construction materials, by first being dried, then placed in recycled 40-foot shipping containers and preserved by being "smoked", as it was subjected to incomplete combustion of charcoal production. Wood unsuitable for construction was used for charcoal production. To honour Pueblo tradition, it was however necessary to eliminate the equipment tracks left in the forest by the brush-clearing vehicles. Mulch made from shredding the very small-diameter wood was inoculated with a native mushroom spore, then spread on the equipment tracks. Remarkably, just two years later, no tracks were to be found. The mushrooms are gathered as food by tribal members, while the mushroom substrate and waste, rich in amino acids, serve as feedstock for the newly introduced bison herd. With sufficient livestock feed and ongoing support from Taylor and Haspel, the Sam Family now supplies buffalo meat to local commercial markets.

What started as an effort to reduce the risk of fire that would typically result in burning or landfilling of culled wood, became an example of sustainable forestry through the creation of an integrated biosystem around mushrooms and feed, one that generated jobs, highly nutritious food, an animal feed industry, and high-quality construction materials. The Picuris Pueblo experience is an example of economic development based on natural systems, integrating what is locally available, and building on traditional values and practices.

This is a good example of how an entirely new economic paradigm emerges when old practices are replaced with something new that cascades nutrients and energy. Remarkable solutions emerge from reinterpreting the nature and function of energy and nutrients, allowing us to achieve greater resource efficiency, to build competitive local industries, and to adopt innovations that generate jobs and create added value. This is how ecosystems evolve to ever-more efficient systems, requiring ever-less energy expenditure for ever-more species. It is an all-inclusive cascade that leads to abundance at every level.

Bagasse, a Sweet Solution

The massive volumes of agro-waste our food industry produces can also be deftly handled by mirroring ecosystems. Take the case of sugar mainly sourced from cane. The commercial cane sugar content of sugar cane is around 10-15 percent. Thus, each tonne of sugar produced accounts for only a small portion of its source biomass. The rest, waste known as bagasse, is typically incinerated. Natural systems seldom use fire as a source of energy, whereas our now very sophisticated economies around the world use fire as the primary source, much like our caveman ancestors! Burning bagasse provides a cheap and available fuel source, but the only component that really supplies energy is the lignin. The rest, composed of hemicellulose and cellulose, just contribute to the carbon emissions when burned, as they incinerate without contributing useful heat.

Were we to use bagasse to produce paper, paper products, and cardboard, as has commenced on a small scale, it would clearly be a better outcome. Even though this tropical fibre does not fit the current supply chain management model, which is based on massive worldwide plantings of pine and eucalyptus, a quick calculation produces some astonishing figures. At the annual rate of 15 to 30 tonnes per acre, bagasse provides 100 to 200 tonnes of fibre in the seven years it takes the fastest growing pine trees to reach maturity. In terms of fibre, sugar cane handily tops the volume produced by trees from temperate climates.

Considering the potential value of using bagasse projects involving paper and packaging, allows us to begin to see how we can use what is renewably generated while building viable clusters of industries. It is our adherence to a wasteful industrial logic that leads to us using only the sugar in sugar cane and then burning the bagasse, at the high cost of damaging levels of carbon emissions. It is the same allegiance to short-sighted accounting that causes us to extract only the cellulose from pine trees to manufacture paper – and waste the remaining 70-80% of the tree. There are many other examples, such as the harvesting of coffee beans, leaving a staggering 99.8% of the total biomass as waste. The latest studies on solid municipal waste in the USA indicate that for each dollar spent on handling household waste in landfills, US$ 70 dollars per tonne are spent ondealing with the waste from agriculture, mining, and industry!

Imagine if we produced food like the rest of Nature does, cascading through living kingdoms from plants to fungi to animals to bacteria to algae, and back again in different directions and combinations, according to specific habitat … The only energy sources needed are sunlight and gravity, which are readily and freely available! Here are the glimmerings of a new economy, rooted in robust models that cascade nutrients, and generate food, habitat, employment, energy, and currency in renewable ways.

An Island in the Sun

The Canary Islands of Spain are one of the most popular destinations for European tourists. Many of the islands offer tourists beautiful and dramatic coastlines and sunshine all year around. The island of El Hierro, however, is quite different. It suffers a chronic water shortage and over the past centuries thousands of islanders emigrated, as the lack of water threatened the livelihood of the whole community. When the Spanish and Canary Islands governments proposed building a civilian rocket launching base for satellites and space probes to generate jobs through military expenditures, the population voted against it, due to significant environmental, social and economic concerns. The proposed project did, however, ignite the passion of the citizens to create their own prosperity, and a vision emerged to achieve self-sufficiency in energy and water. The vision was clear, but the pathway to reality was blurred.

It was Javier Morales, the Vice-Mayor of the island, who, when realising that nearly US$ 10 million of hard earned cash was needed to purchase fuel to deliver energy to the island and the desalinisation plant every year, proposed an alternative. He conceived the idea to use ten years of such guaranteed expenses, to mobilise the capital to invest in a US$ 100 million renewable energy program. It took 17 years to translate the vision into a reality but by 2014 the island began to generate electricity from five majestic wind turbines, with the excess power used to desalinate and pump fresh water more than 700 metres up to a sealed volcanic basin. When there is no wind, hydropower is generated as the pumped water rushes back down the mountain under the force of gravity.

However, the vision for this grand undertaking did not stop with providing the means to generate cheap, renewable energy because as a result of this system, the islanders now have double the amount of water at half the cost. This shift in the economics of water had an immediate and lasting impact on the local economy. It stimulated many industries that were lost over time due to low rainfall and high fuel costs associated with desalinisation of sea water. The slaughterhouse re-opened, the cheese and yoghurt factory now converts goat and sheep's milk into higher value products, organic bananas and pineapples are now grown, increasing the food palette, and the local winery has again started production. The economy thrives, unemployment is low, and the young who were tempted to emigrate now find that this island offers what they want: a challenge and a chance to make a difference.

*****

Clearly it is not only effective but essential for governmental and industrial leadership to seize the moment. At the same time, a new economic model will only succeed if it fosters business initiatives at grassroots level. It is here where the capacity to inspire the uninspired, to reach the unreached, and the opportunity to work communally with others (who often are neither considered nor given a chance), offer the core perceptual shift for ways in which we can make a difference in this world. Empowering young people, especially those in global pockets of unemployment and poverty, can achieve enormous economic impact. The constructs of scarcity are unappealing to those who must endure it. If you are without a job, hungry, abused, or frail, sustenance is more than polite conversation – it is a matter of immediate survival. If we operate the way natural systems do, it is entirely possible to create more jobs while increasing productivity and improving resource efficiency. You will never hear of unemployed trees, fish, maggots, mushrooms or gusts of wind!

How can we achieve abundance as a society? How can we continuously obtain renewable sources for food, shelter, livelihood, and wellbeing? In mirroring the successful methods found in natural ecosystems, we can begin to choose models with a generous scope, a propensity to cascade, a goal of planetary and species stewardship, and a future of perpetuity. Therein lies true economy. As we begin to grasp the fullness of this paradigm, the image of a Blue Economy rises like a phoenix from the ashes of the economic instability caused by a blind commitment to globalisation. It is an economy which, while cutting costs, draws strength and inspiration from Nature.

5

CHANGING THE RULES OF THE GAME

Today we have a temporary aberration called "industrial capitalism" which is inadvertently liquidating its two most important sources of capital – the natural world and properly functioning societies. No sensible capitalist would do that.
—*Amory Lovins*

Oak from Seed

By 2016, the innovations showcased throughout this book had generated an estimated three million jobs. While this is encouraging, it is a mere trickle for a world that needs a vast river of one billion new jobs. Where the bailout of defunct industries and financial institutions may be money down the drain, investments in innovations that are part of a systemic portfolio applied across entire territories, can provide a catalytic effect in one after the other of the world's economies – to bring about the change we all need to sustain ourselves and the communities in which we live.

Even someone without business experience and only a grasp of the fundamental principles of a Blue Economy can have an entrepreneurial chance to succeed. Human beings are amazing; from being born helpless infants we quickly learn and develop, and after just 10-12 months we are walking! If a new solution requires less expenditure or energy, can redirect existing expenditure locally, or can deliver multiple income opportunities where there was thought to be none left, then start-up capital or micro-investments may be all the encouragement needed to make it happen.

Crisis generates a unique degree of freedom to innovate, and a window of opportunity to fast track initiatives and businesses that meet basic needs, where the status quo has no interest to act and no chance to succeed. The ventures we contemplate may be once-in-a-lifetime opportunities to reorient our economy. In inner city, rural, and peri-urban environments, in the North and South, East and West, we have a chance to introduce innovations and business models that respond better to our economic needs than 200 years of industrial progress.

In the last two months of 2008 alone, the worldwide financial crisis caused an estimated net loss of 50 million jobs in emerging nations. A continuing crisis or lacklustre growth, hovering between zero and one percent, could push another 200 million people into extreme poverty, in spite of the Millennium Development Goals all countries have agreed to strive for. The International Labour Organisation reports that the number of "working poor" could reach 1.4 billion, or half the working population of the world's developing countries. The youth of Spain and Greece must tolerate the fact that, in 2016, more than half of their friends under the age of 26 do not have jobs. Even if economic growth were to pick up and maintain itself for years to come, the present model would never be able to absorb such an offer of human capital. How can we condone such a travesty? It has been reported that 3.8 million working Brits do have jobs, but are living in poverty.

How can we abide such loss of human potential? It is with a sense of urgency that we need to focus on the solutions that can make a difference in the lives of many. Achieving livelihood security means individuals can obtain food, shelter, and comfort, provide for their families, and experience a measure of dignity and satisfaction from the contribution of their labour. Innovations that emulate Nature's cascading effect can offer an invitation to a greater and more abundant future, thriving with diversity. The jobs potentially created may well be counted in the hundreds of millions.

New Possibilities, New Perspectives

We may compare economic upheavals that grip the world to what Nature accomplishes with volcanic eruptions and tornadoes. Although such natural disasters wreak destruction and cause tragic loss of life, such extreme, out-of-bounds states also restore the prevalence of ambient conditions. They are the exceptions that confirm the rule. Such exceptions put whole systems under enormous stress, yet they also provide an opening for new possibilities and new solutions where none were evident before.

In economic terms, when a breakdown in the system occurs at such a fundamental level, a completely new pathway to the market becomes available. Innovations that can emulate Nature's cascading effect and that make use of the laws of physics have the chance to succeed because they have little to gain from existing business models. They simply do not operate or compete using the same rules. Batteries containing toxic chemicals can be replaced by water and gravity; medical devices, surgery, and pharmaceuticals can be replaced with pure water and healthy diets and lifestyles, as Las Gaviotas achieved by offering free drinking water to all, and by providing a free bicycle to every child as of the age of six.

Instead of dealing constantly with waste, what Amory Lovins refers to as "unsaleable production", can be used to realise greater income than that generated by the core business of another totally unrelated business. In essence, this is why now, more than at any time in recent history, we have the opportunity to generate millions of jobs while moving away from scarcity, pollution, and waste. Furthermore, there are many resources that are readily available today that have been overlooked, such as thistles and nettles. These so-called "weeds" that grow by the millions of tonnes, are currently destroyed but can be the source of multiple bio-products.

By taking a Blue Economy approach, one that emulates Nature and puts physics to work, thousands of people in hundreds of countries will intuitively grasp the path to implementation and realise the opportunities in what lies before them. Their work will cascade and conjoin with the work of others – and create opportunities for even greater numbers of people. This fundamentally rooted approach emulates Nature's models. Such innovations are benchmarked, and the solutions are real.

These opportunities are tied to the reality that the use of non-renewable resources is a weakness. The use of toxic components is an even greater weakness. Failing to use, or even destroying, resources not considered part of the core business definition are lost opportunities and significant weaknesses. Shedding thousands of jobs does not promote customer loyalty nor build corporate knowledge required to implement innovations; resisting change and receiving government bailouts are simply other forms of energy wasted. They engender no confidence and have no chance of long-term success. Paying excessive bonuses to top management undermines any grain of loyalty that might have survived in both staff and customers.

For the past two decades, prominent and eloquent scholars, academics, and leaders have lectured on and presented many of the breakthroughs described in this book. Introduced by various researchers and with various names, examples of Nature Technology (NT) have been put forth around the world. Many brilliant and enthusiastic researchers and innovators have contributed to the growth and interest in the field. As the first awareness of Nature Technology achieved international prominence, research dollars were allocated to study innovations that could direct business towards sustainability. The media reported these innovations in stories accompanied by marvellous photographs and films. Televised presentations all found large and appreciative audiences eager to know more of the next fascinating flora or fauna performance unimagined by humans.

Yet top business management remained uninterested. With the exception of a few cases, notably in Germany and Japan, market leaders fell short of adopting or promoting any of these technologies. Industry barely paid lip service to the possibilities and hardly responded to proposals. Business executives attended presentations that outlined these marvellous opportunities and voiced their enthusiasm. Yet they returned to their offices to continue business as usual. At Vice-President Al Gore's Expert Panel on Solutions for Climate Change held in New York in January 2008, it was common to hear that although venture capital had its antennas directed towards Nature Technology, most of the proposed innovations were simply "too different to get traction on the ground". Perhaps this is true, for these innovations essentially alter the current business model, and business experts unwilling or unable to adapt will have little understanding and little in common with the emerging approaches.

If we are serious about designing a new economic model, one that is richly inspired by natural solutions that have evolved over time, then it is not enough to attend lectures, read reports, watch colourful documentaries, and contemplate connections. There is a major hurdle that must be surmounted to move from talk to action. The key is to achieve a competitive and strategic positioning of these innovations by vigorous operators in an open economy, mapping a pathway within the competitive environment – one that leads from discovery, to understanding the science, to replacing the present unhealthy and unsustainable production and consumption model, with something better.

How do we transform our present socio-economic downturn, and our present economic system that is so woefully in need of improvements, into a system that:

- promotes life,
- strengthens resilience,
- relies on what is available,
- builds on sustainable practices,
- works with the flow of physics,
- offers innumerable opportunities to learn,
- adapts to changing conditions,
- responds to basic needs,
- builds community,
- instils a sense of responsibility beyond oneself,
- generates jobs,
- creates multiple revenues, and
- provides challenges?

We risk that our children will be confronted by the results of the same mistakes we have endured: wars waged, human rights violated, worldwide hunger, chronic diseases and rampant poverty, as society at large remains distracted and disengaged. There is a great need to encourage the freedom to improve, the liberty to rethink and re-imagine, to finding solutions that are just, equitable, and stabilising. Whether theirs are fresh, young faces in posh Manhattan preschools, or faces streaked by grime and hardship in the favelas of Ecuador, the new generation is easily inspired by opportunities that are alive and present around them. Why are our business leaders missing out? Are there enough entrepreneurs with the will to transform our economic systems so that, as a society, we can move beyond unsustainable rampant consumerism and exhausting the resources available to us?

The wealth of innovations before us certainly provides an impetus for this urgently needed economic shift. Imagine an economy without a scarcity consciousness, a limiting belief in lack. Imagine an economy inspired by the abundance of Nature, one that evolves to sufficiency, where moments of stress catalyse abundance, where the abiding impetus is to realise ever more creative ways to stimulate innovation. Imagine an economy that encourages new generations to achieve greater success than their parents ever did – greater even than their parents could imagine, greater than they could ever dream of.

Why the old business approach won't get us there

Although applying the cascading model may be most attractive to innovative business organisations with broader and stronger social missions, the opportunity to generate jobs in the new economy will no longer be based on the time and motion studies that brought us 19th and 20th century labour productivity. New job generation opportunities will emerge from "eco"-facture, not "manu"-facture, shifting from production that reduces the need for things to be made by the hand of man to rather be made by the forces of Nature, and to one that provides greater employment while reducing the impact on the environment. The new industries that emerge will utilise processes that conform to the same physical rules that Nature follows.

Harsh chemicals, refined metals, and other polluting and non-renewable materials will be replaced by solutions achieved through simple physics – gravity, pressure, and temperature. Eco-facture will replace energy-intensive and toxic processes with ambient temperature operations that make use of natural variations of pressure, and other principles of physics to produce goods – like making a Kevlar alternative from spider silk at room temperature. Waste will return to being considered a resource. Locally available materials will be incorporated into materials streams. Market standards will be transformed, and creative ideas will take precedence over out-dated and stagnant business norms where the status quo rules out changes to revenue streams.

Many companies today still operate under established management school doctrine that does not encourage people to think "out of the box" – which given current times, is sorely needed. The traditional business model delivered a lot of wealth and lifted many into middle class. It is based on a set of core principles, outlined below, that although these once brought growth and prosperity, they now hinder progress in meeting the critical needs of our time. Our challenge is not only to get out of the box, but also to find a way to leave all the boxes behind and work with the landscape of these management principles, while replacing old limitations with new opportunities.

Many years ago, Mr Soichiro Honda, founder of Honda Motor Company, was asked if he had done a SWOT analysis (strengths, weaknesses, opportunities and threats) when considering whether to evolve from a motorbike manufacturer to an automobile producer. He responded, "If our team had run that business case analysis, we would never have ventured into the car business." He quickly added, "I simply made a list of the weaknesses of the world's biggest carmakers – and that list was quite long," he concluded with a smile.

MANAGEMENT PRINCIPLE 1: CORE BUSINESS DEFINED BY CORE COMPETENCE

Graduates of business schools around the world follow the axiom that any initiative must subject itself to a thorough business analysis, producing detailed reports and mapping out clear-cut strategies for ways to succeed, and how to fend off major competitive forces. Corporate CEOs and managers are trained and expected to operate within well-defined fields that have clear parameters for success. If a company is not competitive, it is not viable; if it does not generate sufficient cash flow, it will fail to exist. Achieving market share means consumers repeatedly buy a product when offered at the perceived ideal combination of cost and quality. However, once mainstreamed this model resists change, and often excuses collateral damage to the environment and even to society at large. The blinders of a core business approach can even disconnect managers from social ethics, creating a moral double standard. Remarkably, businesses that do "less bad" are lauded for doing good, but in reality less bad is still bad and can be avoided entirely.

The concepts of core business and core competence have dominated management directives for the past half-century. If a new approach emerges, that falls outside the scope of a core competence, such as a fishery operation expanding to produce haemoglobin, it is extremely difficult for management to accept. Furthermore, a new technology cannot be brought to the market solely on the basis of core competencies. Even though a market leader may be persuaded that a new technology is an opportunity to gain competitive edge and market share, there is no guarantee this technology will be approved for development. Often entrepreneurs outside of so-called market leaders or incumbents are more easily engaged by these new fields. The shift in technological platforms and the need for new competencies favours the start-up company, as it does not require experience in previous technologies used in the industry.

Take the case of the pacemaker. For 50 years this surgically implanted medical device has been the solution to irregularities in cardiac rhythm. A battery located near the collarbone powers the pacemaker. Current stress-filled lifestyles will lead to the need for millions of pacemakers – at a minimum cost of US$ 50,000 each – in the years to come. While everyone is focusing on developing more efficient batteries, locking the technology into a toxic and materials intensive option, the next generation of cardiac rhythm solutions requires neither surgery nor battery and is inspired by the heart of the whale. Based on an innovative application of nanotubes, the cost of this new intervention technology could be as low as US$ 500 dollars; the cost of the nanotubes is not more than a few dollars. Instead of introducing better batteries that continue to rely on surgery, the focus is now on a system that requires no batteries at all.

The introduction of a nanotube conductor that channels electrical current from healthy tissue over afflicted areas of the heart, was inspired by studying the channels of cells that provide conductivity around and through the heart of the whale. This is a knowledge base that is foreign to pacemaker manufacturers. No mainstream medical technology company has the foundation on which to build this new business. This innovation requires a conductor, carbon tubes, communication capabilities, natural energy sources, and chip designs. Such a retooling implies a deep chasm of unknown factors, making market leaders disinclined to invest. This sort of technology advancement would further require new staff, components, and business planning – comparable to the creation of an altogether new business division. Although challenging, it would present a significant opportunity. Most challenging of all, adopting such an innovative approach could very well undermine the lucrative income stream enjoyed by medical equipment companies, who would be likely to find ways to push back.

Who would venture into the unknown, particularly during a recession where the industry is required to focus on cost cutting? Would you expect industry giants like Boston Scientific or Medtronic to lead the way? If a top business executive has made the decision to acquire, at great expense, a gadget with guaranteed revenue potential from a proven and successful technology, why would they promote research funding or approve an investment that would undermine it? Who would accelerate the shift to this non-surgical approach when the revenues generated would be only a fraction of the cash flow each operation generates for the whole medical system, including companies with core competencies in surgery, anaesthesiology, pharmaceuticals and especially batteries?

The answer is obvious: no one who benefits from the market today. This creates the technological and institutional lock-in, blocking real innovations that can lead to multiple benefits a better common future, and are aligned to sustaining our amazing planet, as we have grown accustomed to it from market entry. The well-being of the client, and the lower cost to the insurance companies are not served by this blockage. Early moves were being made with Dr Jorge Reynolds and, against all odds, Boston Scientific supported the implant of a nanotube in a human patient by a medical team at the famous Mayo Clinic (USA) on October 8, 2016. While this is not a fully fledged testing programme, it is a first attempt to get the greatest scientific instrumentation companies in the world thinking about a battery-free world.

Another example is the innovative use of the physical properties of vortices. Currently, industries that desalinate, de-scale, and purify water depend on chemistry and reverse osmosis. Chemicals like chlorine kill bacteria, other acids de-scale, and a pressure of up to 800 PSI separates salt from seawater to create potable water. New technology is proven to utilise mounting pressure in a vortex to convert calcite to aragonite. Ever higher vortex pressure ruptures bacterial cell membranes, while the increased water density naturally achieves 4 °C, thus expelling salt, leaving the centre of water flow pure and clean. This is a fundamentally different approach than that taken by market leaders, although some market leaders, such as Nitto Denko, Siemens, and GE, may be ready to pursue these new developments. It requires not only forward thinking but also the appetite to master the challenges of new technology and the willingness to learn new competences.

MANAGEMENT PRINCIPLE 2: SUPPLY CHAIN MANAGEMENT

Supply chain management involves the oversight of materials, financial transactions, and delivery to market as products move from harvest or collection, to manufacture, to consumption. Even though a market leader may be persuaded that a new technology is an opportunity to gain competitive edge and market share, there is no guarantee this innovation will be approved for development. It must fit a manufacturing and distribution system – a supply chain – that predates the innovation and can carry the breakthrough to the end consumer. The strategic management team must make sure that research ideas make sense across all the affected areas of the company, such as marketing and manufacturing.

Many activities within a company need to converge around the introduction of new technologies and processes as well as the associated emerging product portfolios. Lack of a joint commitment from all departments, especially finance, supply chain management, and marketing, could unleash overt and covert conflicts based on personal interests, ranging from career plans and year-end performance bonuses, to corporate policies such as depreciation rules, tax planning, and quarterly earnings targets. In the end, these conflicts often undermine an innovation strategy to the detriment of the business. There are, in fact, remarkable innovations described herein that perfectly fit an existing supply chain model. Even in these cases, other factors mean that developing market share is a challenge that requires enormous fortitude and perseverance.

Here we would take the example of vaccines that traditionally require a complete cold-chain from production to transportation, delivery, and storage at the dispensing medical facility. The supply chain management is based on strict temperature control. If one link in the chain fails, the spoiled vaccines must be discarded and replaced. In developing countries, where access to refrigeration often depends on an irregular electrical power supply, the solution has been to invest in solar or propane-powered refrigeration to eliminate the risk of spoiling vaccines. Yet viable innovative solutions are available. Bruce Roser and his venture companies, Biostability and StablePharma, developed hero-stabilising technology, inspired by the resurrection fern (*Polypodium polypodioides*) and a microscopic invertebrate, the tardigrade, or water bear. These companies offer a freeze-drying system using tardigrades for preserving vaccines, applying this innovation with off-the-shelf equipment. This could handily facilitate a speedy integration of the innovation into the supply chain.

The previously mentioned fire and flame-retardants produced by Mats Nilsson, that are made of natural food-grade ingredients, have successfully integrated the supply chain for use in particle board (for furniture or housing), polyurethane (widely used in cars and homes), and carpet fibres (for offices, homes and airplanes). There are hundreds of additional applications that need to be developed. Even though he can offer these non-toxic chemicals in gel or powder form, bonding with the materials to be treated requires minor adjustments for each application. The research to make this possible takes time and requires money. Treating materials as varied as latex, nylon, and cellulose requires a detailed understanding of how to bond the food-grade retardants with the production processes for different materials. Lack of major investment funding has so far compromised Nilsson's ability to complete the necessary research and make the bonding specifications each material and process requires. Need we wait decades before halogen and bromine toxins will be replaced by Krebs Cycle-inspired molecules? Perhaps a clear preference, expressed by consumers, would encourage the world's largest homebuilders to test, approve, and utilise this product. One hopes that mainstream companies like Albemarle, Chematur, or BASF, will be ready to move forward with such breakthroughs.

MANAGEMENT PRINCIPLE 3: OUTSOURCING

Innovations that succeed in meeting core competence and supply chain management requirements must also fit with the management principle of outsourcing. Outsourcing is the process of subcontracting to third parties, so that management can dedicate time, people, and resources to its core competence. This requires more than the mere adoption of a new technology by corporate management. The company must act as change agent for all its suppliers and subcontractors. If Daiwa House (Japan), the world's largest homebuilder, decided to replace the fire-retardant chemicals they currently use, it would require developing and testing distinct product variations for each field of application, approval from industry regulators, determination of new adoption specifications, and coordination with the procedures of over 600 suppliers and subcontractors. That would be a significant task.

When this innovative flame-retardant does not contribute additional revenue, only better indoor air quality, then the shift of one technology to another during an economic downturn diverts significant management attention from its perceived core responsibilities – securing sales and improving cash flow. The will to change would come from some greater sense of allegiance to health and the environment than that given to ingrained management principles.

Another technology based on the Fibonacci sequence, common in Nature, demonstrates proven energy efficiencies that could save computer server companies millions by cooling their servers with natural geometry. Not only this, the shape also lends itself perfectly to moving water with low energy and zero turbulence, in fact inducing a laminar flow rather than using turbulence to increase pressure to force flow. Naturalist Jay Harman, while working with the Australian Department of Fisheries and Wildlife, observed the flow geometries of ocean and air currents. His observations led him to formulate what he terms the "Streamlining Principle," which translates Nature's flow efficiencies into streamlined design geometries. What he learned from the nautilus shell and kudu horn, significantly improves the performance, output, and energy usage of a wide range of fluid-handling mechanical movements while reducing noise. He founded Pax Scientific in 1997 and raised capital through the sale of sub-licenses, since the proof that this technology saves energy is beyond debate.

Yet, despite the exemplary performance of the technology, it has yet to be successfully mainstreamed some two decades later. The delays he and his team face are in accessing supply chain management, responding to fast turn-around cycles in the computer industry, and coordinating with the computer industry's worldwide outsourcing. The patents accumulate, and the revenue from advances on sub-licenses continues to provide the cash for further research. But to close the first mega-sale, a fourth obstacle must be overcome: the seal of approval of the Vice President for Finance.

MANAGEMENT PRINCIPLE 4: CASH FLOW AS KING

Even though new products may reduce costs by saving money or energy, while simultaneously benefiting the environment, they may not automatically produce sales. In standard business practice improved margins are great, because they generate additional cash with which new investment can be funded. But shelf space is expensive for consumer goods, and fast-moving consumer products, heavily advertised in the media, mean that the cash flows faster.

This is particularly relevant in periods of economic downturn and financial crisis, where giant international companies with a wide portfolio of products, are dramatically reducing the number of their offerings and brands, limiting their catalogue to products that have the fastest turnaround, and not necessarily the highest profit margin. The overall cash flow is much greater on a product with daily sales and a five percent margin as opposed to a 50% margin on a product that sells only once a month. Just-in-time inventory turnover eliminates holding products in a warehouse, freeing the capital locked in stored consumer or industrial goods. Fast-turnover goods are attractive to investors and shareholders, especially industries that manufacture and deliver basic necessities like food-related and health-related products not as subject to up-and-down economic cycles.

Part of the aftermath of the 2008 financial crunch was that credit was hard to get. When a technology like Watreco's vortex-based device to remove air from water might save 10-12% of energy usage as explained previously, corporate financial management will conclude that this reduction in energy cost does not justify committing scarce cash. The money spent to introduce this innovation may take years to recoup. That is sufficient to derail a lucrative purchase decision. Even outside of periods of economic downturn, innovations providing energy savings of even 20-30% are unlikely to be adopted for similar short-term reasons. Given this context, the idea of securing investments out of the savings new technologies offer is often not a viable approach, unless it is actively supported by government policies. Innovations must offer more than energy savings; simply costing less and saving more is not good enough, given the entrenched structures and technologies in place and the disturbance associated with changing. Market leaders have the confidence to make the necessary capital investment, only when much more additional revenue can be assured.

Innovations have largely been constrained to cutting costs, even with a 'green' agenda. This must be complemented by a portfolio of balance sheet, profit and loss, and cash flow operations that convince the Vice President for Finance of the validity of the proposal. When the concept of paper making from crushed stones was scientifically demonstrated, it did not take long for mining companies to adopt the technology, even though it is far from their core business. These companies could easily see the value in converting rock refuse and dried tailings from mines into raw materials for rock paper that requires no water and cuts the capital expenditure as well as the long term risk of a mine. As with all Blue Economy case studies, the value creation does not stop there… the elimination of the need to build a deposit or a dam by using the rock for another process reduces the need for cash up front by 25% – thus rendering the project easier to finance with lower risk. The acceptance is swift since the innovation generates multiple cash flows (ore and paper) and this speeds up decision-making.

MANAGEMENT PRINCIPLE 5: "CROWDING OUT"

Even when the corporate strategist, the supply chain manager, and the finance director have endorsed an innovation, the marketing team remains to be swayed. Inventors and innovators must develop a unique selling proposition that gets a product into the catalogue and on the shelf, while successfully communicating its "story" to prospective consumers. In an atmosphere of concern about scarcity, the on-the-shelf reality is that everyone operates in a market characterised by oversupply. Our present variety and choice of consumer products is aptly described by the French proverb, "*l'embarras du choix*," meaning being spoiled for choice by an 'embarrassment of riches'.

With so many alternatives, success is not a given – even when a new product is better and cheaper, or even greener. The first difficulty is getting attention, and the next is attracting purchasing dollars. This is mainly due to the fact that established market leaders pursue a strategy known as "crowding out". This means that a product based on the same technology is made available with minor variations, absorbing all the possible shelf space, or responding to slightly different industrial requirements. The idea is to give buyers the sense that they have exactly what they need. This does not leave much room for a new arrival.

Products and services are standardised; production and distribution are streamlined and simplified. Diversity is reduced to marketing gimmicks and packaging design – whatever is underneath is much the same everywhere. There is essentially only one diesel engine on the world market, although it is used by dozens of carmakers. The electric motors for home appliances are nearly identical everywhere in the world. Such manufacturing processes universally consolidate market share into the hands of a few, whose goals are economies of scale: producing more of the same at an ever-lower marginal cost. Once an item is mainstreamed, the associated and secure money flows inhibit and discourage change.

The adhesive products market superbly illustrates this dilemma. There are hundreds of glue and sticking solutions on the market, dominated by giant companies such as 3M. Henkel, a German company, markets adhesion products derived from plant starch and face significant barriers to competing with the mainstream products as the market is effectively inundated with "solutions", solutions that already have proven performance and existing acquisition processes. The world demand for adhesives and sealants approaches US$ 50 billion in annual sales. The adhesives and sealants sector in Europe alone invests US$ 200 million in research and development each year. This is huge market with lots of research power concentrated in the hands of a few, who already have such a breadth of products, that it is difficult for a new product, however creative and however appealing, to build a niche and crowd others off the shelves, gain space in the sales catalogues, or acquire the attention of buyers. An article in *Time Magazine* or *The Economist* may provide some visibility, but as long as there is no actual accompanying order form, it will make little difference. Despite the many solutions that could someday replace the unsustainable products now for sale, present market leaders are disinclined to endorse such change.

This brings up another aspect to developing and maintaining market share that can threaten or obliterate a product on its path to the mainstream market. "Suffocation" can pre-empt the necessity for crowding out. Once a new product is selling in a niche market, and is perceived as a threat to the market standard, the giants of industry may act to acquire the emerging business and its patented technologies. The inventor will be offered a favourable buyout, and the new technology may simply be buried, never reaching consumers, simply because it disrupts an existing cash flow and profit margin.

Why has it been slow to shift?

So many solutions, so little time – where do we start?

Over and above the range of synthetic solutions already competing in the market, there are numerous known innovations inspired by natural systems. The gecko is the popular new arrival, while Velcro™ has successfully created a multi-million dollar niche of its own. The paper wasp, native to central Europe, has pincers that enable it to break down wood mechanically (physics first). It then eats these pieces and mixes them with aqueous digestive juices. This chemically shortens the length of the fibres. On drying, water evaporates, the cellulose fibres form a mat, and the adhesive hardens. The nest is ready.

In contrast to paper wasps that use a water-based adhesive, the adhesive used by honeybees for comb building contains wax. Wax is a liquid at a bee's body temperature. Only on cooling does it solidify and adhere. Bees' wax hence meets the ideal requirements for modern adhesives; it is solvent-free but can be applied as a liquid. Barnacle larvae can bond to virtually any hard marine material. The bonding is achieved through a secretion from cement glands. This secretion is a reactive adhesive possessing a high resistance to water. New adhesive is constantly secreted to ensure that the bond remains intact.

Such competition in the glue and adhesion sector alone illustrates that opportunities using natural solutions abound. Thus, even an alert management team can have a difficult time choosing which innovation to support. Where do you start if your research department has hardly any biologists or biochemists, and the marketing and production strategies remain bound by the straightjacket of core business based on core competence? The only way forward is to redesign the business model and go beyond the mere substitution of one technology with another.

A fascination with 'Green' that missed the big picture

While many of us would consider ourselves positive and pro-active, consumer enthusiasm and the desire of concerned citizens to contribute to solutions for sustainability can end up an obstacle to embarking on real change. In our quest for green solutions we are keen to quickly embrace what seems an obvious path towards sustainability, though in reality it may not be such a good idea after all. In 2006, Europe rushed to promote biofuels, only to realise that this sudden massive demand for raw materials, spurred by consumers wishing to buy green fuels, would affect the availability of corn grown for food. Instead of maize corn for human consumption, farmers planted field corn – suitable for livestock or biofuel manufacture. Prices for this staple food increased, making food security in the developing world even more difficult to achieve. The rush to secure corn supplies helped the world's largest traders and processors of agricultural output achieve record profits, yet it caused enormous hardship elsewhere. The United Nations issued a warning, and corn and palm oil were discouraged as biofuel sources.

Hence, if we can be mindful of the larger picture, we can avoid too readily embracing a seemingly obvious solution – only to later discover compromising harm. For instance, we ponder the rationale of consuming delectable organic shiitake mushrooms cultivated from felled oak forests in China. We also rightly question the sense of biodegradable soaps made of fatty acids, derived from palm trees planted on denuded land where rain forests once stood. The conversion to biodegradable soaps in Europe and America destroyed the habitat of the orangutang. When ecologically minded companies developed a line of biodegradable soaps derived from the fatty acids of palm oil trees, their success in taking market share incited the major market players to follow suit. To meet burgeoning international demand, millions of acres of rainforest were cut down and replaced by cultivated palm oil trees. Such unintended harm is a hard way to learn that biodegradable does not equate to sustainable. Green solutions that put the livelihood of the poor and the life of primates at risk are morally and ethically unacceptable, and are just another form of greenwashing. As long as we are ignorant about the impact, it is an unintended consequence. The moment we know, it turns into collateral damage, and that cannot be condoned under any circumstance.

"Green" solutions that have (less) toxic inputs or processes and unintended side effects, should not be in line for sustainability awards. It is irrational to offer congratulations for doing less harm, especially when the damage is inflicted upon the whole ecosystem on which life depends. The ethically correct choice is to achieve greater benefit not by inflicting less damage, but by inflicting no damage at all. Substituting asbestos with halogen- and bromine-based fire-retardants, for example, does not offer a real solution. A less toxic solution is still a toxic solution. We must seek out solutions that neither pollute our food chain nor our personal environment. We can adjust our thinking and increase our ambitions. The argument that a little toxin load does no harm, relies on the pretence that something proven detrimental, mutagenic, or carcinogenic can be tolerated in minute quantities. There is no diagnosis such as "a little bit of cancer" – one either has cancer, or one doesn't. The same applies to the notion of making as much money as possible by whatever means, then reserving some of that gain to do something special for society in order to being lauded for being 'socially responsible'. Such a compensation game is unethical, although unfortunately widely played.

The inability to see connections beyond the obvious is a major challenge we must surmount when designing the Blue Economy. Several innovations have succumbed to flawed or short-sighted processes. A new molecule for controlling bacteria used toxic solvents in the production of the synthetic analogue. The first hydrophobic/hydrophilic sheets manufactured to capture dew in the desert used a chemistry that created a potential health hazard for workers and consumers. Compact florescent lighting provides major energy savings and is widely accepted by consumers, yet the mercury used in manufacture is a toxin. It is released into the environment when the light bulbs are discarded and not recycled. We cannot, with a clear conscience, defend saving energy while releasing mercury into the ecosystem. I am not here to accuse, I am writing this book to demonstrate that everyone can do much better.

Where to now?

When the markets soften and margins are under pressure, it may be that the last thing established management wants, is anyone in the research or product design departments promoting a creative new idea, especially one "inspired by Nature". Within this context, it is a challenge to introduce innovations, even those with many applications. While we may lament the difficulties in convincing market leaders of this brilliance, we may more reasonably be delighted that such innovations will generate enormous numbers of entrepreneurial ventures and sustainably based jobs. The inaction of today's market leaders may turn them into the dinosaurs of tomorrow, leaving tremendous opportunities for those who are ready to change the rules of the game. Of course, it is possible that mainstream management may be convinced to think out of the box. We all know from our own experience that when you are desperate, you are more willing to try a new approach. After all, why do 99% of the men diagnosed with lung cancer stop smoking? And, why did they not stop before? The reverse is true as well: once you are exposed to hundreds of opportunities, why would you let all go by?

Re-imagining the future requires entrepreneurs in science, engineering, social affairs, business, environment, and culture. It requires drawing back from an economy where the engine of growth is indebtedness, which is loaded upon our children and grandchildren, squandering those future generations' material resources. Perhaps now, as we continue to voice our desire for change, having witnessed the tsunami-like destruction wrought by greed, lies, and blindness, we may find that government, business, and industry are ready to alter their perceptions and allocate the resources to support and develop a Blue Economy. Perhaps now they can move forward with the will to respond to the needs of all – with what we have and what we can share with those who have not.

6

NATURE'S MBA (MASTER OF BRILLIANT ADAPTATIONS)

Do not expect the earth to produce more;
do more with what the earth produces.

A standard MBA (Master of Business Administration) confers a status to the holder that makes them desirable as business managers and leaders. They have learned to analyse transactions and interactions that help pinpoint cost reduction for labour and raw materials, maximise cash flow, increase market share, and fine-tune supply chain management. Unfortunately these experts, who are today's dominant business leaders, seem on the verge of disconnection from the habitats and inhabitants of our planet. What once seemed like a logical and sophisticated approach to improve prosperity, is now its most dangerous threat. Worse, their narrow focus on one core business blinds them from recognising viable opportunities outside their sphere of business or knowledge that can give us the 'mid-course correction' that pioneering sustainable business leader Ray Anderson called for. Our production systems are out-dated, incapable of responding to the basic needs of all. They must either evolve or be replaced by ones that thrive by functioning harmoniously with all life, promoting diversity, and ensuring food, shelter, health, and livelihood for everyone.

It is with this conclusion that we turn our admiration and attention to Nature's MBA – Master of Brilliant Adaptations.

Ecosystems offer tremendous inspiration for devising economic models capable of responding to the needs of all at the scale that we now face. Natural systems always change, always evolve, always grow and even resurrect. That is their power and their beauty. When we pay attention to Nature's MBA, we can begin to understand how to integrate innovations into multifaceted models, cascading nutrients and energy, supplying energy from integrated and renewable sources, designing structures that capture and utilise what is minute and transform it into what is grand – into networks that become so effective that nothing is wasted and we have a net energy gain.

Industry is resistant to continuous change – despite it being a certainty. Predictability is the name of the game. The model of core business and core competence pursues productivity in a manner that actually inhibits the businesses' ability to follow the natural path of evolution and change. This is in fact the logic by which industry arrives at solutions based on standardisation and genetic manipulation. Once you know how to alter genes, you believe you know how to predict outcomes. Where industry leaders prefer a predictable production system that uses harsh chemistry to stabilise molecules indefinitely, and genetic modifications that stifle natural evolutionary tendencies, natural systems offer a different solution. Water is the solvent; molecular bonds are temporary in order to permit high biodegradability for natural feedstock and high stability for mineral feedstock, so that molecules can be combined over and over again. Genetic modifications naturally occur in the realm of bacteria, as this is part of their evolutionary pathway; every other form of life is very slow to adopt genetic variations.

These differing frameworks explain why natural systems are always changing while industrial systems are inherently resistant to change. To avoid change and to provide more of the same, industrial systems create global standards that apply everywhere – under the pretext that this reduces costs. In contrast, ecosystems source everything locally. They satisfy their needs with what is readily available. Since ecosystems thrive on local biodiversity, standardisation is of little use. After all, biodiversity is based on – as the word implies – diversity while it enjoys a stable presence of minerals that can never be destroyed, only transformed in different combinations. This helps elucidate why new business models based on bundled portfolios of innovations will be implemented through thousands of entrepreneurs, each of whom will find their niche and their chance making best use of the local conditions. Industry's need is to control and standardise, to merge operations and capture economies of scale, while externalising all costs outside their narrow focus just to make more money? The fact that only a few varieties of tomatoes and potatoes are commercialised, while there are hundreds, even thousands of varieties, and that our main crops are primarily wheat, corn, and soy monocultures, explain why soils are depleted and disease infestations meet little resistance, requiring a constant search for new genetics. This practice is self-defeating.

If we observe Nature, we see that ecosystems evolve towards ever-higher levels of efficiency and diversity – due to contributions from all players. A 500-year-old cedar tree and a majestic bear may be the most remarkable inhabitants we notice when hiking in the Rocky Mountains, but a closer look shows that millions of other species, mostly invisible to the naked eye, are not only contributing but are critical to the whole system. Evolution implies a constant trend towards greater efficiency and greater diversity. May new economies, shaped by entrepreneurs at all levels in business, science, culture, and education, do the same.

As Fritjof Capra has pointed out, ecosystems are networks of networks. The same management principles can be observed layered within each network. Ecosystems are indeed all about connecting, about harnessing and nurturing the contribution of those in the system to ensure the health of the overall system, while operating within clearly defined boundaries, where nutrients and energy are endlessly cascaded and the laws of physics are followed without exception. Following a cascading model and capitalising on the principles of physics make it possible to respond to basic needs, in every location, with whatever is locally available. Instead of contrived scarcity and shortages, what we see in a Blue Economy is abundance – of food, energy, jobs, and revenue. How many communities would oppose this? Given the potential outcome, how many entrepreneurs would refuse the risk of bringing such innovations to the market?

We can all imagine what it would mean to have the benefit of a simple technology for purifying water, one that replaces the use of chemicals with a purely physical effect, as the vortex has been documented to do. Everyone can understand what it means for food security when coffee waste, or other agro-waste, turns into protein-rich mushrooms, contributes income from both the waste and the mushrooms, and then provides amino-acid-rich left-overs as high-quality animal feed. In this way we are building up social capital and eliminating abuse. When a poor family, or an orphaned child, can provide their own food, they will no longer tolerate abuse. There will be no need to sell girls into prostitution rings in order to survive. We are turning a globally traded commodity like coffee into a resource for food security. Food security offers people dignity. Surely everyone can understand such value.

Empowering Entrepreneurs

The model for a Blue Economy is based on what is real. While job losses and youth unemployment are dramatic in the industrialised world, the reality we must confront is that the present economic disarray leaves no place for the one billion new arrivals, especially those from developing nations, entering the labour market. The inability to imagine meaningful jobs and provide worthy challenges to a whole generation equates to telling the young that there is no future for them, that their generation is lost. Over a billion people go to sleep hungry every night. Nearly two billion have no access to safe drinking water, including millions in Europe and North America. Worse, the current economic system is based on the bankrupt notion of scarcity, where much of the growth achieved is funded by debt perpetually carried over to future generations – who will have to contribute the taxes to cancel our debts of over-consumption. Shortages and deficiencies are considered the logical base and a necessary evil from which a more efficient allocation of resources will evolve. This same scarcity mentality also instigates debate and social resistance to innovation, because it portrays such change agents as threats to job security, by proposing to reduce labour expenses of businesses.

Thus it will require creativity and inclusiveness of entrepreneurs in science, social affairs, business, engineering, ecology, and media to move us towards a Blue Economy. Natural systems can build local entrepreneurship much as evolution embraced innovations through diversity. *There may be no greater power for change than the young at heart, ready and willing to assume the risk.* It requires as much clarity of purpose as it requires perseverance. Fortunately, it does not require experience in a given sector, nor a lot of money. It does require maintaining a solid ethical underpinning, and knowing how to generate cash flow against all odds.

As we have noted, innovations outlined in this book may prove hard for mainstream businesses to adopt. Big companies, content with producing more of what has proven successful, may lack cutting-edge competencies, or may be unwilling to commit the initial capital necessary for a new approach. This is a major advantage for committed entrepreneurs. Basing their actions on solid science and their vision on social and emotional consciousness, they can implement and develop these innovations to create waves of change that infuse every business sector, shifting entire markets towards sustainability. They will succeed by developing successful partnerships, taking advantage of institutional aggregation, and achieving market viability by garnering consumer support across a wide socio-economic stratum. Market success will stem from the availability of better products that cost less than their competition. We need to collectively prepare the next generation of leadership to understand that it is possible to create a company without money or experience – this is, in fact, the only way fundamental innovations have found their way to the market.

A time of crisis, when market leaders are stressed, and some are even on the edge of survival, is perhaps the best moment for the young and the young at heart to set their minds on a new business model. Practically speaking, there are not too many careers available when millions of jobs have been lost and well-paid jobs for graduates are the exception rather than the rule. In addition, and contrary to expectation, the barriers to market entry are actually lower in a downturn. In a relatively stable economy, innovations do not easily find their way to market. However, when the entire economic framework is in a state of turmoil, decision makers latch onto any object that seems stable or that stands out. A major firm may be disposed to accept products and methods with a fundamentally new or different approach.

The task of an entrepreneur is literally to create, to manifest or bring into being, something new. His or her task is to be the carrying force that brings an idea into substance, to be the agent between thought and realisation. Even when well funded and passionate about entrepreneurship, you remain alone. Market success depends on partnerships and teamwork. One of the ways to succeed with the introduction of these innovations is to build partnerships with change agents who have the power to influence the market and tip the balance. Innovations do not necessarily flow into the market, nor are company executives and investment bankers the only players who shape the market. Market breakthroughs are often brought about by change agents. Though numerous innovative consortiums exist (consider the role of media, grassroots activists, and NGOs), there are established ways to create pressure effectively.

For example, insurance and re-insurance companies have their finger on the pulse of today's market, tabulating trends in the world economy through the monies they must pay out when disasters occur. Insurance companies are an obvious leverage point for change in the market, especially when savings are substantial. They closely follow a wealth of statistics, which is one of their core competences. No one knows how to crunch numbers better. In fact, a decision on their part to object to business as usual is based entirely on the simple science of statistics. Insurance companies, along with consumers, institutional investors, local communities, and local governments, are the stakeholders who drive decisions that stimulate innovation beyond the steady pace and comfort zone of industry.

To illustrate this, let us consider how insurance companies earn money offering fire insurance policies. When the number of infant deaths by fire became a concern based on statistical data, insurance companies and industry manufacturers lobbied for the adoption of requirements specifying the use of fire and flame-retardants. The risk of fire damage statistically decreases when any fire and flame-retardant is used. A lower incidence of fire means an increase in industry's profit. A few decades later, when their statistics indicated an increase in male infertility, allergies, and even cancer at a young age, and these statistics can be scientifically linked to the fire and flame-retardants in use, then the insurance industry could once again stimulate change by urging lawmakers to accept a new standard or a new solution, while restricting (even against the will of the industry) the agents suspected of causing such conditions.

Insurance companies and their expert statisticians know all too well that correlation does not prove cause and effect. Rather, it is the reversal of the burden of proof that changes the business model. To achieve a secure angle, the company must demonstrate that it has considered all options and has concluded that negative effects could never occur. For change agents, it offers another lever for securing faster acceptance of breakthrough innovations. In our case in point, consider that insurers could earn multiple revenues by selling product liability policies to the makers of toxic fire retardants. If emerging evidence were to link a particular chemical to a specific illness, the liability insurance premium would increase – perhaps to a point where cost pressures would spur management to change even faster than legal guidelines dictate. The cost of insurance and the reluctance of re-insurance companies to cover the risks would force the company into action.

Insurance companies could further augment their revenue potential by integrating data from each of their separate risk businesses. This would provide a formidable base of information with obvious pathways for shifts in industry – encouraging innovations on the recommendation of insurance companies. Health insurers could link toxicity beyond the Ames test, which assesses the mutagenic potential of chemical compounds. They could rank the chemicals suspected to cause health problems, suggesting substitutes.

Three Levels of Sustainability

All too often industry finds natural substitutes for effective but toxic products, and then manufactures the natural replacements in the traditional "heat, beat and treat" mode that is responsible for significantly excessive pollution. When industry finds solutions in biology, it reverts to cloning and genetic manipulation to secure "predictable" results. Thus, the inspiration from Nature to find substitute molecules for the market's standard bearers requires more than the simple shift from one molecule to another. The molecule and the manufacturing system must be inspired by natural processes to create the desired convergence toward sustainability. A Blue Economy approach follows physics and learns from Nature in order to inform materials selection and production methods. At its core, the approach initiates a generative and regenerative cascade of implementable innovations. We thus have sustainable product, sustainable manufacture, and sustainable whole systems. In terms of business and economic benefit, this creates competitive products, competitive processes, and competitive business models that go far beyond core business practice.

Nature works at ambient temperature and pressure. Even abalone shells and spider silk, which are stronger than the bullet-proof ceramic Kevlar™, are methodically assembled, the former layer by layer, the latter by pressure and moisture control only. The shells are made from calcium carbonate and proteins, materials that are completely locally sourced. Silk is made from protein. These processes are sustainable. The manufacturer could argue that Nature produces too little, too slowly, and that industry standards require efficient, timely, and predictable results. It is true that the time needed to manufacture ceramics in an oven at a temperature over 1,000 °C is considerably less than the time needed by the abalone. However, a ceramics company purchases mined materials. These materials needed to be found and then mined. A permit was needed to extract the resources. The materials mined must be shipped around the world, processed (at high pressure and high temperature to speed up and standardise operations and product output), and delivered in the appropriate form. When we take these factors into account, beginning with the search for the mine to the arrival of the calcium carbonate at the ceramic production facilities, the time and efficiency advantage is less obvious. It is worth noting that whenever mining is part of the production process, natural systems will perform faster and at a fraction of the energy cost that mining has grown accustomed to.

One Innovation, Multiple Revenues

The innovations described herein clearly have the potential to generate multiple revenue streams. The market turns around money; money is thus a medium of exchange. Innovations that generate more market applications have greater appeal, and are thus most likely to be embraced by established businesses and entrepreneurs. The opportunity to generate multiple revenues is very attractive since it mobilises parallel investments for several niche markets. This reduces the risk of innovation. Nonetheless, these are still high-risk investments. The terms may not be appealing for the inventors but the need for cash may be so urgent that they accept an investment agreement.

In a downturn, cash is king. Those who have billions to invest can easily set the terms of the deal. Investors who want management to focus on the single most promising application often prefer the model of a core business with a single revenue stream. Any investor will hire people with MBAs to assess a new technology's chances for success. Entrepreneurial companies wishing to raise venture capital must reveal a very long list of "things that can go wrong". At the same time, hardened Silicon Valley venture capital companies will listen to a presentation of one innovation with dozens of possible applications. Without exception they will ask for the one application that guarantees to gross US$ 100 million dollars within three years and ask the inventors to downplay all other opportunities that combined could be a multiple of the US$ 100 million dream factory.

While risks are inherent to business, those associated with the majority of the innovations considered and reviewed in this book have been calculated, mitigated, and are much lower than usual for the market. In fact, these innovations can reduce risk because they alter the fundamental business model. The achievements of a platform technology where basic parameters have been successfully applied clearly reduces risk and offers potentially better returns than funding a narrowly defined niche. Such a vast potential for sales implies that investors reassess the risk in light of these multiple revenues. This is the key advantage to nearly all the top innovations we describe.

We need not look far to demonstrate this fact. For example, there are 37 known commercial applications for the vortex. There are over 20 for seaweed furanones that control the proliferation of biofilm by jamming bacterial communication (see Chapter 8). Savings are hard to miss in replacing a US$ 50,000 surgical procedure with a US$ 500 non-surgical intervention that provides permanent heart monitoring without batteries and at a fraction of the cost. Instead of selling a pacemaker one million times per year, the medical industry can sell monitoring patches a billion times a year.

The silk polymers developed by Oxford Biomaterials (see Chapter 7) are already under development in five different companies, each with separate financing. Peter Steinberg's Australian start-up developing antibacterial applications for furanones, had a comparable strategy of spinning off potential applications for agriculture, consumer, industrial, medical equipment, and therapeutic markets before its technology portfolio was merged with another company. Each of these in turn may raise diverse funds for mobilising niche solutions such as anti-corrosion products, antiperspirants, or a potential cure for cystic fibrosis. All derive from the same platform technology. Similarly, Watreco, the start-up company built around Curt Hallberg's mathematical interpretations of a vortex, brings solutions to the market as varied as saving energy in ice making, speeding percolation on golf greens, de-scaling pipes, and pumping air into fish farm tanks. These venture companies exemplify entrepreneurs who are ready to move businesses forward.

The power of these technologies to provide multiple cash flows through multiple applications reduces risk and dramatically increases the value of the intellectual property, potentially allowing inventors to sub-license technological applications to raise capital to focus on applications that drive their interest and stimulate their curiosity. The power to overcome obstacles requires partnerships. Although inventors and marketers have different goals, a winning coalition can begin with solid leading-edge science and build on the sharp competitive analysis of entrepreneurs. The world of risk capital is ready to finance people with good ideas. What is needed now is the capacity and willingness to bring innovations to the market. Innovations with the potential to generate multiple revenues in diverse markets are attractive. If these cash flow generators change the business model, then businesses that develop these innovations not only meet an important need, they will be pursued as investment and entrepreneurial opportunities.

Cascading Resources in a Community

Such innovations can also empower communities to respond to their own needs, especially in societies under major stress. They offer the foundation and the means to grow initiatives into movements, achieving market share despite adverse conditions. Communities that have neither money to trade nor capital to invest are often regarded as less responsive to the introduction of new ideas. Yet the achievements of Father Godfrey Nzamujo in Benin, Chido Govera in Zimbabwe, and Paolo Lugari in Colombia demonstrate that this is not true. The design and implementation of these integrated biosystems have converted economically non-viable communities into successes where money flows and circulates while capital grows. Half of the world's human population lives in rural or agricultural settings. Developing nations with rural and agricultural populations can greatly benefit from integrated biosystems complemented with bio-refineries – such as the method of conversion used in Las Gaviotas for collecting resin from harvested trees, locally processed with renewable energies from the region into different products, with all waste from the process used in the production of construction materials. Integrated biosystems will also permit industrialised nations to dramatically reduce their negative impacts on the environment and society while increasing their material productivity.

Real Opportunities, Real Solutions

This shift in business model that is becoming more evident and necessary, develops from our growing understanding of Nature's

MBA – how natural systems rely on the forces of physics, rather than consuming ever more resources, the very things needed to maintain survival. The impact is surprising. The results are compelling. There are vaccines that need no refrigeration, heart rhythm devices that need no surgery, vortex technologies that de-scale water pipes without chemicals, algae that defeat bacteria by turning a deaf ear, or silk that cuts with razor-sharpness – the list is long! You will find more than 100 case studies illustrating this on <www.TheBlueEconomy.org> website.

The replacement of something that is chemically toxic and clearly unsustainable with what is nothing more than a natural process may well help solve some of the biggest challenges of our time – while opening a window of opportunity for a portfolio of completely new products and services.

This opportunity to replace "something toxic" with "something natural" – to replace a toxic or non-renewable material or process with one that relies merely on physics and natural processes – is particularly exciting. The capacity to reduce risk by generating more cash flow makes products and services competitive. This is where it will foster a new wave of entrepreneurship. This is how millions of sustainable jobs will be created, fundamentally shifting old model products and out-dated production methods to innovations and processes based on the scientific understanding of already proven solutions – ones that encourage the next generation to become innovators. The billions of years of experience accumulated in the evolution of ecosystems and species do count when it comes to perfecting solutions and providing alternatives for different environments. These are proven solutions that have had to evidence resilience and flexibility in order to survive – as the human race must now do on our small blue planet.

In past decades, the goal of environmentalists required everyone to pay more and invest more to save the environment or reduce pollution. Few were prepared or willing to adopt this means to effect that goal. Even government tax levies and fines for polluting practices did not noticeably promote responsible stewardship. We even continue to allow, and even applaud, the use of palm oil farmed on destroyed rain forests in Indonesia for cleaning up rivers in Europe! And how supportive are you of an economy where everything that is good for your health and that of the Earth is expensive, and thus only for the few who can afford it?

A Blue Economy approach allows us to change all this. It allows us to achieve better results and create multiple revenue sources while building social capital and community resilience, at lower costs. Those who profited in the past from poor choices can now rationalise investing in new solutions that will strengthen economies and communities from the roots upward. The driving force of success could well be thousands of entrepreneurs with boundless enthusiasm and commitment, supported by millions of entrepreneurially thinking people across society, in government, NGO's, universities, etc., that more than compensate for any lack of capital or experience. Moreover, innovations that achieve strong market success in the future will be those that address basic needs. This is what management wizard Peter Drucker claimed in the 1980s: "The needs of the poor are opportunities waiting for entrepreneurs."

When manufacturers choose to replace a toxic process with a less toxic alternative, they are simply "doing less bad". That is the option taken when billions of dollars are poured into less toxic though longer-lasting batteries. These batteries still rely on mining, smelting, and harsh chemistry, with an overwhelming majority ending up in landfills that pollute the environment, poisoning ecosystems while posing a long-term health hazard to us all. Many will argue that a halfway measure is at least on the right track. Yet this is nothing short of a duplicitous moral standard. We all have the urge to do more good. Let us not accept that doing less bad is good enough. This is the basics of ethics.

Current scientific literature offers insights into thousands of possible breakthroughs inspired by ways that natural species have solved challenges to procurement and survival. Though fewer have revealed the entirety of their process, the possibilities remain and the mysteries can be solved. We still have to understand how each breakthrough emerges in a network of networks. Time will permit us to understand and implement innovations that will dramatically shift our methods of production and consumption toward sustainability. This relies on a new generation of MBA graduates who can design business models that emulate Nature – as the Master of Brilliant Adaptations.

In the following chapters we will further explore the framework of the Blue Economy from the basis of existing contributions and solutions that are at work right now. A Blue Economy is what will apply the achievements of ecosystems to economic systems, through the ingenuity of communities. Implementing a Blue Economy will indeed ensure that human systems, in fact all living systems, can attain the stability and security that will safeguard and maintain their evolutionary and regenerative path.

The MBA Comparison

	Nature's MBA -- Abundance	*Core Business MBA -- Scarcity*
1.	Everyone has a job to do and contributes their best.	Unemployment is part of the system.
2.	Thousands of small contributors; many opportunities for entrepreneurship.	Power concentrated among a few. Multinationals rule.
3.	Everything is used: cascading of nutrients, matter and energy.	Minute parts are used. The rest is wasted, abandoned in landfills, indiscriminately. incinerated.
4.	Predictable physics provides the first source of power.	First source is non-renewable fossil fuels. Climate change and acidification is guaranteed.
5.	Water is the primary solvent. Chemistry has limited, secondary use.	Heavily reliant on chemistry. Aggressive solvents are used to create covalent links.
6.	Biodiversity is time and place specific. Biology is characterised by exceptions.	Biology is cloned.
7.	Diversity flourishes and continues to evolve.	Standardised and predictable output.
8.	The constant of change is the basis of evolution.	Resistance to fundamental change. Innovative technologies are considered disruptive.
9.	What is locally available is put to use.	Centralised manufacture requires global sourcing.
10.	The basic needs of all are met.	Vast numbers of the population are left out even when a majority lives in wealth.
11.	With few exceptions nearly all models are non-linear.	All calculations are linear.
12.	All materials degrade over time, but transform and reconstitute.	Covalent molecular bonding gives us components that do not degrade for centuries, even millennia, even those with a one-time use.
13.	Everything is connected, evolving in symbiosis.	All is a stand-alone. Synergies are discouraged, except in finance.
14.	Clean air and water are free and abundant.	Everything can be sold for profit, even basic necessities like water.
15.	One initiative generates multiple benefits. for several partners.	One project equals one cash flow, only for the progenitor and controlling partners.
16.	Risks are shared.	Risk hampers innovation.
17.	Material and energy utilisation are permanently improved; taxation does not exist.	Taxation to redistribute wealth unsuccessful due to tax havens.
18.	Optimise the system.	Maximise one critical success factor.

19.	Negatives are converted into positives.	Negatives are mitigated at high cost, or ignored, or passed on, unresolved, to future generations.
20.	Economies are based on scope.	Economies are based on scale.
21.	Generate value with what you have.	Cut costs at all costs

7

HOW ETHICS CAN REINVENT FISHING

Recycling and renewables are not enough to steer us towards sustainability.

In doing our best to do what is best for our planet, we are often confronted with the harsh realities of our own short-sightedness. The production of palm oil, used in biodegradable soaps, leads to the destruction of large areas of rainforest. How can we possibly defend the cleaning up of rivers in Europe, knowing that it is destroying the habitat of the orangutang in Asia? Vegetarians who promote the consumption of mushrooms certainly reduce the footprint of their protein consumption by substituting animal protein (and animal feed) with fungal protein. However, few mushroom-lovers realise that shiitake farmers around the world are fast destroying oak forests in order to boost the output of shiitake mushrooms. This implies that attempts to not eat animal protein could well destroy natural forests. We very often do not realise the unintended consequences of our deeds. We therefore need to learn to think in terms of connections – searching for and seeing the broader impact of what we are producing and consuming.

While we can easily be concerned about our lack of understanding, and the subsequent errors it leads to, we do have a lot of engrained routine thinking that does not allow us to fundamentally change our approach to business and the way we live. Let us take the case of fishing. We should assess a few realities of this industry from a deep ethical perspective.

Firstly, we overfish – we take more than can be sustainably harvested. Secondly, while harvesting the fish stocks we want, up to 70% of the catch's biomass is fish and sea life that we do not want. This is not by any means efficient, but current fishing techniques do not permit us to differentiate. Thirdly, we drag nets around the ocean, often scraping mile long dragnets along the sea floor, destroying ecosystems and killing a wide array of sea life that can take years, even decades, to recover. To make matters worse, a medium-sized fishing vessel will consume 250,000 tonnes of fuel per year, nearly always subsidised by governments. And, apart from needing energy to drag the nets, a lot of power is consumed to feed the compressors that drive the ice machines to store the catch on board. Even worse, these vessels (and the processing of their catch) consume more water than certain communities will ever have access to.

While this is standard procedure worldwide, and the problems are well known, it is difficult to change behaviour in a world of dwindling resources. While everyone desires more of the same, it is exactly that 'more of the same' that destroys ecosystems beyond repair. And while all parties debate the harsh realities of unsustainable fishing, there is one reality that everyone overlooks: the catching of female fish with eggs! No cattle farmer in the world will send his cow for slaughter a few days before a calf is to be born. There is no fruit farmer who will prune trees in the weeks before the fruit ripens. Yet fishermen around the world think nothing of catching females with eggs and submerging them in freezing water or putting them on ice, along with all the other fish. This is one of the most unsustainable acts of modern times and yet, this practice has never been debated – nor are any attempts made to redress this anachronism.

So, if we agree on a basic ethical position that *females with eggs should always be protected, irrespective of the species*, then it becomes clear that we need to change our fishing model. We simply cannot allow fisheries to continue catching fish indiscriminately and inhumanely submerge them in ice water. These freezing temperatures lead to a rapid release of acids as the fish's system attempts to counteract congelation, causing massive stress to the fish and affecting the taste. In addition to this unethical behaviour, the dragging of nets and the production of ice represent more than half of the energy required to operate a fishing vessel, with the balance needed for the propulsion of the boat. If we eliminate the production of ice, and find another way of catching fish than with nets, then the energy requirements of any boat will shift dramatically.

The design for a new fishing method starts with a catamaran, powered by electric engines. Fish are caught in nets by making use of rings of bubbles andair curtains – just like whales and dolphins do. The fish are then preserved in cold water tanks with temperatures ranging between 2-4 °C degrees. Energy consumption drops dramatically. The boat is equipped with four fixed sails, especially designed for the currents and winds of the region, inspired by the unique designs of the BMW-Oracle ship that won the America's Cup. When there is no wind, the masts drop and convert the sails to solar panels capable of generating electricity to power engines. The goal is to quickly process all fish into value-added products. It is here that an innovative ecographics system allows for checking each fish for eggs.

This breakthrough technology, much along the same logic as pregnancy tests that have been performed for decades, leads to the identification of pregnant fish. Each female with eggs is immediately released from her state of hibernation and placed back into the sea, securing the repopulation of fish stocks. We lose sight of the fact that a female fish weighing half a kilogram is able to carry up to 500 eggs, whereas a one kilogram fish could lay as many as 3,000 eggs. An average female fish in her lifetime could have more than 5 million offspring, whereas a tuna can have up to 40 million and a sunfish 300 million. And while all fish do not hatch, it is a remarkable demonstration of how Nature promotes life.

This exponential growth in reproductiveness is the main reason why the catching of mature or breeding females is so counterproductive. The experience on the island of El Hierro in the Canary Islands (Spain), where the fishing community took matters into their own hands to sustain their future, demonstrates that fisheries that had once crashed can be revived to flourish. Amazingly, a group of over 40 fishermen decided on a set of rules for their industry that saw the fishery recover in just two years. Measures included no net-fishing at all (using hook and line only), the protection of female fish through the creation of a self-imposed UNESCO Biosphere zone known as La Restinga and an increase in minimum catch sizes set by the EU. By placing ethics at the core of the industry, this group of fishermen now have access to an exponential growth in productivity, fish-catch size and revenue.

As always happens once a direction is chosen, a cascade of additional innovations emerges. A boat that requires no ice, nor any power to drag nets, can operate with electric power only. When the boat is sailing with wind, it can even generate power from the wake by applying the same principle as a hybrid car that recovers energy from the brakes – in this case from the turbulence caused by sailing. This new vessel design is the most sustainable and while it offers opportunities to cut out fuel altogether, it also creates an opportunity to translate the subsidies associated with fuel for the fishing industry into financing for new vessels. It is indeed possible for every government around the world that reserves state funding to support fishermen, to convert a subsidy into an investment – one that leads to higher efficiency and proven sustainability.

With the new catamaran design allowing operation without fuel, the subsidies committed for years to come can now be converted into a net present value that takes subsidies (and corruption) out of the equation – and puts renewable energy options squarely on track. The new design of the vessel, which enables checking each fish for eggs, now enables the processing of the entire catch on board the boat. In this way more revenue is generated from the Omega-3 oil, collagen and fishmeal that is produced from all process leftovers after filleting the fish. This design in addition allows for processing with seawater, thus saving fresh water on shore. It also enables the sale of the processed catch prior to landing. This system cuts down on intermediation by middlemen, ensuring that the fishermen, who risk their lives out on the ocean every day, generate at least double the income of their standard revenue. In some cases, especially due to harvesting of essential fatty acids in the form of omega-3 oil, their income can increase five-fold.

Each new boat will benefit from start-up funding, due to the elimination of subsidies. It will also enjoy lower risks, due to the generation of more income with available resources. This breakthrough design is driven by the simple yet powerful statement that when it comes to sustainability, female fish carrying eggs should be protected at all costs. This can be done by identifying them in the catch and giving them a safe refuge in order to breed. This particular drive towards sustainability generates better income and more jobs, while eliminating the dependency on fossil fuels.

The most important result of this paradigm shift is, however, that more cash flow circulates in the local economy, generating a multiplier effect that creates growth by nurturing and using available resources sustainably. An added benefit is that once the multiplier effect kicks in, and activity and innovation increases, one sees a reverse of the 'brain-drain' where young, educated people rather return home, or no longer leave to find work in the cities or even in other countries. The design of new fishing boats will see highly qualified Moroccan engineers, wanting to contribute to this innovative business development, return to their homeland to contribute to the re-industrialisation of the economy. This could even extend to include the local construction of the fishing vessels, a sector that may have been considered long gone and impossible to ever recover. It will require a deep ethical shift in fishing – the protection of breeding females – to lead to the relaunch of industries we could not even have imagined before.

The decision to move beyond merely reducing our negative impact on the environment and society, and to embark on doing more good, is in the end an ethical decision. If one is ignorant about the impact of one's choices, then there will be unintended consequences. Should you knowingly cause a negative impact, then you are responsible for collateral damage, and should be held accountable. Unethical behaviour is knowing that you can do good, but refusing to do so. Such behaviour may appeal to certain people in the short term but it stands to destroy our hopes for a long and prosperous future for generations to come.

8

PULP TO PROTEIN

Give me a place to stand, and I will move the Earth!
—*Archimedes*

In times of upheaval, positive minds look for solutions, wherever they can. There are always areas of growth even when the overall economy is considered to be in decline. Health care, food production, renewable energy and pollution control are four areas where there is consensus that increased expenditures are certain, even in rough times. Few markets better exemplify growth potential than the burgeoning worldwide demand for edible and medicinal mushrooms.

Ever since a middle class with purchasing power emerged in China, demand for the fruiting bodies of shiitake (*Lentinula edodes*) and other fungi has been explosive. Double-digit growth rates have been the norm for over two decades. Europe and North America are also discovering the unique nutritional and medicinal effects of several mushrooms with unfamiliar names such as "Judas ear" (*Auricularia auricula*), "enoki" (*Flamminula velutipes*), "maitake" (*Grifola fondosa*), or "reishi" (*Ganoderma lucidum*). Soon these words may well become part of our daily vocabulary, just like "espresso," "latte," "sushi," and "pizza".

Demand for fungi has risen ever since cultivation of these delicacies started, and so has the number of jobs required to meet that demand. Wu Sangong, a 13th century farmer-scientist, initiated the Chinese foray into healthy protein from fungi, one of the five kingdoms of Nature. The shiitake capital of the world is Qingyuan, located in the Pearl Delta of Guangdong, China. Qingyuan is smaller than the San Francisco Bay Area, yet this region employs over 120,000 people farming shiitake mushrooms, with a market value in the West of over one billion dollars. According to Prof. Shuting Chang, the mushroom expert who taught at the Chinese University of Hong Kong for years and made major contributions to the international success of mushroom farming, the total export value of Chinese mushroom cultivation topped US$ 20 billion and supported 1.2 million jobs in 2012. Fungi such as *Volvariella volvacea,* also known as the paddy straw mushroom as it is grown on rice straw, has clearly contributed to food security for China's large population. This fact has surprised Western food and population experts.

In Nature nothing happens in isolation. Life is divided into five kingdoms: Animals, Plants, Fungi, Protista, and Monera (also known as bacteria). These five kingdoms of Nature cascade energy from the one to the other. We employ this concept by feeding items from the Plant Kingdom, in the form of plant material such as grain, soy, fruit, and vegetables to poultry, pigs, fish and cattle, members of the Animal Kingdom. Their food source is complemented by protein from mushrooms, the Fungi Kingdom, which prodigiously convert plant waste, especially straw, into food. Bacteria, the Monera Kingdom, are also mobilised. For instance, manure from animals is converted in digesters to become a growth medium for algae, from the Protista Kingdom, which are farmed in shallow, open-air ponds.

Annual US demand for tropical mushrooms is barely 200 grams per person per year. Consumption in Canada is already double that amount. Hong Kong reaches an amazing 65 kg per person per year. If US consumers were to eat as much fungi as Canadians, this would translate into an additional two billion dollars in revenue. If the US population were to shift its food habits to match those of Hong Kong, the tropical mushroom industry would top most other businesses in the world at today's market prices for petroleum and mushrooms. The significance of this order of magnitude is that mushrooms are traditionally farmed on agricultural waste, which is widely considered a burden and often simply burned.

The biomass from plant husks, cobs, or straw on which mushrooms thrive contain no protein or polysaccharides of any importance – yet mushrooms are rich in protein. Based on dry weight, some varieties of oyster mushroom compete with meat for concentration of protein as well as all the essential amino acids. Interestingly, white button mushrooms (*Agaricus bisporus*) remain the most consumed species in the West, although they have the least protein and require pasteurised horse manure to grow. Some countries even import this animal waste from overseas to locally farm the white buttons. Imagine, we have international free-trade in horse manure to produce low quality protein! This is neither a sustainable nor a competitive business model for achieving the nutrient needs of an expanding world population.

The interplay of natural systems is capable of securing a cascade of protein from multiple sources, and is thus free of reliance on a single source. This provides insight into how we can provide worldwide food security with what is locally available. Mushrooms convert plant waste into edible fruiting bodies. The portion of the fungi that remains in the substrate after harvest is called mycelium, and being full of essential amino acids is highly nutritious for animals. Animals in turn generate manure that bacteria digest, enriching the soil so plants and microorganisms thrive. The cascading of nutrients from one species, belonging to one kingdom, to another species, belonging to another kingdom, is an ecosystems marvel. That is why there is neither starvation nor unemployment in an ecosystem. Everyone is busy contributing their best, gaining sustenance from something that was waste for another, and satisfying the basic needs of all.

The business model for the production of tropical mushrooms is simple. Firstly, handbooks prescribe that a fibrous biomass is sterilised under pressure and high temperature, although many know how to skip this process saving the energy cost, as has been demonstrated by the washing technique of Ivan Milenkovic of Ekofungi, based in Belgrade (Serbia). Most of the time the growing medium consists of dead or dying biological matter. Next, mushroom spores are introduced in small quantities. Since bacteria have been largely eliminated by the sterilisation or washing process, the mycelium expands into the substrate in a relatively short time, over a matter of just weeks. Once the substrate is fully populated, a thermal or water shock is applied. This causes the fruiting bodies to emerge. Mushrooms typically reproduce quickly when their survival is threatened. What we refer to as "mushrooms" are actually the offspring – the fruiting bodies of the fungi.

The Chinese reuse all straw waste to grow straw mushrooms. Unfortunately, several straw crops have been genetically modified, as has been the case with rice, to have short stalks and thus much less straw. Elsewhere in the world straw is burned, generating massive quantities of air pollution. Burning rice straw is a horrendous problem in Egypt, affecting the health of upwards of 20 million people along the Nile Delta. Those who study massive population needs have yet to emulate the Chinese wisdom of converting straw into protein, and the mushroom substrate into animal feed. In fact, countries such as Egypt have adopted genetically modified short-straw rice, and at the same time have experienced a shortfall in food security, relying on imported wheat to make up the difference. It is in preventing such shortfalls where we see the obvious business opportunities.

Current mushroom farming practices are not always sustainable. Where oak is used as the preferred growing medium, it is logged, shredded, and converted into a high quality growth substrate for shiitake, one of the priciest and healthiest mushrooms on the international market. The rapidly increasing demand for shiitake strains harvest capacity of oak forests throughout China.

Over the past twenty years, innovative and efficient farming of local and tropical mushrooms has evolved to a low cost, competitive, year-round business. The innovations are multiple and have led to the creation of a new business model for production and marketing. The model of mushroom farming inspired by the cascading of nutrients in ecosystems has been benchmarked in Africa, Latin America and recently in Europe. An increased Western demand for exotic mushrooms, coupled with a price trend towards greater affordability, would be critical to securing widespread adoption of this high protein cholesterol-free and fat-free food source. Increased demand would spur cultivators to search for more abundant waste materials as a growing medium. Since mushroom farming is relatively more labour intensive, this waste-to-food chain would create thousands, even millions of jobs. Entrepreneurs working locally to realise this potential would create job opportunities, particularly in areas where accessing the employment market holds greater challenge.

The Buzz about Coffee

At the turn of the 21st century, mushrooms overtook coffee as the second most widely traded commodity. Now a new opportunity emerges that will increase the value of both: mushrooms grown on coffee waste. There are two waste streams related to coffee. The bulk of the waste is generated on the farm and is known as "pulp." Brewing coffee produces a second waste stream known as "grounds." From the time the beans leave the farm to the moment they finish brewing in coffee pots, 99.8% ends up as waste and only 0.2% is ingested. While this currently contributes mightily to the waste management issues noted earlier, there is now a positive and creative approach that cascades waste streams generated by both farms and coffee shops into nutrient streams for mushrooms. This opens up an unparalleled opportunity. The farmer earns about one-tenth of a cent on a coffee shop espresso that sells for three dollars, a mark-up factor of 3,000! Given that the annual world consumption of coffee in 2015/16 was 151 million bags (one bag is 60 kg), the total biomass that is left to rot is a shocking 28 million tonnes. If the value realised from the coffee bean can be replicated or even surpassed with the potential value of the waste from coffee harvest and production, it would be a genuine bonanza.

Mushrooms grow on ligno-cellulose. The massive waste generated in the process of converting coffee from a berry on a bush to a beverage in a cup, consists mainly of ligno-cellulose. Better still, coffee is a hardwood, like oak. In 1992, Prof. Shuting Chang from Hong Kong demonstrated through scientific research that coffee is an ideal substrate for cultivating mushrooms, especially the oyster and shiitake varieties. Even the medicinal and highly prized reishi thrives on coffee grounds. This means that if all coffee grounds and pulp were converted to a substrate, we could add 25 million tonnes of protein to the world's food table.

From farm, to roaster, to consumer, the coffee bean is a perfectly monitored crop. Seldom will you find any agricultural product that is subject to more stringent quality controls. When the coffee beans are processed on the farms, the husk is removed by way of fermentation, before being roasted to perfection. When coffee is then brewed, the hot water or steam passes through at a high temperature, sterilising the ground beans. All this is to great advantage for the purpose of growing mushrooms, as it simplifies the mushroom production process. The steamed and moistened grounds, returned to the packaging it arrived in, could be directly inoculated with mushroom spores without the added necessity of sterilisation. This would further reduce cost and readily supply local entrepreneurs. In addition, since the caffeine stimulus in the coffee grounds encourages some mushrooms to fruit faster, using grounds would generate a better cash flow than the typical mushroom farm. This corresponds perfectly with our economic ideal: less investment, more cash flow; one initiative, multiple benefits. This translates to lower cost, faster output, and better cash flow as well as higher customer loyalty, through a more natural product that is farmed sustainably.

A venture that converts waste into a highly nutritious food that is cheaper and healthier for everyone is attractive in challenging times. From a business perspective, the best message is that this method offers improved cash flow, which interests investors and bankers. After Prof. Chang undertook the first scientific studies, Carmenza Jaramillo spent six years studying the utilisation of coffee waste to propagate fungi for CENICAFE, the research institute of the Colombian Federation of Coffee Farmers. She published more than 20 peer-reviewed scientific papers in international journals to report and document her findings. Dr Ivanka Milenkovic from the University of Belgrade scientifically analysed the use of the mushroom substrate as animal feed and found no loss of meat or milk production. Clearly this Pulp-to-Protein method has major economic benefits.

It is unfortunate that currently coffee pulp is simply left to rot on the farms, often with the excuse that it is good fertiliser. The 16 million tonnes of organic waste annually left to decompose on coffee farms and in landfills, produces millions of tonnes of greenhouse gas. The Pulp-to-Protein approach reduces the need to harvest wood. This allows trees, particularly hardwoods such as oak, to continue to fix carbon from the atmosphere, which slows the adverse effects of climate change. Feeding waste back into the nutrient cycle simplifies waste management and cuts methane gas emissions from rotting biomass. The integration of mushroom and coffee production leads to a dramatic reduction of every negative. In combination, two negatives become a positive.

When we look at coffee from the perspective of global development, we realise that the use of pulp on coffee farms would offer many advantages that would offset the negative impact that has tainted this monoculture cash-crop for decades. What we see in the current model is that coffee as a cash crop provides a living for farmers and their communities only when market prices are high. The moment the price drops below a certain threshold, farmers, their families, and their communities suffer. Significant declines in coffee prices result in the onset of poverty so severe that many *cafeteros* plough their coffee bushes back into the soil, turning to subsistence farming with two cows per acre on their plot of land, and little or no chance of ever making ends meet. Unable to feed his family and prepared to do anything to save them from hunger, the farmer moves with his family to a shantytown at the edge of an urban area, joining millions of others looking for jobs that pay little and offer only a bleak future.

At the end of the 20th century, Vietnam became the world's second largest exporter of coffee, creating economic havoc in many countries, particularly in Africa. However, as soon as coffee and mushrooms become a unified ecosystem, the dichotomy between cash crops and food security evaporates. We can envision a potential end to poverty in the coffee growing regions of the world – from a nutrient cascade involving plants, fungi, and animals. Each pound of farm waste generates at least half a pound of protein-rich food for the farming family. Because the mushroom substrate is an excellent (and free) animal feed, farmers will be able to afford and maintain livestock, which will further augment their nutrient needs and food security. It is a unique opportunity to observe how the waste of a cash crop like coffee can provide local food security and many additional benefits that then buffer the economic turbulence of an internationally traded commodity. These farming techniques resonate with the young, the unemployed, and the disadvantaged, as well as with hardened MBA graduates who see an opportunity to generate cash from what was previously considered waste. A decade of field experience in Zimbabwe gives us a brilliant demonstration of these benefits.

Multiple Benefits of the Pulp-to-Protein Model of Coffee Waste to Mushroom Nutrient

For Consumer and Producer		*For the Planet*	
Richer	coffee provides the ideal nutrients and growing medium for mushrooms	Lower Energy	coffee grounds are sterilised, no further processing is necessary
Cleaner	both brewing and inoculation require only hot water	Less Methane	grounds used won't decompose in landfills so less greenhouse gas

Faster	caffeine makes mushrooms grow faster	Less Grazing Required	post-harvest substrate is a high-quality animal feed
Cheaper	raw materials are free	Less Logging	coffee is also a hardwood and an ideal substitute for oak
Healthier	mushrooms are protein-rich and cholesterol- and fat-free	Less Landfill	coffee shops waste removal costs and contribute less to landfill waste
More Secure	waste from the cash crop secures food for the region	More Food Security	waste from the cash crop secures food for the region

The "Orphan Teaches Orphans" programme, started by Chido Govera, herself orphaned at the age of seven (and now my adopted daughter), teaches other orphans how to grow mushrooms using locally available agricultural waste, including water hyacinth, an invasive species that proliferates throughout much of Africa. Water hyacinth has been named "Public Enemy Number One" in Zambia, and is fought with chemicals and by biological control with non-native insect species like the weevil that is imported from Australia. Yet one kilogram of water hyacinth can provide the nutrient base for up to two kilograms of mushrooms. Chido collects wild mushrooms during the rainy season and has mastered tissue culture techniques for the production of mushroom spawn. With Chido's inspiration and guidance, other orphaned girls, who have often suffered much, now not only find the will but also acquire the skills to provide sustenance and a livelihood for themselves. Having food security motivates many of them to think beyond food and build a future free from abuse and suffering.

Pulp to Livelihood

Based on results obtained in Colombia, each coffee farm undertaking mushroom cultivation could generate a minimum of two new jobs. With an estimated 25 million coffee farms in 45 countries, this translates into an additional 50 million jobs worldwide, while providing food security not only for the workers but for their families as well. If we include other waste streams such as straw, cobs, clippings, and water hyacinth, we are quickly edging towards truly amazing numbers. The capacity to provide local food for local populations increases farm income and farm stability. Instead of expending time and money to gather a subsistence diet with only the most basic of nutrients, a considerable quantity of healthful and protein-rich food, as well as animal feed, can be derived from mushroom production.

This is only one tributary of the cascading model of the Blue Economy, which provides an economic stimulus to generate jobs, especially in rural areas. If there were jobs on the farms that pay, provide food, and ensure that generations of expertise and tradition are used to their full potential, then few would be tempted to leave to fight for survival in the slums of the nearest metropolis. By now thousands of women living in villages in Zimbabwe, Ghana, Tanzania, Congo, Cameroon, South Africa and even in India, have been trained in using this simple methodology. Chido has created a special training centre, "The Future of Hope" in the vicinity of Harare, the capital of Zimbabwe, to institutionalise this health and food security programme.

Along with the direct benefits mentioned above, there are other tributaries of this Blue Economy approach, such as the creation of inner-city jobs. World-wide, coffee grounds are produced in hundreds of thousands of inner-city coffee shops. From the coffee shops of the Arab cities of the Middle East, to the *kohi shoppu* of Tokyo, to the traditional French cafés and that of the voracious American coffee culture across the USA, converting coffee grounds into mushrooms could mean a potential 100,000 additional jobs in urban zones. Pioneering efforts have been tested and proven effective in Rotterdam by Siemen Cox and Mark Sluggers and their start-up company RotterZwam, as well as that of Nikhil Aurora and Alex Velez of the San Francisco Bay area, who decided to forego consulting careers and create their coffee/mushroom company BTTR Ventures. They were trained and inspired by Ivan Milenkovic (Serbia), Carmenza Jaramillo (Colombia) and Chido Govera (Zimbabwe), all three entrepreneurs that translated the science into action. It is not difficult and therefore it is no surprise that more than 5,000 initiatives have emerged over the past decade. Knowing that orphans in Zimbabwe can achieve results with hardly anything but local waste, the assurance of success in the city is robust.

Jobs are only sustainable if income is generated. Income is only sustained when value is added. The core of this proposition is producing healthy food at a lower cost, with greater availability.

The years of experience of mushroom production on the market, demonstrated in urban and rural settings, that the lower prices for mushrooms create proportionally more demand, sustaining the farmer's livelihood and growing the business. Calculations using research data and hands-on experience indicate that the income potential from cultivating mushrooms on a coffee ground substrate is vast. Considered together, and solely on the basis of coffee waste, the inner-city and farm-based production units could produce an estimated 25 million tonnes of additional nutrient-rich food for human consumption. This is more than half the protein provided by the entire world's fish farming. And we know today that we can do the same with used tea leaves (provided no sugar was added). It is a secure revenue stream and a major resource for a global food market that is under severe stress due to the population explosion.

Cascading nutrients and energy – and not genetic modification – is what will allow us to respond to the basic needs of people.

Waste has always been unpopular. Aside from what we contribute to the "waste stream" on a personal basis, massive-scale disasters have turned our attention toward nuclear waste, petroleum spills, and chlorine pollution. Waste has been universally branded as negative. Imagine that waste now generates jobs and healthy food. This can only be good news! Since coffee pulp and coffee grounds make such an ideal substrate for mushrooms, and generate all the benefits just described, it should be touted and become part of coffee's image: Coffee makes for healthy food and secure jobs. Coffee could be associated with energy efficiency, sustainable livelihood, climate change mitigation, and even nourishing food at lower prices. The social capital would be substantial and widespread. Considering that it all started from something once considered "waste," coffee can hardly be positioned more positively. Whose waste is it really?

It would be an admirable act of corporate social responsibility if the coffee traders of the world – from Neumann Kaffee Gruppe to Nestlé Foods – were to ensure that all the farms they buy from convert all their on-site waste into an ideal mushroom growing medium. If the proponents of fair trade were to provide their farmers with the technical assistance necessary for converting waste to mushrooms, with whom would farmers prefer to trade? Cascading coffee waste could become a strategic tool for positioning long-term supply contracts with farmers, importers, and roasters.

To go one step further, traders and consumers who already support the organic and fair trade movements can be made aware that the real arena for fairness, the real opportunity for growth and development, can come from the 99.8% of the coffee harvest that has little value for those who harvest, purvey, and consume the bean. Such a viewpoint goes far beyond organic and fair trade. It permits the coffee trade to embrace sustainable development to its fullest extent – further than anyone has ever imagined. The label "organic" only certifies the absence of chemical fertilisers and sprays. It does not tell the user anything about resource efficiency. The label "Fair Trade" secures a fairer reimbursement for farmers, but does not secure the added value for the environment. Few coffee drinkers realise how little of the biomass generated at a coffee farm is consumed, or the wastefulness associated with their consumption habits. If consumers are educated to add a requirement for "resource-efficiency" to "organically grown" and "fairly traded" labels, and traders and distributors help foster a Pulp-to-Protein model on the farms from which the beans they market originate, such collaboration would bring about self-sustaining communities that experience food and livelihood security rather than malnourishment and despair. What incredible potential might be redirected for the benefit of the poor, the jobless, and the environment!

The Pulp-to-Protein initiative is based on the power of ecosystems, and builds on worthy organic and fair trade initiatives. It creates value for 100% of the nutrients. If fully developed in all coffee-producing communities, by turning a waste stream into an income stream, this business model could generate a staggering 1.5 million times more revenue than coffee produces today. Imagine 1.5 million times more revenue! It is in this spirit that entrepreneurs creating a Blue Economy will look at all waste streams, and succeed either by eliminating them altogether or by converting them to tributaries that cascade for providing a livelihood, food security, and abundance for all.

The Pulp-to-Protein Machine

Farm jobs	1 acre farm = 2 jobs x 25 million coffee farms worldwide = 50 million jobs
Inner-city jobs	10-15 coffee shops = 1 farming unit = 10 jobs x 21 000 coffee shops in the US + 100 000 ~ worldwide = 1.2 million jobs

Results	25 million tonnes of fresh protein worldwide in +45 countries 5x sales increase 2000–2010 – worldwide 51.2 million jobs

Let us do the math on this: If we are using the total biomass, and not only the 0.2% that ends up being ingested, we improve the material use by a factor of 500. If we generate as much value-added as a coffee shop in any major city does, where a cup of coffee contains 3 grams of ground coffee beans, that brings the farmer an income of one-hundredth of a dollar (one cent) but is sold for three dollars, then we are looking at a potential 3,000-fold increase. If we combine the two opportunities (factor 500 and factor 3,000) then we realise that coffee has potential revenue that is 1.5 million times the current revenue! Imagine how much better that cup of coffee would taste to the informed consumer when he or she realises that their purchase helped train another coffee farming community to achieve self-determination, sustainability, as well as food and livelihood security. The invigorating effect of the coffee would be enhanced with the flavour of satisfaction and the aroma of success – and without any additional expense. The consumer has the power to channel his or her dollar towards paying those who deliver products sustainably and equitably, using what is locally available, providing food for all, and empowering communities around the globe.

Mushroom cultivation programmes have been field-tested and fully realised in countries ranging from Colombia to Zimbabwe, from the USA to the Netherlands. The Colombian state of El Huila has over one hundred coffee-to-mushroom companies and is rapidly replacing illegally grown crops with nutritious food. The conclusion is that this system works. The expertise is fully prepared and readily available. The power of a just and sustainable economic model is that it generates greater value for all stakeholders. The Pulp-to-Protein business model is not about investing more to save money or to recover the additional expense, but about reducing costs for everyone – while generating a great deal of additional revenue. When waste becomes nutrient, it creates value that can be measured in jobs, cash flow, and profits. Green business and fair trade are stepping stones. Economies that cascade like ecosystems achieve the goal of providing multiple benefits for diverse partners.

From Waste to Superfood

Continuing to explore the potential of our Pulp-to-Protein model, let us imagine an entrepreneurial enterprise that makes coffee and coffee consumers healthier: an infusion of medicinal mushroom with that espresso or latte. Most mushrooms are rich in protein. Reishi and shiitake are prized nutritional varieties that are also medicinal marvels. In ancient times the wild red reishi was exclusively reserved for the Emperor of China. Although little is published in the way of clinical trials, the beneficial influence of these mushroom varieties for health conditions, ranging from diabetes to hypertension, is time-tested in Traditional Chinese Medicine. If the costs of these exotic mushrooms could be reduced using the production system just described, a helping of *Ganoderma* in that morning cup could be offered to customers wishing for an instant immune-system booster. It could even remove the acidity from that energy drink, balancing the pH naturally, and enhancing digestion.

This arithmetic is attractive for all the parties involved. Beyond the first mileposts of employment, income, and nourishment, if Starbucks Coffee were to offer its worldwide customer base a healthy *Ganoderma* infusion for their coffee, it would initiate a massive increase in demand for this mushroom, the name of which means "one thousand lives" in Japanese. If only a hundred customers each day at the 19,000 Starbucks coffee shops around the world were to order a Ganoderma shot in their espresso, macchiato, latte, or chai, at say US$ 0.50 a serving, it would annualise to an impressive additional revenue of US$ 365 million.

Consider further that were Starbucks to help develop the Pulp-to-Protein programme on their coffee farms and in urban areas, it could easily donate 10% of their increase in revenue, or US$ 36.5 million per year, to fund the effort. This would handily pay for itself in terms of social capital and tax-deductible expense, to say nothing of the employment, income, and nourishment made possible from a market consuming approximately two tonnes of *Ganoderma* per day. Such a sum represents $25 per pound of mushrooms for the coffee farmer. Where the cash transfer, of the total value in coffee itself, is one to the farmer, and 2,999 to everyone else, for *Ganoderma* the terms of trade could tilt towards one for the farmer and ten for everyone else. This would generate a net cash infusion into rural and inner-city economies that would effectively stimulate supply and demand, build consumer confidence and social capital, and provide opportunities for jobs and education, seldom seen or mentioned.

Negative branding of waste, through publicising blacklists of the worst polluters in the world, has caught the attention of the public at large. With the Pulp-to-Protein model we have nothing less than a complete re-branding of waste. A product negatively associated with exploitation and poverty could be transformed into a means to eradicate injustice and generate livelihood security. The chance for such a positive accomplishment comes at an opportune moment. Positive branding marks a shift in the focus of the business model. Entrepreneurs who are prepared to take up these business models can play a critical role in society by empowering their clients to speak out, using their purchasing power.

Tea could quickly engender a Pulp-to-Protein initiative of its own as well. The amount of tea biomass that is ultimately consumed in a cup of tea is only half of what is consumed from coffee, a mere one-tenth of a percent. Fruit tree clippings are another possibility for exceptional mushroom growth medium. These hardwood species may lack the added stimulus of caffeinated coffee grounds but are nonetheless a quality wood – that should not be incinerated, as is the current practice. Ivanka Milenkovic from Serbia tested apple orchard clippings as a growth substrate for mushroom cultivation. Not even the coldness of winter weather seemed to slow the mushroom growth. In field-tests, goats were observed consuming the substrate residue after harvesting, even before scientists established its amino acid content. As noted earlier (in Chapter 3), bison in New Mexico share this appetite.

There are endless possibilities, and resources abound. The key is simply to uncover value in waste. Water hyacinth, an ornamental plant from Latin America that creates havoc in tropical lakes, rivers, and dams, proliferates on the massive flow of nutrients from soil erosion and excessively utilised fertilisers that accumulate in water bodies. Instead of trying to obliterate this invasive aquatic plant, it could be harvested and converted into a growing medium for mushrooms, in the same way that Chido Govera is doing it in Africa. Whereas foraging ruminants would not eat the water hyacinth itself, the mushroom substrate remaining after harvesting would make an ideal feed. Merely with the waste from coffee, tea, hardwood clippings, water hyacinth, and straw, astronomical volumes of nutrients can be derived.

Ecosystems inspire us to look beyond conventional models to cascading models, where waste of one becomes raw material for another. Generating multiple benefits for diverse partners is a fair and positive Blue Economy model – one that evolves towards ever-greater levels of efficiency with ever-greater diversity. This is how rainforests are regenerated from depleted savannah. This is how a cash crop like coffee could not only provide food security and meet basic needs for clean water, fresh air, and healthy soil, but also could substantially augment local income and increase social capital. While the creation of 10,000 jobs may today be considered a massive success, there are 25 million coffee farms that could benefit from this model, creating employment for 50,000 more people! Given the magnitude of these possibilities, perhaps even Nestlé, a giant in the coffee trade business, may reconsider its rejection of an undertaking that, in the past, seemed too far outside its core business definition. With more vision, and perhaps the greater goal of profitability – along with food security and environmental stewardship – a compelling story could be told.

Drink it – Eat it – Wear it

Opportunities are vast and innovation often lies around the corner, provided we are open to ideas that go beyond status quo. Grandma knew all too well that when her refrigerator started emitting a foul smell, coffee grounds placed in it would resolve the problem. Jason Cheng, the founder of Singtex Corporation (Taiwan) turned that observation into a business. He produces textiles with a small percentage of coffee grounds mixed in, which control odour and block UV jointly. While we knew coffee eliminates smells, finding out that it has the capacity to block the sun with a protection factor of 50, came as a surprise. The complex processing of coffee, starting from a bush that originated in Ethiopia, to a fermentation process that was developed in Colombia, and a roasting technique that was perfected in Italy, provided this Chinese innovator with a tailor-made ingredient. Today, Singtex delivers odour-abating fibres to more than one hundred textile companies, including market leaders such as Nike and Adidas, pioneers like Patagonia and innovators like Ecoalf from Spain. These synthetic fibres include 5% fine coffee grounds. The coffee-enriched fabric eliminates odours, even after the wearer had a good run or climb. It retains this ability even after multiple washes. Timberland now lines the inside of the shoes it produces with this odour controlling tissue, attaching the "Drink It, Wear it" label.

Synthetic fibres have a value of US$ 1,500 per tonne. Functional fibres command a premium price. Coffee waste has no value. Jason Cheng started collecting coffee grounds from the local 7-Eleven stores but soon ran out of supply. Here is another opportunity: There is an opportunity for the instant coffee makers of the world: to set up a recycling plant for PET bottles next to the extraction unit that isolates the soluble part of coffee using steam only, and process these with coffee grounds doubling the income of the factory. The Buendía instant coffee factory in Chinchilla, owned by the Cooperative of Coffee Farmers of Colombia, is seeing light at the end of the tunnel. The 20 tonnes of waste coffee, which is presently incinerated, would double the income of the factory, while responding to a pressing demand from the market.

Once we start on this pathway of cascading nutrients and energy, and identify opportunities, it seems that the innovations are unstoppable. Crises are opportunities. It now even offers the chance to imagine re-industrialising entire regions using waste streams that render the primary sector competitive again – and is providing farmers with a decent income. We now have to thank Jason Cheng for putting coffee into textiles, knowing that the physical chemistry is so strong that it even works after washing and drying.

9

A NEW FUTURE FOR SILK

> **When one tugs at a single thing in nature, he finds it attached to the rest of the world.**
> —*John Muir*

Topsoil on the Cutting Edge

Centuries ago, the Chinese were confronted with a growing demand for food and a limit to the fertile soil available. As they searched for ways to acquire additional arable farmland by regenerating topsoil, they observed and reflected on the materials and processes that natural systems use to make arid land fertile. They also realised that farming and animal husbandry often failed to maintain the flow of contributory elements, causing fertile land to degrade and become barren, arid soil. What they discovered, and the strategy they devised, changed the course of their civilisation, and if we are smart it will do the same for ours – by enabling us to use an ecosystem approach to change economic models and business strategies for modern products as diverse as aeroplanes and razors.

The mulberry tree (*Morus alba*) thrives in most of China's typically arid soil. The wild moth caterpillar (*Bombyx mori*), more commonly known as the silkworm, feeds on mulberry leaves and its droppings fall to the ground, attracting bacteria and micro-organisms, which quickly produces nutrients that enrich the soil. Over years, centuries, and even millennia, the density of the newly created, healthy topsoil increases by about one millimetre each year. This equates to the formation of 15 to 25 tonnes per acre of organically enriched topsoil annually.

This natural symbiosis between caterpillars and trees, and the contribution they make to soil fertility, promised food security for China's expanding population. Hence, China undertook a large-scale planting scheme. As dynasties rose and fell, soil fertility was regenerated and maintained. Previously infertile land became productive without tilling, ploughing, or irrigation. Farmers intercropped with cowpeas and groundnuts. Throughout history, Middle Eastern and European countries have also planted mulberry trees, and benefited from the positive effect on soil fertility and erosion control. The Italians planted vineyard borderlands with mulberry trees to stem erosion on vineyard slopes, as did the Turks.

These natural methods to generate topsoil were in time forgotten as attention diverted from the practices of sustainable farming to commercial monoculture. A lucrative industry and enormous wealth emerged from producing one of the legendary artefacts of human culture: silk, the natural polymer spun from the threads of the cocoon of the silkworm.

According to Chinese legend, the idea to use caterpillar polymer as silk thread is attributed to Chinese Empress Si-Ling-Chi (Lady of the Silkworm), who, one afternoon, as she sat under a mulberry tree to sip her tea, had a cocoon fall into her cup. She noticed the strong, smooth threads of the cocoon uncoiling, and began pulling them from her cup. She was fascinated and enthralled as a thread over a thousand feet long emerged. It is said that Empress Si-Ling-Chi first developed the uses of silk for clothing and for wrapping fruits and vegetables

– a proven preservation technique. Her husband, Emperor Huang Di (the famous Yellow Emperor), has been credited with the invention of methods for raising silk worms and spinning silk thread. Emperor Huang Di is also said to have taught humankind to manufacture objects in wood, ceramics, and metal, and to have ordered the construction of the first boats and wheeled vehicles.

As the legend implies, silk is a serendipitous discovery. It is a by-product that originally had no value compared to the strategic long-term importance of soil regeneration and the fertilisation of arid land. More recently, the introduction of synthetic polymer textiles made from petrochemicals, not only replaced a renewable (silk) with a non-renewable (petroleum), but it also deprived intercropped farmland of millions of tonnes of fertiliser.

The popularity of stronger and cheaper synthetic polymers decimated silk production. Consequently, the planting and care of mulberry trees became obsolete. The millennia-long tradition of regenerating topsoil fell into oblivion since its by-product could not compete in the modern market. Worse still, while plastics and polymers made inroads into every stratum of consumption, the land not only lost its source of nutrients and soil replenishment but also required petrochemical fertilisers to boost levels of food production. This increased the energy input needed to achieve a harvest, and furthered dependency on fossil fuels while increasing greenhouse gas emissions.

The loss of topsoil currently represents one of the greatest challenges to food security for the world's future population. Ethiopia, a mountainous country with highly eroded soil on steeply sloping land, loses an estimated one billion tonnes of topsoil a year, carried away by rain and wind. This is one reason Ethiopia always seems to be on the verge of famine, never able to accumulate enough grain reserves to provide a meaningful measure of food security. In dust storms alone, two to three billion tonnes of fine soil particles leave Africa each year, inexorably draining the continent of its fertility and biological productivity, while depositing enough dust in the Caribbean seas to cloud the waters and impact coral reefs. The farming practices brought to Africa by European colonisers were not adapted to the continent's climatic conditions.

Some farmers build the soil they sow. Most, however, simply rely on chemical fertilisers, pesticides, and intensive irrigation. Using modern farming practices, from one to ten tonnes of topsoil per acre are lost annually. However, soil losses of as much as 125 to 250 tonnes per acre are common. Losses of 750 to 1,800 tonnes per acre due to soil runoff from a single rainfall have been recorded. In South Africa, some seven tonnes of topsoil can be lost for every tonne of grain harvested. When all these factors take their toll, farmers are persuaded by the promise of higher yields to look to petrochemical fertilisers and genetically modified seeds, although such promises are often short-lived or misleading.

Over a five-year period, Prof. George Chan extensively studied integrated farming systems around the millennia-old Chinese tradition of using mulberry trees and silkworms. He assisted farming communities in more than 70 countries to realise the practice of nutrient cascading by planting mulberry trees and introducing silkworms to build topsoil. The application of Prof. Chan's topsoil-generating techniques has inspired agriculturally based industries in Namibia, Japan, Fiji, and the USA to adopt their own nutrient-cascading strategies. As a result of drawing on an ancient Chinese tradition, modern food production can now be transformed.

Silk for Carbon Capture

Natural silk contains upwards of 30% carbon but when replaced by petrochemical fibres the carbon fixation from silk production and the growth of mulberry trees is lost. It also ends the associated topsoil regeneration. Just this one case demonstrates that the air pollution and greenhouse gas emissions are only part of the problem when it comes to petroleum. The substitution of a renewable (silk) by a non-renewable (petroleum) eliminates natural carbon sinks. The ecosystem then loses efficiency since it is incapable of replenishing soil nutrients. It therefore requires additional input in the form of fertilisers. This releases more greenhouse gases, especially since nitrogen-based fertilisers are one of the biggest sources of nitrous oxide (N_2O). According to the Intergovernmental Panel on Climate Change (IPCC), even though this gas is released only in small quantities, its impact is huge. The emission of one tonne of N_2O equals the emission of 310 tonnes of carbon dioxide (CO_2).

Traditional farming techniques work in harmony with the delicate interconnections in Nature that characterise an ecosystem. With silk production we see a shocking example of how these positive cycles are decimated when replaced by monoculture and synthetics. The fertilisers and plastics proffered as symbols of modernity are in reality case studies of how production and consumption systems have devolved from sustainable to unsustainable.

Wallace Carothers, the chemical engineer who invented nylon for Dupont, could not have had any idea that his petroleum-derived fibre would unravel a web of life that had harmoniously enfolded industrial production in a nutrient cascade, benefiting land and agricultural cultivation over five millennia. It is fair to say that in our quest for modernity we have demonstrated considerable ignorance concerning the impact of our inventions. Consider Dr Thomas Midgely, who invented lead additives for gasoline that have lead to serious health concerns and have been banned in most countries. Then there is Freon for refrigeration, which achieved its goal of stopping refrigerators from exploding, but also destroyed ozone in the atmosphere before it was be replaced. How can we now expect that government and industry will be able to solve the challenge of climate change, unless they gain an understanding of the thousands of connections that can be destroyed if the full implications on the system are not understood? Once we grasp the elegant interplay of physics and biochemistry in ecosystems, we can model more breakthrough innovations that open up ever more possibilities for progress and sufficiency. It is up to all of us to see the complexity of our amazing planet and to conspire to create new opportunities.

The Geometry of Silk

Recognition of the problem is also a key to its solution. There are hundreds of species that produce silk. Ants, wasps, bees, mussels, and spiders are among them. Only one, the Chinese silkworm, has been domesticated. Sophisticated instrumentation makes it possible to analyse all the different silks produced at the nanolevel. Scientists are beginning to see how these natural polymers can outperform some of their synthetic counterparts and even some metals, such as titanium, which is considered to have the highest strength-to-weight ratio of any metal. As Janine Benyus points out in her book *Biomimicry*, if we can learn how to manufacture biocompatible polymers as these other species do, under ambient conditions, with available nutrients, it opens a new world of possibilities and a potentially virtuous cycle of soil regeneration and climate stabilisation.

While on a Smithsonian mission in Central America, Oxford University Professor Fritz Vollrath encountered a species of golden silk orb weaver spider (*Nephila clavipes*) that spins a one-metre diameter web of a beautiful golden colour. He was fascinated by experimental evidence suggesting that the colour served a dual purpose, both attracting prey and providing disguise. After decades of research he came to understand spider silk and its remarkable qualities of resilience, strength, and flexibility. He realised that the extraordinary performance of the spider's silk is due to its geometry at the nanoscale. Geometry is part of mathematics. In this case, Vollrath used it to determine how the crystalline and non-crystalline structure of silk creates variation of strength that often out-competes metals and designer plastics. By merely controlling pressure and humidity in the rear abdomen at the moment of spinning, the golden orb spider is capable of producing seven different types of silk.

The Joro spider (*Nephila calvata)* outperforms many others in terms of tensile strength and versatility of its silk under changing conditions. The extreme toughness of spider silk stems from the controlled folding of all the proteins that compose the silk during spinning. This protein folding is largely dependent on the precise extraction of water, accomplished with no more than the pressure in the spider's abdomen. Professor Vollrath's comparisons between spider and insect spinning provided further insights into the range of different extrusion processes.

Spiders have a remarkable ability to recycle their webs, reconditioning it to meet new requirements. A spider will ingest the portions of its web it wants to renew, converting the polymers back into their original amino acids. How can we not be impressed by this ability? It models one of the best recycling programmes ever designed for a polymer! How does this compare to the "disposable" plastics of our modern life, that continue to accumulate in a massive floating continent of plastic waste in the Pacific Ocean, one which is toxic to ocean life?

The domestication of spiders is, however, very challenging. The species are aggressive. Even if such defensive behaviour were overcome, their productive output is low. They simply recycle too much, reprocessing their web into a new variety of silk adapted to the changed circumstances, with little need for additional production. These limitations compelled Vollrath to compare the structure of silk spun by the mulberry silkworm with the structure of silk spun by the golden orb spider. Using the basic amino acids as building blocks, he and his Oxford team replicated the spider's recipe in order to structure silk from the silkworm to match that of the silk from the spider. The processed polymer they developed is a silk with properties identical to those that make the spider's version so unique.

Professor Vollrath is engaged in the design of a systemic approach to the production of biocompatible polymers from renewable resources, very much along the lines of the original Chinese strategy for regenerating topsoil. Building on his visionary research, Vollrath has established business entities that are manufacturing these polymers and identifying markets where these biocompatible products can outperform and underprice petroleum-based polymers and expensive metal alloys. Instead of generating collateral damage, as is the case with products that produce copious pollution and generate greenhouse gases, these products can help reconnect our economy to the original purpose of China's silk production: regeneration, renewal, and abundance – of soil fertility, harvest capacity, and carbon capture.

Over a century ago, the annual output of raw silk hovered around one million tonnes. Current production fluctuates in a range below 100,000 tonnes per year. With the exception of luxury fabrics such as those made by Hermès, the future market for silk will not be textile or clothing manufacture. It cannot compete in price with brand-name petrochemical synthetic polymers that hold greater market share in the textile industry. However, it notably outperforms expensive metals such as stainless steel and titanium by a factor of 6, in price and performance. Titanium has become the standard structural material for jet engines, spacecraft, desalination plants, medical prostheses, orthopaedic implants, dental implants, sporting goods, and mobile phones. Although the aerospace industry uses up the largest portion of processed titanium, consumer goods increasingly include titanium in stainless steel manufacture, as well as many products ranging from bicycle frames and jewellery to implants and prostheses.

It is here that we can spot a potential strategic shift in the business concept that could give rise to new economic development opportunities. The production of titanium from metal ore consumes large quantities of magnesium, chlorine, and argon gas. Titanium must be welded in an inert atmosphere to protect it from contamination with oxygen, nitrogen, or hydrogen. Both the energy inputs and the use of scarce and mined resources are significant, so that the end products have high price tags. Processed and cured titanium has a high tensile strength-to-density ratio and high resistance to oxygen and seawater corrosion. Because of these desirable qualities, customers pay more and ignore the collateral damage to the environment. When we contrast a life cycle analysis of titanium, with the simplicity of mulberry leaves transformed into silk, at relatively ambient temperature, pressure, and moisture levels, silk clearly emerges on the positive side of the sustainability index. We quickly understand how we can move these industries towards sustainability. Companies willing to take advantage of Vollrath's nanoscale insights for controlling silk's geometry will find that these biocompatible silk polymers are an ideal substitute for high-performance metals.

A Close Shave

An ubiquitous example of our unsustainable consumption is the razor we use to remove hair. There are few activities more common than shaving. Hair grows year in, year out. Cave paintings show that even prehistorically men scraped off unwanted hair using implements such as stones and clamshells. During the Bronze Age, humans developed the ability to forge simple metals and began to make razors from iron and bronze. Early Egyptians shaved both their beards and heads, a custom eventually adopted by the Greeks and Romans, particularly soldiers facing hand-to-hand combat: a lack of locks meant one less handhold for an enemy.

A modern shaving blade, manufactured in the early 21st century, uses almost twenty times less metal than the first disposable ones introduced by King C. Gillette over a century ago. While this confirms the drive towards material efficiency, lowered cost and thus greater affordability, it results in less incentive to extend a product's useful life. As Gillette increased profitability and market share, the overall volume of individual razors, as well as the total weight of metal waste, increased dramatically. An estimated 10 billion throwaway razors annually contribute 250,000 tonnes of valuable metal to landfills. Most unfortunately, the latest models have increased the number of blades from two to five or even six. Here we witness a rebound effect that undoes the material efficiency gains of the past fifty years.

Razor blades are exposed to high levels of moisture and must therefore be made from a special corrosion-resistant steel alloy or titanium. The grade of steel must be hard enough for the blade to hold its shape, yet flexible enough for it to be processed. Carbide steel is preferred because it is made using carbon, silicon, manganese, chromium, and molybdenum, with the remainder being iron, and a finishing layer of titanium. The steel is heated to temperatures of 1100°C, then hardened by quenching in water to a temperature of around -70 °C. The steel is tempered at 350 °C. The blades are then stamped to form the appropriate cutting edge at a rate of 800-1,200 per minute. Because the blade is so small, a special metal and plastic support structure is required to hold it inside the cartridge. Just like titanium, stainless steel is part of a production and consumption pattern that is unsustainable. This entire process offers only a few clean shaves and then the razor ends up in a landfill.

The shaving industry now has a choice. Rather than market growth by volume, they can turn the razor business into something that contributes to solving the environmental and employment crisis while offering something better and cheaper. A razor made of silk will cut through keratin (hair) but will not slice the skin since it rolls hundreds of fine threads over the surface of the skin, in effect a miniature version of a hand-pushed lawn mower. The technology is here. Its fine-tuning and production are just a matter of time and money. The fact that silk can be substituted for mined ores, dramatically reducing carbon emissions and even sequestering carbon, reveals an ideal cost/benefit structure. At US$ 100 per pound for processed silk, each silk-blade razor would cost less than a dollar, yet its performance and feel would be equal to that of the latest industry versions.

Smooth as Silk

Because the manufacturing is a trade secret, another use of unsustainable polymers, namely cosmetics, has escaped consumers' attention. After water, polymers represent the second largest category of ingredients in cosmetics and personal care products. A diverse range of polymers are used as film-formers, fixatives, thickeners, emulsifiers, stimuli-responsive agents, conditioners, foam stabilisers, skin-feel benefiting agents, and antimicrobials. The market value of synthetic polymers is currently US$ 15 billion, and steadily growing. Polymers have replaced many cosmetics ingredients formerly derived from natural sources. While it may be difficult to visualise how silk can replace stainless steel in razors and aeroplanes, our tactile association with the softness of silk makes it much easier to imagine how silk could be a main component of skin and hair care products. Using silk nanotechnology products as substitutes for synthetic polymers could be a most promising and highly profitable direction for the cosmetic industry to take.

It will take only one market leader such as Clarins or Shiseido shifting from synthetic to natural polymers to garner the attention of all the major players in the market. The first application would likely be sunscreen products, since silk could provide a dual functionality. Silk polymers would give structure to the cream and at the same time dissipate ultraviolet rays. Silk could also be a biocompatible replacement for titanium, in the expensive titanium oxide creams that are marketed to protect against ultraviolet exposure.

The hair colouring market is a second area where naturally produced silk nanostructures could quickly gain market share. Greeks and Romans used highly alkaline soap, boiled walnuts, and henna to create different shades. Although such colour tinting products are kinder to our body, they do not retain their colouring over time. The colouring products made from harsh chemical polymers provide more permanent hair colour. Published research linking cancer to the prolonged use of hair dyes has, however, prompted the US Food and Drug Administration to study the potential toxicity of these colouring agents. Fortunately, new insights on silk polymers have made it possible to develop biocompatible products that can obtain and hold a desired colour. Silk polymers and other biologically derived renewable raw materials could handily replace toxic hair dyes – and at the same time release a cascade of positive health and ecological effects.

Biocompatible Medical Uses

Silk thread has been used worldwide for many years as a suture in intricate surgical and ophthalmological operations. It is suitable for this purpose because of its fine, soft fibres and tensile strength. It is also easy to tie yet difficult to untie. Its protein composition makes it compatible with the human body, eliminating the need for surgical removal. Other medical applications have been commercialised: anti-hay fever masks, gauze pads, and bandages for dermatological disorders are made from silk. The development of technology to dissolve silk fibres and make film from silk protein has opened the way for research and development for use in artificial skin, blood vessels, tendons, and nerve regeneration, as well as contact lenses, catheters for surgical procedures, and anticoagulants. All these applications employ the biocompatibility and permeability of the silk.

Presently, when knee or spine tissue cartilage is damaged and cannot regenerate, an artificial knee made of titanium is surgically implanted. Another product being developed by Professor Vollrath and his team is a porous silk scaffold with mechanical properties that nearly match those of human fibrocartilage. The silk scaffold is inserted in place of damaged cartilage and stimulates cell growth on its porous, biocompatible surface, regenerating the cartilage using the body's immune response. A natural system with biocompatible components can successfully strengthen an existing structure, as opposed to a system with expensive and incompatible components that require immunosuppressants to overcome rejection. The world market for biocompatible devices already approaches some US$ 20 billion annually, with an annual growth rate of over 10 percent. Silk sutures will soon be complemented by silk-based wound dressing, replacement joints, and orthopaedic implants – all stemming from insights into how natural systems perform.

The demand for medical devices made from silk offers a high-end proof of concept that these products are financially viable – even under present economic conditions. Professor Vollrath and his team have succeeded in bringing silk-based products to market. The opportunities for these technologies to become available worldwide will substantially stimulate the demand for silk. If the research is done for products as complex as these, making razors or cosmetic ingredients from silk polymers will be easy. It is just a matter of putting our minds to it! And who will do that? Will Schlick, Gillette, or a consortium of entrepreneurs transform a surprisingly unsustainable consumer product into a quality product that sequesters carbon and is as smooth as silk in performance? As stated before, at its peak, a hundred years ago, the annual volume of silk production had reached one million tonnes. If the demand for silk to make razors and cosmetics were to reach just 100,000 tonnes over the next ten years, imagine the beneficial effect this would have on increased soil fertility.

Merging the Arts

China has an exceptional silk cultural tradition. It has an equally exceptional tradition in bamboo. Silk has been defeated by cheap nylon, as bamboo weaving has been by cheap automated mass production. Bamboo weaving has, however, now re-emerged as an art form, one in which shapes and forms that retain their shape for decades, if not centuries, without the use of metal or glue, are created by hand, These forms are now covered naturally with a blanket of silk by caterpillars working for months on end. For instance, a baby's crib, made to measure, is painstakingly covered in silk by thousands of silk worms. These insects (that we call worms but are in fact caterpillars), do so in an attempt to create a cocoon, as a safe place in which to pupate. Raw silk has a few unique features: it is a virus, bacteria and fungus free product – offering an environment that every parent would like to offer an infant. Whereas silk and bamboo as a stand-alone art would not stand up against the global onslaught of competition, the two combined offer a product that is unique – outcompeting whatever is available today.

The added appeal of this approach is that it does not eliminate any industry jobs. The number of jobs potentially lost will be far outnumbered by the number of new jobs created – a total of 1.5 million jobs for each 100,000 tonnes of additional silk harvested. Applying a sustainable model that uses silk instead of plastic is more competitive, has greater marketing appeal, generates topsoil, and cuts carbon emissions. This is the Blue Economy we seek to bring to the centre stage of modern society.

10

FROM THE MIGHTY TO THE MINISCULE

The sun, with all the planets revolving around it
and depending on it,
can still ripen a bunch of grapes
as if it had nothing else in the universe to do.
— *Galileo Galilei*

Only a Heartbeat Away

While we rightly worry about human-induced climate change, humanity is hovering between two killing fields: children dying of malnutrition from shortages of the most basic nutrients, and adults dying of malnutrition from an excess of the wrong foods. A diet of artificial and refined food and a lack of exercise combine to create a terrain that leads to a lessening of quality of life and a shorter lifespan. The unconscionable truth is that we know this! Until we act and this pattern shifts, regular monitoring for heart disease will remain a necessity as heart disease takes a higher toll of lives than any other single malady.

Medical researchers have tried to address this for decades, and have found ways to apply technology to beneficial effect in helping correct heart malfunction. Dr Jorge Reynolds is one of these researchers. Having studied electronic engineering at Cambridge University and graduating in 1953, he devised a way to correct an irregular heartbeat by modulating an electric current, one that was sourced and transformed from a car battery, and attached to two diodes connected to the heart.

Between 1954 and 1964, Professor Reynolds developed a prototype version of a pacemaker that could be placed into the heart to correct heart function by keeping it beating regularly. Even though the device was the size of a car battery on wheels and required continuous connection to the post-surgical patient, over 1,700 patients were aided by his invention. In fact, in 2013 five of these patients were still alive. His prototype pacemaker is on display at the Museum of Science and Industry in London. In the 1960s Prof. Reynolds transferred all his patents and protocols to a third party for further development and dedicated the rest of his life to research. He was looking for a better way to get the human heart to keep working efficiently. His curiosity and research led him to study the heart functioning of other mammals. When he began to study the whale's heart and circulatory mechanism, he was fascinated by what he found.

Energy from Whales

The whale was once a land mammal, one that returned to the ocean, evolving into the largest and perhaps the most intelligent animal living on Earth. In the 18th century, the whale was sought after for its blubber. Whale oil, rendered from whale blubber, was globally harvested and traded. Its uses ranged from lamp oil for nighttime illumination to cooking oil. Whales were hunted to near extinction. It took another 250 years of human development for us to realise that the real marvel of the whale is not its blubber but rather its capacity to generate six to twelve volts of electric power merely by way of an electro-chemical process using potassium, sodium, and calcium. This is remarkable since whales rely solely on krill and small fish for their nutrition and energy. This biochemical capacity to generate electricity is a phenomenon that has been studied extensively by Prof. Reynolds, who has monitored the heart function of whales non-invasively for over three decades.

Prof. Reynolds wondered how the heart of this magnificently large mammal adapted throughout its remarkable physical and physiological transformations. With each pulse, over a lifespan of approximately 80 years, and without any maintenance or intervention, the whale's heart, bathed in blubber, pumps 250 gallons of blood along 100 million miles of arteries and veins. As the whale's muscles, valves, veins, and the arteries had evolved over time, Reynolds pondered on how the whale was able to distribute electric current to its massive physique and coordinate the pulsing rhythms at a scale one thousand times greater than the heart of its dog-like ancestor. There are no known cases of cardiac arrest among whales. Yet if a human heart were to lie in so much fat, it would simply stop working.

Prof. Reynolds posed these key questions: What do we stand to learn from this? What clues are there? No one could offer any answers, so he embarked on an intensive quest to learn everything he could about whale and other mammalian hearts. Wishing to record and graph the whale's heart, he designed an ECG recorder to attach to a whale and transmit heartbeat data via satellite to his research centre in Bogotá, Colombia. One may imagine the difficulty of designing and fabricating the machinery, and setting up electronic data transmission, but the real feat lay in how the recorder was attached. Jorge Reynolds did this by hand, one whale at a time, working from an open boat in the ocean waters. This was science on the edge!

Prof. Reynolds' career in heart research now spans five decades, and his fascination is not limited only to whales. He has recorded ECGs from over 200 animals, some as small as a fly, as elusive as the pink dolphin of the Amazon, or as curious as a grazing iguana on a Galapagos island. To date Prof. Reynolds and his team have compiled a list of over 10,000 whale ECGs, using advanced sound filtration systems, originally designed for military use, as underwater audio-phones. This greatly facilitated the research, as it eliminated the need to physically attach the equipment to a whale. The team eventually gathered so much data that Prof. Reynolds could accurately map the functioning of a whale's heart. Further remarkable data was revealed from medical dissections performed on dead beached whales. Scientists postulate that the whale has channels of cells that appear to be solely dedicated to guiding electric currents in and around the heart. These currents coordinate the electric flow and are capable of adjusting their pathways to bypass damaged tissue.

Prof. Reynolds' curiosity drove his research far beyond observations of heartbeat. To comprehend how potassium, sodium, and calcium combine to power electric currents at the molecular level, without either metal wires or batteries, he studied the entire genesis and transformation of the whale heart, beginning with its embryonic materialisation from the time of conception. He mapped his findings onto a three-dimensional virtual heart. Using off-the-shelf AutoDesk engineering software, he gave other scientists and cardiologists access to open source information that could be mapped before their very eyes.

His observations made him rethink pacemaker fundamentals. By now a practically ubiquitous device prolonging millions of lives, the pacemaker replaces the body's natural capacity to generate electric currents with a battery-powered device that connects to tissue in the depths of the heart. Hundreds of thousands of these devices were, however, plagued by defects. This fact pushed Prof. Reynolds to think beyond the obvious. He hesitated at first – because of the simplicity of his idea. Inspired by the physiognomy of the whale, he thought about recreating the cell-thin channels that bring along electrical currents, to improve the distribution of current throughout the human heart. He envisioned replacing the existing device, one that he had helped invent, with a nanoscale carbon tube that serves as a bridge, having the same power as a pacemaker. Instead of replacing the natural function of the heart, the tiny carbon coil would simply channel the current from healthy tissue to damaged tissue. Here was a revolutionary idea: to build on the existing power generation capacity, and simply improve conductivity!

The second revolutionary concept was based on his realisation that the whale, like all other mammals, and even some insects like the fly, generate and conduct current with neither battery nor wiring. Our planet's diverse living species have learned to generate the electrical power they need, using quite an extensive collection of energy sources: gravity, temperature differential, acidity (pH) differential, kinetic energy from muscle movement, piezo-electrical energy from movement of the heart and blood, energy derived from CO_2, and physiological biometals. Prof. Reynolds' studies concluded that all these species' applications work and that they have been proven over millions of years.

He designed a series of new medical devices that operate like everything else in Nature – that is, without cables or a battery. He focused on how whales generate a continuous flow of electric pulses from the minuscule supply and fine coordination of chemical reactions produced with a combination of potassium, sodium, and calcium. The medical devices and physiological monitoring systems he produces, rely only on the sources of energy that already exist in and around the body.

The first such application Prof. Reynolds designed, the nanopacemaker, is a minute device of only 700 nanometres in length (that is 700-millionths of a millimetre) that is controlled by the latest microprocessors. It takes its inspiration from the whale's conductivity channels and has proven its viability in the laboratory. After Medtronic ran and monitored animal studies of his prototypes, a team of surgeons from the famous Mayo Clinic (USA), with the support of Boston Scientific, implanted the first successful nanobridge in a human patient in October 2016. It functions as expected, and works without the need for a battery.

It is easy to understand why the market leaders in pacemaker manufacturing and sales, companies such as Medtronic, Johnson & Johnson, and Boston Scientific, would challenge this innovation. They are earning on each surgery performed. This is in conjunction with the pharmaceutical industry that will garner great profit from the supply of medicine for the rest of the patient's life. How would the leading pacemaker manufacturers react to an innovation that eliminates a guaranteed income of at least US$ 50,000 for each patient diagnosed with a treatable cardiac arrhythmia problem, and another average of US$ 50,000 for a lifetime supply of medicine? All these expenses could be reduced to a US$ 500 procedure. Placement of the nanowire is done via a catheter and does not require general anaesthesia. Since patients are not likely to require any continuing medication, the total cost for medical insurance companies drops by a factor of 200. Insurance companies should therefore be keenly receptive to this innovative application.

Healthy, Battery-Free Electrical Current

Our industrial system is oriented to the use of immense size and power. Thus it is not surprising that the minuscule electrical charges generated by natural systems are dismissed as trivial. Self-winding watches and flashing lights in children's shoe soles are on a short list of familiar commercial applications. Yet the human heart and brain function by way of micro-currents. No one is wired or carries a battery, except when a pacemaker has been surgically implanted or a hearing aid is fitted into the ear. Simple, naturally generated electrical current is powerful enough to continuously regulate the flow of blood through the heart every day. Over a single lifetime, the energy the body produces, sourced from the core elements in food, is sufficient to lift a 40-foot shipping container from the harbour in Mumbai (India) to the top of Mt. Everest!

On a wider scale, Prof. Reynolds' research and subsequent innovations may well herald the end of our dependence on chemical batteries that end up in our landfills and pollute our environment. By eliminating the need for a battery, we would also be eliminating pollution and toxic waste. Batteries offer convenience, but they are a major source of demand for mined materials, and are seldom fully recycled. It is no secret that metals from batteries do pollute and are health hazards.

There are over 40 billion batteries manufactured and sold each year. The vast majority of smaller "disposable" batteries simply becomes waste. Worse still, is that this trend is accelerating. Batteries are one of the double-digit growth segments of the market. Even Sweden and Germany, two countries with great societal discipline, do not recycle half of what is used, while in South Africa it is estimated that only 6% of batteries under 1 kilogram in weight are recycled. Because their low cost, availability, and size make recycling them easy to dismiss, these smaller batteries most often collect in landfills. In South Africa, over one-third of all handheld batteries, weighing over 8,000 tonnes, are sent to landfills annually. Another daily occurring tragedy is that we fail to realise the adverse impact such a tiny device has on the health of our planet – and ultimately on our own health. The metals it contains are indiscriminately dispersed into the ecosystem on which we depend for critical resources like drinking water and fertile soil.

We also fail to consider the high energy cost of battery power. If we compare the cost per kilowatt hour of a battery to the cost of the same energy from a socket at home, most of us would be surprised to discover that we are paying 100 to 500 times more for battery power than we pay for electricity in our homes. Industry analysts who have come to this realisation are now avidly searching for the most efficient battery. Billions are being spent by governments and private investors to find the longest-lasting and least-polluting battery that will give consumers the convenience and flexibility of electricity when they need it. While huge amounts of money are spent, we seem to have collectively forgotten that any battery made of metals (especially heavy metals) is taxing the Earth's resources beyond its capacity to sustain future demand. Worse still, it increases the demand for mining as well as the unregulated dispersal of metals into the environment. Batteries may be a convenient source of energy but the economic and environmental costs are beyond reason. Not only has Prof. Reynolds and his team significantly reduced the cost of a life saving procedure, they have also eliminated the need for toxic batteries to be manufactured. This type of innovation is creating a bright future, rather than destroying it little by little... The time has come for us to design a battery-free world and make use of innovative nanotechnology to power our gadgets, from pacemakers to remote controls and all hand-held devices.

The Furore over Furanones

The first living species on Earth were bacteria. Photosynthesis by bacteria emerged at least 2.8 billion years ago, well before plants existed. While scientists call single celled organisms "Monera" we call them "bacteria," "bugs," or even "germs". Bacteria are everywhere and just about everything we know finds its origin in bacteria. Our eyes, nose, ears, and taste buds are all associated with these first living creatures. Few of us seem to recognise that we exist in symbiosis with bacteria. While we like to think that our ancestors were apes, we are really nothing more than the great-great-great-great grandchildren of bacteria! Knowing that we cannot digest food without digestive bacteria makes it even more curious that we want to obliterate them all.

Ever since microscopes made it possible for us to see these nucleus-free single cell organisms, and science and industry convinced us of their evil intentions, we have been on a quest to exterminate them. If we are so determined to kill them, using the harshest versions of chemistry and antibiotics (originally based on the biology of the fungus), then we find ourselves ... killing ourselves. We "disinfect" our bathrooms and kitchens, and even our skin, with chemicals that are not conducive to life. Assuming that we brush our teeth twice a day, there are still probably more bacteria living in your mouth than there are people living on Earth. Our preoccupation with killing bacteria is one campaign that is certain to fail. Bacteria are a basic and ubiquitous form of life that in fact comprises almost 10% of our bodies by weight.

Failure is certainly the result we are likely to achieve with our excessive use of bactericides. Not only are many of these chemicals linked to a higher incidence of cancer and an array of unhealthful and physiologically disruptive side-effects, our desire to eliminate these microorganisms, in fact, spurs them to mutate faster. As they have no nucleus, bacteria pursue genetic modifications at will. It is our chemically loaded killing spree that has put these miniscule but mighty organisms on an evolutionary path towards becoming super bacteria. Our immune systems, already continuously stressed by being forced to cope with increasingly ineffective chemical bactericides, and functioning without the benefit of the helpful bacteria eliminated by the same chemical overload, cannot keep up. The double whammy of chemical attack and depleted natural defence mechanisms exhausts our body's ability to respond effectively.

Since trying to kill bacteria may in fact kill us, it is worth observing how the second form of life on Earth – Protista, which includes eukaryotes like slime moulds and micro-algae, ancestor of seaweed – adapted to bacteria, the first form of life. Considering that the ocean, from which life emerged, is literally a soup of bacteria, killing bacteria did not make sense to the newer micro-algae. Had the Protista developed a poison potent enough to kill all bacteria, it would have annihilated every other form of life, including itself.

As seaweed started populating the oceans, they quickly found their surfaces colonised by bacteria. Bacteria slowly build a biofilm, just like those that line our digestive system, cover our scalp, and populate our tongue. If the colony gets out of control and bacteria sense they have a quorum, they may decide to take over the host.

How did seaweed then cope with the need to compete and the challenge to survive? To survive as a recently arrived species, seaweed needed to become better at mastering its environment. *Delicea pulchra*, the red seaweed found between Tasmania and Japan, perfected a way to jam communication among bacteria. Instead of endangering their own long-term future and attempting (ineffectively) to eradicate bacteria, *Delicea pulchra* simply learned to "deafen" the bacteria temporarily by creating a small molecule, named a "furanone," which occupies a bacteria's receptor and makes it impossible for the bacteria to "hear" other bacteria of the same genus.

This is a brilliantly effective solution. Bacteria use chemicals to communicate with each other. If they do not receive specific molecules, because the necessary receptors are already blocked – by a molecule from seaweed – bacteria do not have a clue where other family members are. Under these conditions it is difficult for bacteria to work together to form a dominant biofilm. Better even, existing biofilm disintegrates when there is no communication to coordinate joint action. If there is no biofilm, there is no longer any danger of infection.

Scientists Peter Steinberg and his colleague Staffan Kjelleberg, who conducted breakthrough research on *Delicea pulchra* at the University of New South Wales in Sydney, Australia, quickly understood the value of their discovery: human-induced superbug mutations could be replaced by seaweed-inspired bacterial controls! The potential applications they envision give them many choices of where to start applying their knowledge and expertise.

As their findings would apply to controlling the spread of bacteria, a broad range of industries, including private housing, commercial buildings, transport, agriculture, consumer products, medical devices, and pharmaceuticals could benefit. The industry roadblocks are, however, quite daunting. A naturally occurring substance that inactivates bacteria communication and thereby eliminates their proliferation, threatens the antibiotic cash cows milked by big pharmaceutical companies who benefit greatly from the rampant prescription of antibiotics for just about any health inconvenience. Moreover, the investment and approval procedures are such that bringing a new medical innovation to market can literally take years, if not decades. If it were not for lengthy and complicated government approval procedures, furnaces may have already replaced antibiotics and bactericides.

Meanwhile, other fields less burdened with approval processes are readily apparent. Consumer goods and industrial and agricultural applications represent vast potential for this significant platform technology. Consider deodorants, currently manufactured with questionably safe ingredients including titanium and zinc. Body odour is caused by bacteria feeding on perspiration. A furanone-based deodorant would result in fewer bacteria and consequently less odour.

Then there is the brushing of teeth, a part of our daily routine. The amount of bacteria in our mouths is impressive. Although bacteria contribute to the digestive process and to our ability to taste food, they also cause bad breath and tooth decay as they feed on food residues in the mouth. If furanones were present, no bacteria-laden biofilm could form. Thus a furanone rinse would have a major refreshing effect.

Agriculture is likewise affected by biofilms. Seeds could be protected from bacterial contamination by simply dipping them in a furanone bath.

Cut flowers, which decay under a bacterial onslaught, would remain fresher longer when held in furanone-infused water.

Heating and cooling systems in buildings are at risk for the creation of biofilms, including the worrisome accretion of *Legionella*. This bacterium is difficult to eliminate because it lives in a host. The doses needed to kill the host will likely expose the building's occupants to an excessive chemical burden. The alternative is to install filters and replace the filters regularly, further increasing handling costs and downtime. In all these applications, furanones offer a remarkable alternative to the toxic chemistry in widespread use today.

British Petroleum made the headlines in 2006 as a result of their leaking Alaskan pipelines. Few people realise that the corrosion commonly affecting pipelines that transport oil, gas, or water is induced by bacteria. Every two weeks, the entire pipeline is shut down and flushed with acidic chemicals to kill the accumulation of bacterial biofilm on the interior. Since it is known that even these measures are not powerful enough to remove all the corrosion-causing microorganisms, a pigging machine is used to scrape the surface and remove these accumulations. Could furanones trickled into the pipelines possibly, simply and safely, deal with this problem?

Reverse osmosis production of fresh water from seawater is adversely affected by the accumulation of biofilm on the membrane filters. This reduces their effectiveness by more than 50 percent. As is the case with oil and gas pipelines, entire water purification systems need to be shut down to kill bacteria with chlorine. The drawback is that excessive use of chlorine chemically degrades the osmosis membranes, reducing the life of a system and increasing costs.

This handful of applications is only a fraction of the possibilities. The real future of furanone use, and Peter Steinberg's core fascination, has always been the application of his insights to pharmaceutical and medical devices. Cystic fibrosis and tuberculosis are two biofilm-based illnesses where a colony of bacteria slowly and steadily overwhelms the host, eventually with fatal results. As soon as the bacterial biofilm is formed, antibiotics attain far less effectiveness. A thousand-fold dosage increase is sometimes required. Imagine the impact of a seaweed-inspired synthetic analogue. As bacteria in the biofilm are rendered incommunicative by the furanones, individual bacteria dissipate and disintegrate since they do not sense a quorum. Ultimately the supra-structure becomes non-functional and the individual bacteria can be more readily eliminated by the body's natural maintenance processes.

The understanding that furanones do not obliterate but rather functionally impair detrimental bacteria, offers in itself, a fresh insight as to how we could improve health and treat illness – without stimulating the evolution of superbugs that defy our own immune system. If Steinberg's medical applications ever reach the market, it will break ground for hundreds of different applications. The reasoning is impeccable, the performance is demonstrable, and the cost of production is likely to be competitive, since effective concentrations of furanones appear to be just a few tens per billion. The technology company was taken private again, and the patents were sold to Unilever. It is now an anxious wait to see if this conglomerate will put this natural technology to use.

If we take an educated guess at evaluating the net job potential, we must consider that the production of furanones will replace the volume production of chemicals that are proven occupational and health hazards. Thus, employment in the manufacturing sector would have neither loss nor gain. Improved material efficiency can be estimated at 20-25%; for example, reverse osmosis membranes and pipelines would function longer, more efficiently, and with lower maintenance costs. The most important job generation is, however, likely to come from exploring the bacteria-defeating product possibilities of a remarkable species, silently at work.

Some Possible Uses of Furanones

Housing and Building	Air conditioning, Water supply
Agriculture	Fish farming, Food preservation
Industry	Food processing, Micro-electronics
Transportation	Oil and Gas
Pharmaceutical	Cystic fibrosis, Tuberculosis
Medical Devices	Urinary catheters, Syringes
Consumer Products	Deodorants, Mouth and tooth hygiene, Skin care

Miraculous Maggots

The spread of HIV/AIDS, malaria, and iodine deficiency disorders (IDD) throughout Africa has caught the attention of Western health experts. A number of philanthropic US foundations are aggressively funding the quest for solutions. The reality that is, however, overlooked, is that more Africans are adversely affected by a lack of basic wound care than by these debilitating diseases. Poor wound care leads to infections, gangrene, and amputations, all precursors to social marginalisation and shortened life expectancy. If a basic treatment were more widely available, especially in rural villages, subsequent larger problems would be avoided. Though it sounds incongruous, one surprising (and successful) wound care technique comes from insights into how maggots ensure hygiene.

In Nature, when an animal dies and begins to decompose, flies arrive in swarms. They feast, and then lay their eggs. The maggots that hatch quickly consume the rotting flesh. With the flesh consumed, there is no opportunity for bacteria to proliferate. The maggots either grow into flies, or are devoured by birds, fish, or other species having the highly acidic digestion needed to quickly absorb the 80% protein content of the maggots.

The use of maggots in delicate wound treatment is historically well-documented. Healers in ancient Mayan culture and Australian aboriginal tribes regularly used maggots for wound healing. Napoleon's Surgeon General, Baron Dominique Larrey, reported the use of maggot treatment for wounds during France's Egyptian campaign in 1799. Hygienic conditions in war campaigns certainly left much to be desired. Maggots were an important and effective form of field therapy. The widespread use of maggots for wound therapy diminished prior to World War II, following Alexander Fleming's discovery of penicillin in 1928.

More recently, with the acknowledged dangers of antibiotic-resistant bacteria, medical doctors have sought to re-introduce maggot therapy. Worldwide, over 4,000 therapists in 20 countries use maggot wound therapy. Dr Stephen Britland from Bradford University (UK) pioneered research into the capacity of maggots to effect wound healing. Advanced Gel Technologies (AGT) aims to complement the products developed by ZooBiotic Ltd, based in Wales, which started as a government services provider and is now one of the world's largest suppliers of live maggots for wound therapy. His research found that maggots do more than simply clean wounds. Maggots produce enzymes that stimulate cell-growth through the release of slight electrical charges. For the maggots, even antibiotic-resistant bacteria are nothing more than competitors for food. Left to do what they do best, maggots perform exceedingly well.

However, modern hospital conditions require sterile conditions, and maggots are not traditionally associated with bacteria-free hygiene (nor are all modern hospital settings). One of Britland's innovations has been to devise a way to collect the active wound-healing ingredients that maggots produce offsite without harming the maggots. This procedure is quite simple and not much different from what happens when one inadvertently takes a few gulps of salt water when swimming in the ocean – making one vomit up one's stomach content. Maggots are collected then immersed in salt water to induce disgorgement. The procedure is fast, cheap, and easy. This scheme, as proposed by Advanced Gel Technologies, would allow wound therapy to be accomplished using only the enzyme-rich regurgitated matter, without the disconcerting sight and sensation of maggots consuming necrotic bacteria-laden tissue.

Maggot therapy favourably compares with vacuum treatments, where leg ulcers are locally isolated in a low-pressure environment to facilitate cell growth. The use of maggots for wound therapy eliminates the need for antibiotics, as no bacteria remain once the maggots have eliminated the dead tissue. Antibiotic resistance thus becomes a non-factor. Clinical trial results demonstrate that maggot treatment is on par with the performance of the strongest antibiotic regimens; this is in itself a remarkable testament.

Aside from the key benefit of healing with a low risk of infection, another major advantage is hospital cost savings for patients who are not critically ill but nonetheless require nursing care to protect them against infection. This is of particular importance for the treatment of burns or ulcers contracted by diabetic patients. When Britland's research team received funding from the British government to develop and commercialise this therapy, it was because the medical records clearly demonstrated a dramatic Health Services savings for wound care treatment. Money is saved by reducing the length of hospital stays from an average of 72 to only 14 days. Hospital stays were also often prolonged because of unhealed leg ulcers requiring amputation. The biggest expense in maggot wound therapy is the rearing of the maggots, as they dine high on the food chain, being fed meat. Fortunately, they are not particular, and will dine on any portion of a carcass or any slaughterhouse waste available to them.

Considered in the context of Africa's health care challenges, maggot therapy could greatly contribute to the successful treatment of wounds. It is a lack of treatment that causes major health problems. When wounds are not treated, ulcers remain. The World Health Organisation estimates that the lack of wound care in Africa generates as many fatalities each year as malaria. It seems this problem should be easy to resolve. However, the cost of delivering the necessary products to remote areas is high and therefore ineffective. A cascading model that utilised inexpensive raw materials, delivered output, and generated cash flow and jobs could easily be configured. In fact, the system benchmarked at the Songhai Centre in Benin (introduced in Chapter 3) demonstrates how this can be accomplished. Maggot wound therapy could become a major health care initiative, while simultaneously generating massive numbers of jobs, without any imported material or equipment.

The country of Benin in Africa is a small former French colony bordering Nigeria. It has a rich history as a part of the Songhai Kingdom, which stretched across Benin and Nigeria before the French and the British imposed boundaries that severed culture and tradition. In 1985, Father Godfrey Nzamujo, a native Nigerian, undertook an ambitious plan to create an integrated farming and livestock operation that would provide food security for the people of the region. In Chapter Three we described how he started the Songhai Centre in Porto Novo, Benin. Like any farming programme that includes animal husbandry and an abattoir or slaughterhouse, maintaining a high level of hygiene was a major challenge. What to do with the offal and the carcass portions that are not readily processed into meat and sausage? When bovine spongiform encephalopathy (BSE), commonly known as mad cow disease, swept across Europe two decades ago, it was attributed to the use of animal waste as feed. European slaughterhouses were forced to incinerate all their waste. Father Nzamujo planned a different approach: let flies feed on it, as happens in Nature – but in a controlled environment.

Father Nzamujo's strategy exemplifies a Chinese farming principle: 'If you have pests, distract them with food that they really like'. Reserve a plot of land to grow their favourite nutrients and the pests will leave your crops in peace. The same applies to flies, which are always a nuisance in any food- processing project. Killing flies with chemicals is like killing bacteria; it is not very effective and any attempt to eradicate them once and for all is guaranteed to fail. Their ecological function guarantees ample presence and supply.

Father Nzamujo allocated a remote site on the Songhai Centre property where all slaughterhouse waste is deposited in small, square containers covered with bird nets to discourage feasting by vultures. The flies arrive and leave their eggs; the maggots hatch and grow. Harvesting is done by filling the containers with water, which causes the maggots to float to the top to reach the air necessary for them to breathe. From there they are easily scooped off each day and fed to quails. The quails flourish and the eggs they produce are exported by air to France where quail eggs are a highly sought-after delicacy.

A portion of the maggot harvest is also used to feed fish, which in turn are netted for local consumption, and the remains contribute to soil amendments that nourish the chemical-free food crops. The Songhai Centre produces organic food. According to Father Nzamujo, "This is easy in Africa, since fertilisers and pesticides are difficult to come by, and even if available they are too expensive." Feeding maggots to fish and quail generates a lucrative return on many levels. However, regurgitated maggot enzymes that can be easily harvested and used for medical wound care generate a value that is a multiple of the whole system. It does not take a mathematician to do the arithmetic in terms of income and jobs. Considering that Africa imports most of its medical wound care supplies, the ability to utilise a locally produced resource represents huge savings. At Songhai Centre, although no more than 60 pounds of enzyme could be collected on a monthly basis, their model holds promise as a major opportunity to lessen Africa's need for imported wound care materials, and to make this ideal application broadly and inexpensively available to those in urgent need of treatment.

There are an estimated 15,000 abattoirs in Africa. Additionally, many animals are slaughtered in small villages. An estimated 200,000 villages process slaughtered livestock locally. If every abattoir in Africa were to complement their operation with a maggot farm, a fish farm, and a poultry farm (chickens, turkeys, quail), it would create an estimated 300,000 to 500,000 jobs by way of the production of maggots to provide protein-rich livestock feed and better, cheaper wound care. There would be no additional expense for raw materials. Only what is currently wasted, or what takes additional energy and effort to dispose, would be used. It would also eliminate the health risks associated with handling slaughterhouse waste. Maggot enzyme collection at this scale would be sufficient even for export. Such extended utilisation would translate into unprecedented medical savings and tremendous benefit to wound care patients, who would regain health and mobility faster and more reliably.

Father Nzamujo took the first step in Benin, now others are following suit. Two brothers,Jason and David Drew, made their money establishing call centres in South Africa. Coming across the soldier fly and its maggots made them rethink their calling in life. Jason, in 2012, wrote the book *The Story of the Fly, and how it could save the world*, and David pioneered the farming of maggots. After experimentation on a farm in Franschhoek, they took production (in comparison to the small scale of 7 to 8 tonnes a month at the Songhai Centre in Benin) to 50 tonnes a day at Elsenburg in the Western Cape, working in cooperation with the University of Stellenbosch. While this may sound like an awful lot of maggots, it only represents 150 to 200 cattle carcasses a day, only a tiny elevation in the mountain range of offal.

Their mission is well articulated: for each tonne of maggots, save a tonne of fishmeal and break out of the protein crunch. The brothers went on to create AgriProtein Ltd in Cape Town (South Africa). They are committed to make a difference – not only for slaughterhouses in Africa but also for fish stocks around the world. Now, the Drew brothers are not on their own with such ambitious missions. By 2017, the valuation of their company passed the US$ 100 million mark, confirming that capital is following. Hilderman Pedraza Vargas, a medical doctor working with the National University of Colombia in Bogotá, has set up operations as well, and as the word spreads, dozens of small-scale maggot farms emerge throughout Africa and Latin America. Large-scale maggot farms are announced in Chile, Argentina, and Australia, and even in Europe several initiatives have gotten the green light from the regulators. The reason for success is simple: it is easy, fast, and while the maggots generate an income 24 hours a day, seven days a week, a lot of good is done as well.

Painless Injections

With maggots offering some inspiration and also garnering a little respect, let us move on to another insect on the short list of irksome pests – the mosquito. For some, a mosquito bite is nothing more than a small nuisance, or the cause of a bothersome itch that may lead to a micro-massage. But for Tetsuya Oyauchi from Terumo, a large Japanese medical instrumentation company, and Masayuki Okano, president of a small metal-pressing company, the painless sting of the mosquito was an accomplishment that piqued their curiosity. Okano wondered, "Why do syringes cause such pain, when mosquitoes are perfectly capable of extracting blood without any pain?"

Most people have an aversion to injections. They hurt. Anticipating the injection causes an anxiety that is almost unavoidable. A few patients will even faint. When the Terumo engineers and researchers learned what it was that allowed mosquitoes to painlessly draw their sustenance, and what it was that caused painful injections, they were stunned by the mechanical simplicity. It was about sizes and cone-shapes. The mosquito's proboscis is finer at the tip and gradually widens along its length. It was once thought that a needle's inside and outside diameters should be kept constant to transfuse medication. Making the tip diameter smaller was thought to make it harder to inject medical solutions, thus limiting how small the tip of a needle could be. But it is the cylinder-like shape of needles that causes pain. Okano-san is known in Japan as the "metalwork magician." Starting with a super-thin sheet of stainless steel, Okano rolled it into a tiny tapered cylindrical cone, sealing it by welding the seam. Oyauchi used his medical engineering expertise to refine and develop what he named the "Nanopass 33 Syringe". Its tip diameter is only 0.2 millimetres, 20% less than needles previously used. Rolling the metal into a cone with a specific contour gives the needle point its fineness. The tip can be superfine and gradually become wider, just like the shape of the mosquito's proboscis. The problem was solved.

Terumo's patent application for a tapered "injection needle and liquid-introducing implement" was granted in 2004. Today, hypodermic needles by Terumo are the standard for diabetic patients' daily needs. In Japan alone, there are some 600,000 diabetic patients who require daily insulin injections. Nearly eight percent of the American population suffers from diabetes, that is some 23.6 million people. Thus, the Terumo needle meets the needs of a large and appreciative customer base. Since it uses less metal there is also a net gain in material efficiency.

The Nanopass 33 needle received the Grand Good Design Award from the Japan Industrial Design Promotion Conference in 2005. Upon accepting the award, Okano commented, "It is fun to make something that doesn't exist in the world, and accomplish something people thought couldn't be done." Like the case of silk, this is another example of how geometry, borrowed from Nature, shapes products and helps solve our needs. While the Terumo needle cannot claim to have generated many jobs, it has substantially reduced the pain suffered by patients needing medical injections. This puts it far ahead of the many other disruptive technologies we condone without a second thought.

Gasless Propulsion

In Nature, ecosystems first use the powers of physics, without recourse to chemistry. The value of this is once more demonstrated by a significant potential application: propulsion gases. University of California researcher Mario Molina, who with Sherwood Rowland received the Nobel Prize for their original work first published in 1974, identified propulsion gases as the cause of the drastic ozone layer deterioration we now endure. Their work led to the banning of the infamous Freon gas and its derivatives, under the Montreal Protocol. Though industry offered a few new variations on propulsion gases, their use exemplifies how "doing less harm" is still very harmful.

Propulsion gases are commonly used for consumer applications, including misting devices for medical dosing of antihistamine or bactericide, and for cleaning and hairspray products. Mist spray technology enables droplet size, temperature, and velocity to be closely controlled. Thus it has other applications such as in the fuel-injection systems of automobile engines. More recently the use of this chemistry has been replaced in some cases, such as for hairspray, by a high-pressure atomising dispenser. It is another of the fine examples demonstrating how the chemical industry found a solution that moved in the right direction, but none-the-less failed to eliminate the unwanted and unplanned side effects caused by inhaling designer chemicals. (We could note here too that patients suffering from cystic fibrosis or tuberculosis may better eliminate the biofilm of detrimental bacteria when seaweed-inspired furanones are effectively blended with air and inhaled.)

Even though the French philosopher Voltaire popularised the old Italian saying that, "The perfect should not stand in the way of the good," it is timely to make a fundamental distinction between the good and the "less bad". The search for a perfect solution should not stop anyone from implementing a good solution, but the search for total risk elimination should remain high on the agenda. In the case of propulsion gases, total risk elimination becomes a practical reality with the help of the bombardier beetle. It has an ability that may help improve delivery of aerosolised respiratory medicines, greater automobile fuel efficiency, reduced emissions from fuel-injection systems, and even lowered risk of explosions in mines.

In Nature, everything has to do with survival – with feeding, procreating and defence. The bombardier beetle (*Brachinus carabidae*) is a rare evolutionary survivor. This amazing little insect has the ability to spray a stinging 100 °C liquid irritant over a distance 10 times its own length. This captivated the mind of Andy McIntosh, Professor of Thermodynamics and Combustion Theory at Leeds University, who was introduced to the bombardier beetle's remarkable feats by Cornell University entomologist Tom Eisner.

Just two centimetres long, the bombardier beetle uses its exothermic spray to defend itself against ants. The bombardier creates its spray by reacting hydroquinone with hydrogen peroxide stored in its fuel glands, producing a blast of steamy liquid. The beetle's one centimetre diameter "combustion chamber" works rather like a pressure cooker. Once again, it is about pressure – physics – more than chemistry. The liquid in the chamber is held under pressure, a valve is opened, and flash evaporation occurs. The valve closes, the chamber refills, and the liquid heats to above the atmospheric boiling point when the chamber valve is again opened. The beetle does this quickly and efficiently, spraying at 400 to 500 cycles per second. "Essentially, it is a high-force steam cavitation explosion," explains McIntosh.

This ingenious mechanical propulsion system, one that perfectly distributes a substance into the air at a particle size of no more than two nanometres, has been modelled by scientists, who can reproduce its action at 20 cycles per second with the same throw ratio. Because the bubbles in the chemical reaction of hydroquinone with hydrogen peroxide are so small, the ratio of the surface area to the volume administered is greatly increased, thus likewise increasing efficiency.

Says McIntosh, "No one had ever studied the bombardier beetle from a physics and engineering perspective. At first, we did not appreciate how much we would learn from it." His discovery has the potential to eliminate the impact of propulsion gases on the ozone layer while increasing dispensary performance. The Swedish entrepreneur Lars Uno Larsson was enthused by this innovation and is taking it from concept, to pilot, to potential commercialisation. The innovation has found its entrepreneur. Once proven, it can inspire others to pursue a wide range of applications.

Bundling Innovations

The combination of several technologies could potentially allow us to completely reconfigure our approach to health care, housing, food and water security and renewable energy provision. The one hundred single innovations, which are summarised in four-page long case studies at <www.TheBlueEconomy.org> and the dozen cases of how clusters of innovation are implemented through a worldwide network, illustrate the wide array of possible applications that are emerging. If one technology motivates us, bundling several innovations will encourage the design of a system that is able to impel our world towards true sustainability. It will also eliminate our dependency on the false comfort of chemistry, a dependency that relies on non-renewable resources and genetic manipulation – with unforeseen and detrimental effects no one can predict. The Blue Economy approach advocates that we rethink our approach to economic growth and development, to seek out and promote solutions that substitute the use of "something" with the use of "nothing", by finding our inspiration from the physics of the natural world.

To achieve this, to even work towards this goal, more contributions are needed. If bacteria-suppressing furanones from seaweed or enzymes from maggots can be administered using a mechanical misting device inspired by the bombardier beetle, then we are truly entering a new era of health care delivery. We will no longer be depositing residues and waste materials with undesirable side effects into the ecosphere – and onto its inhabitants. Instead, we can borrow components perfected over millions of years to achieve a functional, integrated system. The real power of evolution lies in that not only one species' survival is assured, but that a collaboration is emerging, wherein multiple species fine-tune their processes to reach symbiosis, achieving their needs and enhancing the survival of all. This implies that the opportunity for entrepreneurs is not just about creating new batteries or alternative forms of antibiotics but in bundling innovations into sustainable systems. For businesses, for the economy itself, the employment opportunities the Blue Economy heralds point to a solid evolutionary path. The innovations of many will combine to achieve a greater whole, an outcome greater than the sum of its parts.

What we have explored only scratches the surface of the potential. In less than a hundred years of "modern" scientific and technological invention and application, we have achieved diminishing success in conquering viral and bacterial pathogens and other dangers we perceive in our surrounding biota. Yet, any number of Nature's time-tested solutions can inform our ability to overcome bacteria and viruses. Earthworms and the barberry plant are producers of potent antibiotics and have resisted bacterial mutation for millions of years. The bombardier beetle, in surviving against ant armies, deserves admiration and emulation for its exceptional capacity to outwit a species known for its superior swarm intelligence. This alone should further inspire us to respect biodiversity and ecosystems. It should motivate us to go beyond the mere preservation of biodiversity and move toward ensuring that ecosystems continue to evolve without human-induced species loss or change of conditions. It offers a compelling logic for humanity to collaborate with evolution – towards ever more cohesive and adaptive ecosystems. Instead of learning about Nature, we should start learning more from Nature.

Biodiversity and Health

With the loss of biodiversity comes the loss of opportunities to learn from our fellow sentient species and to adapt the solutions they have invented to our mutual benefit. This is particularly the case for the gastric brooding frog or platypus frog (*Rheobatrachus silus*). Unfortunately, this species, native to Australia, did not survive excessive exposure to pesticides, herbicides, and the release of non-native species into its habitat. It could have taught us much about promoting healthy digestion and controlling bacteria. Once the mother frog conceived, she swallowed the offspring, brooding them in her stomach until they were ready to be released into the world. This is possible through control and eradication of acidophilic bacteria and the delicate pH management of the stomach environment. The first phases of the tiny frogs' life occur in an alkaline environment. If the typical gastric acidity persisted and acidophilic bacteria remained competitive, the offspring could not survive.

Our digestive health could have taken great inspiration from the *Rheobatrachus silus*. Stomach ulcers and gastric cancer have been poorly understood for decades. Extreme acidophilic bacteria were not considered the cause of these stomach diseases. Scientists Barry Marshall and Robin Warren nonetheless identified ulcer-causing and cancer-causing bacteria so that the design of an appropriate cure and even a preventive treatment for high-risk patients could be formulated. In 2005, both scientists were awarded the Nobel Prize in Chemistry for their work. Had we the opportunity to further study the gastric brooding frog, we might have learned how to avoid the health hazards of excessive stomach acidity altogether. This knowledge was lost because we were ignorant or dismissive of the impact of our flawed systems on the life around us, and allow waste to be wasted and to end up as pollution. Sadly, thousands of species are still threatened by just such ignorance.

Our beautiful blue planet Earth, endlessly cycling in the embrace of dark cosmos and brilliant sunshine, provides us with the living conditions on which we depend, not only for survival but also for happiness. It is time to actively and consciously link our health to the health of the Earth. It is time to reassess the contributions and genius of our ecosystems, and find ways to adapt natural processes and whole systems solutions to secure livelihoods and survival for all sentient beings on this planet. In so doing we will discover, as has every other species through millions, perhaps even billions of years, new models for survivability, sustainability, and prosperity; models based on a Blue Economy – an economy of support, exchange, and abundance – which provides more with less, and that is conducive to all of life.

11

A RAINBOW OF POSSIBILITIES

The eye is the primary means whereby our understanding may most fully and abundantly appreciate the infinite works of Nature.
—*Leonardo da Vinci*

Light Perception

Visible light is made up of photons, which are packets of electromagnetic radiation that travel in straight lines, reflecting off objects and then passing through the transparent, curved cornea into the eye. As the photons pass through the cornea and the lens, they transition from travelling through air to travelling through liquid. This liquid contains proteins with refractive properties, causing the photons to change direction and further bend to focus onto the retina, which is essentially a sheet of light-sensitive cells. This process is enhanced by the adjustment of the pupil diameter to admit the right quantity of light. Specialised muscles adjust the shape of the lens to improve focus and visual flexibility. Meanwhile, muscles attached outside the eye work to keep the same focal point and to scan back and forth in a coordinated manner. Photons strike a retinal molecule, a modified form of vitamin A. Contact with an incoming photon causes the retina to react by initiating a complex biochemical cascade within the cell that ultimately generates an electrical signal sent to the brain. There, the information from millions of retinal photoreceptors is combined to provide details about contrast and colour. The upside-down images formed on both retinas are mentally combined and inverted and the resulting images are interpreted – in this case, as the words on this page.

Lenses are a key component of the art of light. These refract light, converting or diverting the beam. The earliest mechanical lenses were devised in Assyria some 3,000 years ago. Creatures in Nature, however, have developed lenses hundreds of millions of years ago. The octopus created thin film lenses. The brittle star produced distortion-free lenses. These two marvels of lens technology are indications that our scientific understanding of optics still has a long way to go, and that there is a huge potential for commercial applications.

New applications do find their way to the market in a most surprising manner. In Japan, dragonflies represent lightness and joy. They remind us that we can all produce light and, if we choose to do so, we can reflect that light in powerful ways. The dragonfly's ability to generate energy through the concentration of light has garnered the attention of renewable energy researchers. Concentrated solar thermal power (CST) is a proven industry, highly dependent on subsidies. In the desert of southern Spain, over a thousand mirrors have been positioned that reflect sunlight to superheat water in a central tower, a development and investment of Abengoa. It uses mirrors to focus sunlight onto the water – much as the dragonfly does. By 2050, the solar power harvested using CST is expected to eliminate the atmospheric release of 2.1 billion tonnes of CO_2. Annual CST investments could exceed US$ 100 billion and create almost two million jobs. The financial crisis then hit Spain, and jobs were lost and subsidies evaporated. The technology of light is, however, likely to persist.

Ultraviolet: Light Humans Do Not See

Light does not always bring colour. There is also light from the sun that we do not see at all. Light has different wavelengths. Ultraviolet light has shorter wavelengths than visible light, having a frequency higher than what we identify as "violet" – hence it being called ultraviolet. Ultraviolet light emanates at a higher frequency than the human eye can distinguish. The potentially beneficial effects of UV light exposure are well documented. It can address many skin diseases such as psoriasis.

It stimulates the production of vitamin D, which helps the body absorb calcium to maintain bone strength and lower cancer risk. It provides a natural control mechanism for mites in carpets, rugs, and upholstery. Ultraviolet light treats the water in swimming pools to control bacteria, replacing the use of chlorine, that ubiquitous (and toxic) germ killer.

There are also well-known negatives to excessive UV exposure. It may lead to skin cancer, especially since our protective ozone layer has been damaged by industrial gases like the infamous CFC (chlorofluorocarbon), which we need not have been used in the first place. We recently learned this from studying the bombardier beetle (see Chapter 10). Consumer product marketers promote a variety of protection schemes to counter the perceived risks of excessive UV exposure. These include designer chemicals like oxybenzone, a compound that absorbs UV but is now a suspected photo-carcinogen. In the laboratory, this chemical may have low reactivity, but when illuminated by light, it gets excited and is potentially harmful to biological tissue. Zinc and titanium oxide, inorganic particles that reflect, scatter, and absorb UV rays, were marketed for their UV-protective properties. Recent research at the University of California Riverside, however, indicates that these sunscreens must be reapplied every two hours to remain effective. If not, they unleash free radicals that can cause skin cell damage that may be worse than the UV exposure! It has since been discovered that coffee naturally blocks UV, and this can now be offered as a natural alternative.

In Nature, many species have adapted to prolonged exposure to ultraviolet light and are able to neutralise its effects. Plants, of course must have sunlight to drive photosynthesis. Being rooted, they cannot move into available shade when the sun is too bright. They must create protection. Many animals are also vulnerable to prolonged UV exposure. The mechanisms evolved by plants and animals to protect against these negative effects can provide us with resources, insight, and inspiration.

The edelweiss, the unofficial national flower of Austria, has been studied in detail by the Belgian scholar Jean Pol Vigneron. The edelweiss does not reflect UV but rather absorbs it in thousands of little hairs, avoiding tissue penetration that destroys living cells. Many lichen and fungi exist in high altitude Arctic, Antarctic, or desert areas where UV exposure is extremely high. As a result, they tend to have absorbing pigments. For instance, a novel photo-protective mycosporine has been isolated from the fungi living in symbiosis with *Collema cristatum*, a micro-algae forming lichen. The pure isolated compound prevents UV-induced skin cell destruction when applied prior to irradiation. Some lichens certainly do show better protective traits than others. Research in this field is most promising, as photo-protective compounds offer simple protection, replace toxic applications, and eliminate reliance on mined materials that require massive energy to extract and process.

Certain fruit, such as apples and tomatoes, are notably sensitive to ultraviolet radiation and must protect themselves. They offer us a biochemical recipe that provides better protection than titanium oxide. Tomato skin is rich in lycopene, a carotenoid in the same family as beta-carotene, found in carrots. Lycopene has powerful antioxidant properties and provides a high level of UV protection.

The Evolution of Colour and Perception

The optical mechanisms for vision first developed some 540 million years ago, during the period called the Cambrian Explosion. Suddenly, in less than one million years – a short span in evolutionary terms – and for no reason we understand yet, a broad range and diversity of life began to flourish on Earth. Creatures took on hard body parts, shells and spines, and also shapes and colours of every description. The ability to perceive and visually distinguish surrounding phenomena became a dominant force of evolution. Vision holds a survival advantage for both predator and prey. Food could be more easily identified, predators could be recognised, and mates could be located. Some species evolved bright colouration and intricate patterning to blend with their environment, to warn of their power to defend, or to impress mates.

Cambrian descendants – mammals, birds, reptiles, fish, molluscs, and wonderfully iridescent beetles – have all created their own way of seeing, as well as their own way of producing colour. Poison dart frogs use conspicuous colour to warn predators that they are not good to eat. Venomous coral snakes sport rings of bright colour to advertise that they are not to be messed with. A white milk snake, which isn't poisonous and could be quite safely eaten, benefits from the coral snake's reputation simply by copying its colouration. A cuttlefish changes colour in a millisecond to match its background. A chameleon camouflaged with stripes and spots can stalk its prey without being seen.

Dr Hopi Hoekstra, Loeb Associate Professor of Natural Sciences at Harvard University, studies the genetic mechanisms at work in a species of mouse that adapts to its environment by being sand-coloured if it lives at the beach and dark if it lives inland. Parrotfish are able to alter their gender and appearance from female to male. Female parrotfish are much less colourful than the dominant male. If the male fish gets eaten, the dominant female alters her gender – and displays the brilliant colours of the male. Parrots, the birds, see ultraviolet light. While we only see their monochromatic feathers, to each other they look flamboyant.

Pigments are chemical substances produced by living organisms that appear as colours because they selectively absorb and reflect certain wavelengths of light. Pigments can never add to, but only subtract, wavelengths from a light source. A frog is green not because it has green pigment, but because it reflects blue light from yellow pigment. The white hair of a polar bear's fur, and an arctic fox's winter coat, are in fact clear. There are neither pigments to absorb nor structures to reflect certain wavelengths. Thus, the entire colour spectrum is reflected, making the animal appear white.

The *Cyphochilus* beetle and other beetles have a highly unusual, brilliantly white shell. The *Cyphochilus* has evolved its superb whiteness with scales that are just five micro-metres thick, ten times thinner than a human hair. The random surface structure of its scales simultaneously absorbs and scatters every colour. Industrial mineral coatings, such as those used on high-quality paper, plastics, and some paints, need to be twice as thick to be as white. According to measures for whiteness and brightness, these beetles are whiter and brighter than milk or the average human tooth, both of which have a surface that is considerably thicker.

Many animals acquire their colouration through pigments that they metabolise. Others take in pigments through what they eat, displaying those pigments through their skin. For example, the pink colouration of the scarlet ibis comes from its diet of crabs and prawns that consume red algae. (Imagine if humans could generate colours simply from what we eat!) Nearly all the blue hues we see in the animal world, including the colours of the blue damselfly (*Enallagma civile*), are produced not by blue pigment but by blue light reflected from tiny tissue structures that scatter light and often enhance it. Some species produce colour not by pigmentation but by microstructures in fur, feathers, scales, petals, or other features that reflect only certain wavelengths of light. In animals, the building material for this is often keratin, (what nails and hair are made of).

Birds-of-paradise and hummingbirds have feathers that possess a stunning iridescence, a metallic sheen that is perhaps the most spectacular colour effect of all. The colour effects of the Egyptian scarab and the rainforest beetle have been copied in jewellery for millennia, but have never been industrially reproduced. Some orchids enhance their visual attractiveness by the combination and spacing of gold and silver flecks in their otherwise chemically pigmented petals. A similar effect is found in African violets. Through millions of years of trial-and-error many organisms have perfected methods to enhance attractiveness using metallic colour effects, although no metals are involved. The underlying structures that generate these colourations vary widely from species to species. One exceptional colour producer identified and described by Andrew Parker, is the sea mouse (*Polychaeta aphroditidae)*. This marine animal is covered with iridescent hair and the effect created is sheer beauty.

Colour Pigmentation as Commodity

The earliest known pigments used by humans were minerals. Natural iron oxides produce a range of colours and are still discernible in cave paintings after 20 millennia or more. As early as the Middle Ages, the search for permanent and stable colours drove industry towards complex chemistry and created highly profitable businesses. Two of the first synthetic pigments were white and blue. White was made by combining lead with vinegar in the presence of CO_2. Blue pigment, known as "blue frit," was made with a calcium copper silicate derived from crushed glass, coloured with a copper ore such as malachite.

In the merchandising world of today, just as in the Cambrian Age of pre-history, colouration still serves as an attractant. In the contemporary case, however, bright colours and unique patterns are displayed, more in the hopes of attracting a buyer than a mate. The marketing, selling, and even consumption of products such as paint, ink, fabric, plastics, cosmetics, and food, rely on colouration to stand out. The demand for colour is vast and growing. By 2015, total world pigment consumption had reached nine million tonnes, good for a turnover of more than US$ 24 billion. This means that the average price for a tonne of colour was more than US$

2,600. This is four times the price for cellulose for papermaking, or palm oil for biodegradable soaps. From a business standpoint, colour pigments are a high-end product with solid margins.

It is disconcerting that humans are prepared to adorn themselves with clothing and cosmetics – without ever asking about the ingredients and methods used to create these items. Today, colour pigmentation is created by using cadmium, chromium, cobalt, lead, mercury, titanium, and zinc. In short, it is dependent on mining practices and ore processing that are far from a model of sustainability. Furthermore, the application and use of colour pigments is now highly regulated, since many have been shown to be potential health hazards. Yet none of the modern industry standards require biodegradable pigments. Nor are regulations to be found for when it comes to the disposal of cast-off goods and their metal oxide colour components. Along with batteries, colour pigments make a substantial contribution to heavy metal pollution in landfills. Since these pigments were designed to last and not to fade, thus not to degrade, they can concentrate at dangerous levels of contamination. When indiscriminately dispersed into the environment, they often pollute entire ecosystems.

Colour is indeed beautiful but unfortunately it is a dirty business! From a business standpoint, the most desirable colour is white. Optical brighteners such as chlorine bleach and benzene, the market standards for "brightening" fabric, paper, and plastics, effectively produce visible white because they have very strong light absorption capabilities. These optical brighteners convert the yellowish colour from oxidation to an effect perceived by the eye as white, giving the impression of cleanliness. Clean or not, it is the impression that we value. These optical brighteners are however suspected allergens and are highly toxic. While pigments and optical brighteners may be the best we have, how can we go about managing this in a different way to that adopted by the industry? The hope is that once we grasp how light and colour shaped evolution in the past, we may be able to use Nature's solutions to shape the industries of tomorrow.

Andrew Parker has identified the simple structure responsible for the iridescent colouration of species such as hummingbirds and beetles, and understands how to produce metallic iridescent colour the way Nature achieved it millions of years ago. He has challenged himself to formulate iridescent colours that can be manufactured on a commercially viable scale, and produce a desirable visual effect by emulating the creative ways in which Nature produces colour. He rightly contends that if these vibrant and attractive colourations can be formulated using the physics and biochemistry adapted by animals and plants, it not only represents an important breakthrough, it also offers a strong marketing message. This message will resonate with the growing segment of manufacturers and consumers who are looking for non-toxic and non-polluting alternatives. His goal is to establish a technical research base for a portfolio of innovations that could find applications in multiple industries. Photonic engineering may soon provide colouration results without cadmium, lead, or chromium!

The manufacturing technique may be as simple as the production of glass. If the concept proves successful, the potential is vast. The preliminary trials are convincing. The first application is for cosmetics, a sector with a unique interest in generating colours beyond those offered on the market today. Since cosmetics are about more than only beauty, but also embrace skin health, Parker's work has multiple facets. Companies looking to differentiate themselves with a "fresh and natural" angle in their marketing strategies, will be interested in this innovative approach. Parker's research efforts may well be a milestone in industrial development and a platform for the creation of new industries that are in true harmony with ecosystems. The only challenge remaining is organising supply.

Beyond cosmetics there are applications such as a chemical-free coating for glassware and crystal, which have traditionally relied on lead. A novel crystal figure could be produced, if a piece of glass containing the appropriate microstructure was invisibly inserted into a crystal statue of the whole animal. It would feature spectacular flashes of colour in a much more effective way than can be achieved with glass prisms. This would not only have the same visual effect as the living animal, but the effect would be based on an optical device identical to what the animal uses. The Austrian crystal maker Swarovski has grasped the opportunity and will be the first to meet people's desire for adornment and delight, working with this innovation.

Waste for One, Resource for Another

The location of a tomato processing plant is carefully chosen to minimise transportation from the farm, so that fresh tomatoes can be converted to tomato paste quickly. Unilever, represented (until the business was sold) 6% of the 40 million tonnes of industrially processed tomatoes, averaging 2.2 million tonnes in 2012. With a high volume of tomatoes to process, there are factory waste streams for everything that is not processed and packed. The tomato skin waste generated from this volume of tomatoes amounts to some 30,000 tonnes a year. If the Unilever factories were to add a subsidiary operation that produced a lycopene-based sunscreen from tomato skin waste, then today's titanium-based UV protection agents would be instantly under-priced and outmoded. The renewable available raw material would be free, and using it would in fact save the tomato paste factory the expense of "waste disposal".

It is true that compared to coffee tomatoes generate much less waste. Still, the processing residue is expelled through the wastewater treatment system, using thousands of cubic metres of water. Of the remaining solids, some three percent ends up as landfill. This goes unnoticed, since supply chain managers and corporate policy focus on short-term gain, and do not search for any value from waste. To us, however, these few percentage points should be interesting indeed. Although Benjamin Franklin is reported to have said 'a penny saved is a penny earned', this logic doesn't seem to be applied once an output is considered waste. This is where ecosystems offer solid inspiration, since Nature always finds value in waste.

What Nature teaches us, is that achieving material efficiency isn't accomplished by just one process. There are always multiple functions providing multiple benefits, as the use of tomato skins superbly illustrate. Tomato skins diverted from the waste stream are not only good as an antioxidant and for ultraviolet sunlight protection, they also are the source of a naturally derived, food-safe red colouring that could be utilised in many frozen food products ranging from packaged salmon, to strawberries, to ice cream. Thus, if tomatoes were the core business, the spin-offs in health (UV protection), personal care (cosmetics), fisheries (protein food) and food (ice cream) would fit them into the cascading model that is at the heart of a Blue Economy. Iron oxides and synthetic colour pigments derived from petroleum and mined metals are only offering one product – and a waste stream that is unaccountable. Lycopenes are part of a cluster of utilisable materials that can be rescued from biological waste. Red lipstick made from tomato skins would have a cachet of its own. In fact, if women knew the ingredients presently used for manufacturing lipstick, the tomato skin version would become irresistible.

An entrepreneurial business approach would involve developing lycopene extraction and processing technologies; knowing the lycopene extraction potential from the skins; assessing the volume of UV-protection products the market consumes and at what price; and determining the volume and price of red pigment purchased by the food industry. A tomato skin processing plant established near a tomato processing factory could sell extracted lycopene at a competitive industry price to be manufactured into food-safe pigment dyes and UV sunscreen products. This transformation of waste management to accelerated innovation would profitably generate local jobs, provide lower consumer prices for higher quality products, replace unsustainable business practices, and help secure health as well as reduce exposure to toxins. Such an environmentally sound and financially secure business model can succeed on many levels. Analysing producing tomatoes starts sounding like processing coffee grounds – it gets more interesting the more you look into it…

From a cost point of view, it is considered too expensive to extract lycopenes from tomatoes for the lycopenes alone. This conclusion implies that we would waste the rest of the tomato and that would not make sense, although this is exactly the way industry thinks today. In such a narrow economic analysis, Parker's proposal to derive both colouration and ultraviolet protection from the tomato could never compete with titanium oxide in sunscreen lotions. On the other hand, if the raw material for both is from tomato waste, then we are in business! The generation of two value-adding derivatives (UV protection and colour pigment) from one waste stream is a much improved business proposal, complementing the industrial food production. This logic is not taught in the world's best academic business schools where core business–core competence strategy is locked in with discounted cash flow analysis. Double revenue streams generated from free materials results in a much higher integrated cash flow than what the processing of tomatoes alone could ever achieve.

Thus the entrepreneurial business model could also incorporate use of the tomato seed waste, as well as the skin. Tomato seeds from the larger volume paste processors are either dumped in landfills or sold cheaply to cattle farmers. The nutritional value of the seeds for cattle feed is low – it is a filler rather than a feed. However, tomato seeds are rich in health-boosting trace elements and softening monounsaturated and polyunsaturated fatty acids. Thus a better match of materials to market would be to turn these seeds into products that soothe our skin or nourish our body.

The world demand for processed tomato products – cooked, sliced and diced, canned, bottled, dried, in all its many international flavours – could also meet the demand for safe UV-protection products, cosmetic products, and pigment dyes from the unused tomato peels and seeds. Cascading materials in this fashion offers unique opportunities to develop promising markets, create successful applications, and achieve productive factories. If these derivative processing facilities were located near the primary tomato processing centre, the transport costs would be minimal. This clustering of businesses contributes to cash flow, reduces costs, and generates jobs.

The Biorefinery of the Future

Imagining ways to reintegrate waste streams into nutrient streams brings into focus the outline of a biorefinery. The concept of a biorefinery was originally developed by Professor Carl-Göran Hedén, a member of the Club of Rome and of the Royal Swedish Academy of Sciences. Hedén's idea of a biorefinery involved the capacity to generate more with what has already been harvested or processed. Envisioning a cascading of nutrients and materials, he devised a demonstration facility where all chemicals and catalysts were processed in a closed loop. Lignin, hemicellulose, cellulose, lipids, and essential oils were extracted from one tree species. Revenues were tripled merely by eliminating waste.

In the case of the tomato, we might calculate how many jobs could be generated using the biorefinery concept. The net job generation of this initiative may be larger than expected. The Food and Agricultural Organisation of the United Nations (FAO) reported that by 2010 globally, the area utilised for tomato farming, was 3.6 million hectares. The world output is about 150 million tonnes. The USA alone produces 10 million tonnes. Considered entrepreneurially, we would say that the world wastes around two million tonnes of potential additive, pigment, and oil sources. This amount is impressive and allows us to realise that it is possible to replace metal-based pigments and UV-protectors, without ever stressing the Earth to produce alternatives, and without competing for food, as is the case for corn grown to produce fuel or plastics. The Earth is already producing all we need; we only need to use what is available.

At present one tonne of colour pigment costs an average of US$ 2,600. Tomato-derived natural pigment sources could be made available for roughly US$ 1,000 per tonne, as the materials are from spent product – that is available for free – or only for the cost of local transportation. Inexpensive raw materials would make it possible to produce the pigment at a lower base cost. This new business opportunity would factor out at about two billion dollars. That is the value of what is wasted today, dumped in landfills causing methane pollution in the process, or devoured by cattle that cannot digest it. In Brazil (where Unilever had a processing plant until the business was sold), factory workers live comfortably on US$ 10,000 per year. We could safely state that a turnover like this, in a country like Brazil, could potentially generate 100,000 jobs.

These numbers give rise to a broader debate. Prior to embarking on a guesstimate, it is important to remind ourselves of the market dynamics. If something is expensive yet desirable, demand will generally remain low. As the price decreases, demand will usually increase. Price elasticity studies show that lowering the price of highly desirable products usually generates a greater than proportional increase in demand. If tomato-based biochemistry were available at half the price of the alternatives used today, then it would undercut the dominant products on the market and stimulate demand. While part of the increase would be the replacement of the non-sustainable options now available, the overall demand would also grow.

Worldwide, two million tonnes of tomato waste equates to only 12% of the world's coffee waste. Yet, due to our appetite for tomato sauce, salsa, and pasta sauce, this waste stream could supply every lipstick manufacturer in the world with all the colour pigments it may need. Colour pigments from tomato waste would provide a cheaper, better and more natural product, and one with proven UV protection – while enhancing beauty. And it doesn't taste like tomato!

Using waste streams forms the basis of the new economy that we see emerging. It is already more than only an idea, so imagine what would happen if everything produced were to follow this logic. This is the Blue Economy in action – working with what we have, responding to basic needs first, accomplishing greater sustainability than we ever imagined, generating jobs, and building social capital while competing successfully in the market.

The Biorefinery today

The idea of Prof. Hedén may have been a grand vision at the time but it is now fast becoming reality. Novamont, the first biorefinery, a pioneer in biopolymers, was opened by CEO Dr Catia Bastioli in 2013. Based on a 1,000 patent strong portfolio of intellectual property, her team of engineers studied the infrastructure of a defunct petrochemical plant in Porto Torres, Sardinia (Italy) and concluded that a major portion of the infrastructure could be reused to process a biological feedstock. The question that emerged was what feedstock was locally available? The 1.6 million strong population does not drink enough coffee to power a 360,000 tonnes per year facility; the farmers have long given up on planting tomatoes.

The Sardinians believed that tourism would provide for their livelihood. Thus, 175,000 acres of fertile land was left uncultivated. Then, in the aftermath of the 2008 financial crisis, the tourists stopped coming. It got worse: a few years later during the Arab Spring uprising, the friendly regime in Libya crumbled and the low cost supply of fuel ended. Fuel now had to be purchased at world market prices. Dr Bastioli's team studied all local resources and soon realised that the native artichoke thistle (*Cynara cardunculus*), which invaded the land after it was no longer cultivated, could be processed into protein, animal feed, plastics, lubricants, herbicides and elastomers. ENI, one of the top ten petroleum groups of the world, quickly calculated that the social and environmental cost associated with the closure of their facility could now be turned into an investment.

The effect was profound. The millions that used to flow from the island into the pockets of the oil supplier now enrich local farmers. Thistles are perennials that require no tilling, fertilisers, irrigation or pesticides, and this lowered the barrier to re-entry into agriculture. The lack of capital and the lack of experience, in fact, came in handy. Farming thistles does not compare with farming corn. The creation of value from what was considered a weed, generated a multiplier of growth into the local economy, where readily available material is processed, producing six revenue streams protected by two decades of fundamental research. The concept of the biorefinery now gains credibility, the fantasy turned vision now becomes reality – due to science and the willingness to exchange a certain cost of closure for an opportunity to compete in the bio-based economy. Better still, a joint-venture established in 2013 between Novamont and ENI, Matrica, now offers a solution for the traditional petrochemical industry in Europe and elsewhere, which is forever deprived of low cost access to naphtha, the petroleum based liquid that is the starting stock for most chemical derivatives. The conversion to the processing of coffee and tomatoes already seemed a major leap forward. Society benefiting from thistles processed in an old petrochemical plant really set everyone's minds spinning. And this was only just the beginning of an emerging Blue Economy.

The gain in material and energy efficiency is impressive. The petrochemical plant had processed 2.5 million tonnes of fuel and naphtha into 700,000 tonnes of chemicals. The processing of 360,000 tonnes of thistles could give value to 350,000 tonnes of feed, plastics (including the biodegradable capsules for Lavazza coffee), elastomers, energy, and functional chemicals like the production of the natural substitute for glyphosate. How elegant/ingenious is Nature's revenge – thistles treated with weed killers for decades now provide the raw material for products that will eliminate this toxin from the market.

Jobs are maintained, Nature is put back on its evolutionary path, and funds are made available to undertake the clean-up of Europe's first petroleum cracker, one that was built in 1962. This replacement of a non-renewable feedstock, the revival of farming on a cleared stretch of land, the re-industrialisation and the creation of a social opportunity appealed to investors, civil society, the unions, and the policy makers. It is seldom that innovations can build on consensus. The European Union considers this initiative strategic, and provides strategic funding through the European Bank for the acceleration of this industrial sector. The only ones struggling with this new reality are the economists who have had to get used to multiple benefits, and perhaps also some chemical engineers, who have had to embark on a blend of organic and inorganic chemistry – something new, but challenging.

Should Heinz and Unilever, once the giant tomato processors of the world, neglect these opportunities? Entrepreneurial partnerships have emerged, such as the one between Novamont and ENI. This has taken science and cash flow to the next level, showing that profit can be derived from converting outdated, uncompetitive production plants while responding to the basic needs of all. This includes contributing to a healthy blue planet for all to live on – fully utilising what we already have – including thistles, once considered a weed. Unless companies realise this and join in, untraditional groups will be faced with downsizing, take-overs, mergers and a sure pathway to the closure of most of their operations considered not profitable enough.

The approach to innovation is not only to be disruptive and get out of the box. The speed and the sizeable impact depends on our capacity to provide an exit for the traditional market leaders so that the conversion to the new economy and the better business models advances smoothly and inclusive.

12

AN ECOSYSTEM APPROACH TO ENERGY

If you do not change direction, you may end up where you are headed.
— *Chinese proverb*

The class of fourth grade children in Yokohama, Japan, is excited; each child is given a banana to eat during class, and the aroma is as pleasing as the taste. The teacher also gives each of them a hardboiled egg. They are instructed to cut the banana peel into little pieces with scissors and to pulverise the eggshell. The two are mixed and a little water added. Next, the probes of a digital voltmeter are inserted into the eggshell and banana peel paste. The children exclaim and clap their hands: the voltmeter registers an electrical current!

The reaction in Japan is no different in Brazil, or South Africa – adults are surprised and children are excited. Everyone wonders how this is possible. We are only familiar with modern sources of energy such as steam generators, nuclear power stations, coal-fired electrical power plants, hydroelectric generators, and photovoltaic solar panels. Yet these forms of generating energy are all recent arrivals on Earth. For the previous four billion years no one had relied on any of these modern human engineering marvels. It is as a result of this ingenuity that we today struggle with climate change due to excessive CO2 emissions, struggle to breathe with the air pollution caused by vehicles and industry in many of our cities, and face long-term societal costs for storage and containment of nuclear waste.

We are getting our manufactured electricity needs met via the grid, but remain unaware of the fact that our heart is powered by nothing more than the biochemistry of potassium, sodium, and calcium (as discussed in Chapter 10). A human heart requires just 0.2 volts, built up by the combination of 70 millivolt charges, to regulate the roughly 7,500 litres of blood that flow through all four chambers of the heart per day. There are no batteries and nothing is wired. No copper is needed. Indeed, as a result of our selective diet, evolved over millennia, we ingest a blend of molecules that, amongst other functions, provides a regular supply of biochemicals to make our heart, brain, and nervous system work for many decades without any maintenance required. No power station designed by man supplies energy as reliably as the simple biochemical reactions performed within our body.

Amory Lovins, cofounder of the Rocky Mountain Institute, is among the world's leading creative thinkers on energy. He has often shown that society's centralised energy production, consisting of huge power stations with masses of wires and cables reaching like tentacles into every home, is not the ideal way to achieve a sustainable electrical supply. If we were to take time to observe how natural systems have secured a continuous supply of energy for millennia, we would realise that none of our mainstream power generators apply those principles. Indeed, the collateral damage created by our present energy schemes risks destroying the very life support systems on which we depend.

Today, it is the means of providing energy that tilts the supply equation towards trouble. The massive output of three gases namely carbon dioxide (CO2), methane (CH4), and nitrous oxide (N2O), has had a pervasive impact on the thin band of breathable atmosphere that surrounds our planet. The delicately balanced atmosphere that envelops the Earth is the result of millions of years of interactions with its forest cover. Since less than 30% of the original forests remains, unless we embark on massive regeneration of forests in all climates, the basis on which the atmosphere is maintained, is shifting beyond repair. This had already been outlined by Dr Paolo Lugari in 2002, on the occasion of his lecture delivered to the scientists of Los Alamos in New Mexico (USA). The causes are known. The carbon dioxide comes mainly from burning fossil fuels, the methane from animal waste and rotting biomass from plants, and the nitrous oxide from applying natural gas-derived fertilisers to our agricultural crops. We have created a system much like a huge tanker ship on autopilot. It is hard to stop, takes time to change course, and has no one on board to make the quick decisions required to avoid collision.

The drive towards energy efficiency only started in earnest after the first oil shock in 1974. The Club of Rome, two years earlier, through its report *Limits to Growth,* had warned about the vicious cycle of population explosion, increased industrial output, rising energy demand, and excessive pollution. Nearly all the current alternatives to fossil fuel have major drawbacks. To date no one has been inspired by how natural systems have resolved the issue of energy security over millions of years. Worse still, most of the options being considered make no economic sense. Ultimately, we must go beyond temporary and intermediate options such as nuclear, photovoltaic, hydrogen, and wind power, and we must now embrace solutions proven in ecosystems that continuously renew and refresh air and water, as they have been doing successfully for millennia.

Nations that have opted for nuclear power as their back-up energy source have committed their citizens to cover the risks, often without asking permission. Nuclear proponents should ask the world's leading insurance companies if they are prepared to cover the risks without a taxpayer-funded guarantee. What they will discover is that no insurer is willing to write a policy for a nuclear energy site unless the government agrees to accept full risk, for all time! This generates neither jobs nor value. Considering that governments are prepared to commit all their citizens and their citizens' offspring for generations to come, why does the government not apply the same logic to all renewable energies?

Rethinking the Demand-Side

In Nature, most species meet their basic needs using the resources available to them. How can we model this for our energy generation and consumption? If we consider how natural systems efficiently generate energy, as they have successfully done for millions of years, we may discover the means to cut demand by a factor of 10 or even 20 – while offering greater accessibility. The idea emerges of a consumption system that requires much less external energy, that significantly reduces the need for mining, and that dramatically cuts the pollution from carbon dioxide, methane, and nitrous oxide. The new business model we envision will, in fact, undo some of the collateral damage that has been tacitly tolerated. This is the new approach to demand-side management: intervention on the supply side. If we make better use of what is available, if we retool to achieve greater efficiency, if we learn how to produce sustainably by generating multiple benefits from the same infrastructure, it will mean that we have learned to apply physics in our daily lives to our benefit. We will, at last, be achieving best use of our physical universe. Replacing "something" with "nothing" and reusing waste as raw material means we need less, and have more. Better and more, faster and at scale.

Over time, every species has adapted to refine and conserve the energy it needs to naturally heat, cool, transport, or transform. Bottlenose dolphins and whales know how to reduce drag; bluefin tuna know how to conserve heat. The boxfish with its superb efficiency inspires car design. Antifreeze is made naturally by yellow mealworm beetles; the abalone produces ceramics in cold water. We can include the cold light made by squid, the hibernation chemistry of bears, solid-state energy produced by lichens, frictionless sliding accomplished by the Arabian sand lizard, water harvesting by desert beetles, and the temperature control system perfected by termites. Each adaptation convincingly demonstrates that species can evolve ways to achieve maximal energy efficiency. When the contributions of each are woven into ecosystems that cascade nutrients and energy, we cannot but be in awe of their elegance and precision. Energy is never an objective in itself; it is a means to an end. Most of the time energy provides food and water, creates shelter, facilitates movement (in order to get food or mates) and promotes health. Ecosystems generate energy far more efficiently than our manufactured approaches. Nature teaches us that replacing "something" with "nothing" can bring us the surprising solutions we need for sustainability, and create the industries of the future.

That is the concept: replace "something" with "nothing", or with something so tiny and different that it has no resemblance at all to the system replaced. This is a radically different way to solve our energy problems. It also underscores the business model shift that is required to reduce our dependency on oil and the mined materials that are refined by burning additional fossil fuels.

Recall Fritz Vollrath's silk nano-engineering, discussed in Chapter 9. Where designer polymers, which are plastics, have replaced metals over the past 50 years, they have increased demand for petroleum, the raw material for these plastics. Here again the opportunity exists to use proven, tested, developed technology that mirrors Nature's methods and 40 centuries of farmers' wisdom. Replacing titanium with silk would realise a dramatic reduction in the demand for steel and high performance metals, as well as reduce the need for mining and energy consumption. Chelating bacteria, that can meet demand by recovering metals from end-of-life batteries, are also being researched. Instead of employing smelters that evaporate metals, chelation recovery is done at ambient temperature, using less energy.

Recall Bruce Roser's innovation, discussed in Chapter 5, of using natural processes to stabilise temperature-dependent pharmaceutical products that would otherwise perish. Eliminate the need for vaccine refrigeration and we can shave US$ 300 million off the cost of heath care delivery in developing nations. Such a portfolio of "replacing something with nothing" technologies, applied to our health care delivery system and our food production systems, will further reduce energy consumption. The energy savings would be truly massive, counted not just in what would be preserved but also by what would be reused.

Recall Curt Hallberg's vortex technology, discussed in Chapter 3. The greatest and most reliable source of energy on Earth comes from gravity. We cannot neglect the vast opportunities offered by a force that works 24 hours a day, and not merely when there is sunlight. Just about every living species has adapted to this very predictable force, and uses it to optimally meet its needs. A vortex is reliably generated by gravity, and has the potential to provide potable water with a minimal expense of energy. The swirling force of the vortex, used in applications that would remove bacteria and air from water, would eliminate the need for bactericides and cut energy consumption.

And let us introduce Stefan Larsson, the brain behind fascinating solar systems that function well north of Stockholm. Stefan used to work for Vattenfall, one of Europe's leading generators of electricity and heat, and one of the biggest wind power operators in the UK. He headed their solar research and had the challenging task of designing solar panels that would catch the sunlight even when the sun is only eight degrees above the horizon. And we thought solar research was pioneered only in solar rich parts of the world! Stefan applied alternative logic: if you can make solar work in the north of Sweden, then it will work beyond doubt anywhere in the world. As he deployed optical effects to concentrate sun rays and light using stationary reflectors, Stefan succeeded in getting the systems to work. Then, Vattenfall decided that its future depends on nuclear energy and closed their solar research programme. Ironically, this became the opportunity of a lifetime, and Stefan got the patents and the basics of the lab and, with his partners, created a new venture, Solarus.

It may seem hard to imagine a solar industry in Sweden but as time evolved Stefan applied a simple logic that had been overlooked by all experts who, spoiled by abundance of sun, never asked the obvious question: if solar PV panels work on both sides, why do we only use one side? The specialists will quickly point out that solar on top and concentrated solar on the bottom overheats the panels, and efficiency drops. Then Stefan responded with a second obvious question: why don't we cool solar panels with water just the same way we do with a car engine? At the time when all PV manufacturers raced to reduce the thickness of the wafer, cutting costs by reducing the core material, the idea to put water pipes inside a wafer seemed to come from an outsider, disconnected from the real solar world. Stefan was insistent and built his own version, relying on PV panels from Hitachi. With one-third of the wafer size, he could generate 18% more electricity – while he generated hot water of 60 to 70 °C for free. The combined efficiency of heat and power, using less energy and material, is more than double the performance of the traditional panels. Who had been blinded by an abundance of sun? Necessity is the mother of invention.

Solar on Both Sides

Then, Stefan asked the surreal question: do solar panels work at night? While he had earned some credibility in the scientific world with his innovative multi-layered optical films that capture heat and light from the sun that has barely risen above the horizon, he received a cold response. However, tests demonstrated that the water inside the double-sided solar system cooled down at night. The black cells did indeed radiate all heat out into dark space, and thus cold water could be harvested. Now Stefan's design offers heat, power and chill. Whereas Sweden has no need for cold water, the relevance of this was quickly grasped by Professor Eduard Ayensu from Ghana, a leading scientist from Africa who also worked with the World Bank. He concluded that the use of solar cells at night could replace the refrigerator. A two cubic metre room inside a home would provide natural cooling during the hot summer days. This would eliminate not only the capital costs associated with investment in cooling but also the on-going cost for power. The solar system now offers three benefits. And it has only just begun…

Water, when stored for hours at more than 70 °C, is sanitised. These units offer clean water, a major contribution towards health. Then Stefan and his team reconsidered their structural design and substituted the aluminium frame with recycled plastics. The solar system was adapted to serve as a roof, and since it includes a 22.5 cm-deep air-filled space, it works as insulation in winter and summer. This remarkable adventure to capture sun in Scandinavia now emerges as a revolutionary multi-modal system that offers heat, chill, power, sanitation, roofing and insulation. It also kick-starts a plastics recycling industry. Stefan and his partners never imagined that they could design and produce such solar panels in Sweden, but they did. They then decided to share their breakthroughs with anyone prepared to start local assembly, adjusting the business model to local conditions. The making of solar panels now starts looking like the farming of mushrooms on coffee grounds, doesn't it?

The first factory was set up in Venlo, in the Netherlands, and several investment rounds permitted the design of a plant that brings this technology to communities in Africa (with the Vineyard Hotel in Cape Town, South Africa as the pioneer), India (with Development Alternatives as a strategic partner), and Latin America (with local investors to secure regional funding). A blend of entrepreneurs from Holland and corporate operators from Sweden, took over the professional management with Leen Zevenbergen as CEO and Göran Carstedt as chairman. The company had taken off.

Unlocking 'New' Energies

Is it not curious that what we often describe as an invention, is merely what the ecosystems of our living Earth have been doing for countless eons? When Thomas Edison created the first light bulbs, his original filament was bamboo, rich in naturally occurring iron. A hundred years later, these original light bulbs still work. Contrary to common perception, Edison did not invent electricity – it has always existed, and has been used in cells, for billions of years. Minute differences in pH (potential hydrogen) on opposite sides of a cell membrane generate minuscule currents, often too small to measure. Electric current in natural systems never relies on mined and smelted metals, yet achieves conductivity with practically no resistance. In order to have energy that flows through concentrated metals in a battery, mining is required and this generates massive amounts of pollution, both in processing and post-consumption. Bamboo and whales are two species that have much to teach us about electricity and conductivity.

Nature draws on six main sources of energy to produce electricity: heat, light, friction, pressure, magnetism, and biochemistry. Magnetism contributes the largest portion of electrical production worldwide. Power generators, whether hydroelectric, coal, oil, methane gas, or nuclear, all use magnetism as the actual means of electrical generation. Light acting on solar panels is slowly making headway but at higher cost. Electricity is generated by spinning a metal coil within a magnetic field. Smaller, less powerful, electrical current can be generated directly by heat, pressure, and friction. Chemical reaction in the form of batteries is both the oldest means of producing electrical current and has also had the greatest impact on our modern way of life. Biochemistry is a major source of physiological electric current and the supply basically comes along with the nutrient intake of the particular species – yet it is given hardly any major industrial attention. The biochemical system, as perfected by the electric fish, is a marvel of engineering, and not least in its use of insulation.

Natural systems do not rely on any of the extreme methods that mankind has devised. In Nature, fire and incineration are the exception rather than the rule. Even a 50% dry matter content is not handled by burning. Humans easily resort to burning everything considered waste. It is a policy dominant in agriculture, in industry, and in municipal refuse disposal. Whenever we do not know what to do with something, we burn it. Lately, experts have invented the argument that pyrolysis (chemical decomposition by heating) recovers the energy embedded in complex materials. There are even companies promoting the burning of water! After funding years of research, Nestlé, the largest instant coffee processing company in the world, concluded that burning coffee waste (composed of over 80% water) was the best environmental option!

The exercise of observing natural sources of energy is inspiring. Though we may fully comprehend the law of gravity, few of us pause to question how the constituent components that become apples – before these acquire form and submit themselves to the law of gravity – at first defy gravity. It is this fresh look at the forces at work in ecosystems that provides the right state of mind to search for lasting solutions to our energy predicament.

How does the coconut fill with water? There is no pump; neither does the nut absorb rainwater. How do trees erect their massive structures? Where does osmosis in plants derive the power to trump gravitational forces, pushing nutrient-filled sap upwards through their capillary network? Of course, there is interplay with surface tension and the powerful draw of the moon. The moon is responsible for tidal ebb and flow, another steadily predictable force in the physics of our universe. There are many forces employed by natural systems, in great detail and at minute levels, giving all manner of life the energy resources they have uniquely developed for their needs. This stands in stark contrast with the industrial solutions we have invented and financed. Modern solutions seem straightforward, yet their inherent inefficiencies are vast compared to clusters of natural energy sources. This has led to the waste of so much energy, and this is why we now need to ask, "Where are the real opportunities?"

Electricity from pH

While humans debate the values of nuclear, solar, coal, wind and photovoltaic generation, natural systems cascade their energy requirements among all contributors based on differences in potential hydrogen (pH). A tree generates electric currents from the difference between the pH of the soil and the tree. Potential hydrogen is an important factor in the natural energy equation because it controls the speed of biochemical reactions. It does this by controlling the intensity of enzyme activity, as well as the speed that electricity moves through our bodies. A higher pH means a substance or solution has greater alkalinity and a greater electrical resistance. Therefore, electricity travels slower with a higher pH. If something is acidic (lower pH), the current runs faster. A car battery is acidic. On cold days, a properly acidic battery quickly starts your car. Biochemically, what is alkaline is slow. Compare the lead-acid car battery to an alkaline torch battery. The torch battery discharges more slowly. Natural systems use this interplay constantly, without ever resorting to lead (car battery) or lithium (torch battery). In living species, membranes are the gateways for these flows. Sometimes membranes let electrons pass rapidly, sometimes slowly; it is the management of the differential in pH levels that determines the current.

Electricity from Temperature Differential

Thermoelectricity is the conversion of temperature differential to electricity. In our new energy model, electronic equipment could draw power from the warmth of the human body. In Germany, the Fraunhofer Institute for Physical Measurement Techniques has developed a way of harnessing electricity from natural body heat. Imagine! The difference between the temperature of the human body and the hot or cold environment surrounding it, is enough to generate electricity. Normally, a difference of several tens of degrees is considered necessary to generate enough electricity to nominally power electronic equipment, but the differences between the body's surface temperature and its immediate environment is only a few degrees. "Only low voltages can be produced from differences like these," explains Peter Spies, project manager at the Fraunhofer Institute. This ambient body heat differential capture device delivers roughly 200 millivolts. Electronic devices require at least one or two volts; an LED light will shine with less than one volt.

Yet, the Fraunhofer Institute engineers have found a solution. Instead of searching for ways to create more power – the standard way industry thinks – the Fraunhofer Institute engineers cleverly created circuits needing less energy, a mere 200 hundred millivolts.

They have built entire electronic systems that require neither an internal battery nor a connection to the grid. The system draws energy from body heat alone. Peter Spies is confident that in the future, when further improvements have been made to the switching systems, a temperature difference of only 0.5 °C will be sufficient to generate enough electricity to power a cell phone. This is exactly how natural systems evolved, with ever-smaller currents achieving ever-more – until everything they needed was accomplished – without waiting for a massive surge such as a lighting strike to make things happen.

Peter Spies' breakthrough allows us to seriously consider how to liberate ourselves from the burden of the battery, metals, mining, and the massive energy required in commercial manufacture to produce a consumer product that will shortly become landfill. In a Blue Economy, many instruments could be reconfigured to work without power from a battery or a wall socket. Nature offers endless inspiration.

Seiko, the Japanese watchmaker, in 1999 marketed 500 units of the first watch powered by body temperature. Once fully charged, it operated for ten months. It became one of the most sought-after watches ever made. The power-generating capacity depends on the air temperature and individual differences in body temperature. When worn on the wrist, the watch absorbs heat through the back case and dissipates it from the front of the watch, generating power with its thermal converter. As the difference between the air temperature and the surface temperature increases, the power generation increases. As the difference decreases, the power generation also decreases. Ideally, this is the way we will be working with energy in the future.

Electricity from Gravity and Pressure

Pressure, or technically speaking, piezoelectricity, is another abundant natural source of electricity. "Piezo" is a root word from Greek that means "stress." The main source of compression is of course the pressure of gravity. The weight of a tree can generate electricity from the gravitational stress on rocks in the soil. As a source of energy, stress or pressure works most efficiently with materials that have a crystalline structure. In the past, obvious resources like quartz and diamonds were utilised. Rochelle salt (made from sodium bicarbonate and potassium bitartrate) was the first material used to demonstrate piezoelectric generation. Notably, the molecular composition of salt consists of potassium and sodium, the two key biochemical components powering our heartbeat. Recent insights into piezoelectrical generation added common products like cane sugar, dry bones, silk, and even wood. As cutting edge research explores yet uncharted paths, more sources of piezoelectricity will be discovered. Whereas industrial uses are still undeveloped in much of the world, Japanese industry has given the commercial applications of piezoelectricity a vote of confidence. Numerous applications have nestled themselves into our daily lives without us ever realising that they operate with energy from pressure. The original television remote controls used quartz technology to convert the pressure from pressing a button into an electric current. The echolocation device in cars is also based on this energy source, as is the engine that powers the autofocus of reflex cameras. Simple pressure on the small lever of a cigarette lighter is enough to create an electric spark to light the fuel. Robert Bosch, the German car parts maker, developed the first piezoelectric fuel injection system. This is one of the factors that made the

Volkswagen Jetta a very fuel-efficient car. It outperforms the Toyota Prius, which gained fame in the USA merely by generating electric power from braking and recovering waste power from burning gasoline. Still, the Jetta performs better!

As our understanding of piezoelectricity broadens, a new vision emerges for the design of buildings that could produce electricity using the pressure the structure exerts upon the floor. Quartz crystals occur everywhere in the European Alps, and could be placed under pillars on each floor of a building, generating electrical power exactly where it was most needed. In fact, this application is a direct conversion of the power of gravity. The pressure exerted by the structure is easily calculated based on gravitational force. The potential is huge because the immense weight of a building exerting pressure on crystals could generate several megavolts, certainly enough to power at least the building's lift.

Gravity is our best hope for moving our societies, in general, and our buildings, in particular, towards sustainability. Using the electrical potential of pressure is the means to realise a completely different vision of energy-emancipated houses and buildings. Recall the description of how a design, based on the same principles as the Namibian beetle's water collection method, could produce water on a roof, and how a vortex would clean that water as gravity pulled it from floor to floor. To this we can add electricity generated not from thin-film solar cells that power carbon fibres, but from the structure's gravitational force generating thousands of volts of piezoelectricity. Let our engineers focus on achieving this vision!

These energy insights offer ways that could reduce or eliminate the ever-increasing demand for small batteries for hearing aids, toys, mobile and miniature devices, and cell phones. While venture capitalists have invested billions in funding research for "disposable" batteries that cause less polluting, the real investment return will be in tapping energy sources that integrate seamlessly and harmoniously with Nature and eliminate our dependency on metal extraction.

Another potential source of piezoelectricity is vibration, in particular the spectrum of vibrations we call "sound." Scientists have long known that seismic communication is common in small animals and insects, including spiders, scorpions, and a few vertebrate species, such as white-lipped frogs, kangaroo rats, and golden moles, using a level of sound that humans are unable to perceive. Seismic sensitivity has also been observed in huge marine mammals, such as the elephant seal. Testimonials exist concerning elephants clearly sensing a tsunami forming and approaching, breaking their chains and running to safety. This has sparked the interest of scientists.

In 1997, Caitlin O'Connell-Rodwell, a research associate at the Stanford University School of Medicine, discovered that elephants are able to communicate over long distances with low-pitched sounds that are barely audible to humans. She charted a bold new research direction by proposing that low-frequency elephant calls generate powerful vibrations in the ground – seismic signals – that elephants can feel, and even interpret, via their sensitive trunks, knees, and feet. According to O'Connell-Rodwell, the elephants communicate through the ground, and are able to discriminate very subtle vibrations through their feet.

She has conducted observations of elephant herds at the Etosha National Park in Namibia, and is applying the data collected on animal seismic sensitivity to the problem of hearing loss in humans. People with hearing impairment often develop the capacity for much greater tactile sensitivity in the auditory cortex of their brain than do people with normal hearing. "We want to investigate the possibility that new-borns with severe hearing loss could have their hearing improved by exposure to vibrational stimulation shortly after birth," states O'Connell-Rodwell. One of the basic principles of physics, namely vibration, is at work here, helping to meet the changing needs of a species: creating cells in the brain to compensate for hearing impairment and sensitising a nervous system to perceive vibrations through hands and feet.

The most promising version of a piezoelectric power source is where the pressure created by a voice (yes! sound does create pressure!) generates electricity. If the piezoelectric unit that converts sound pressure to electricity were in contact with your skin, both piezoelectricity and thermal electricity could power your phone. This means the more you talk the longer you can call. We might further imagine the look and design of a hearing aid powered by the wearer's voice to which it connects, supplemented by electricity powered by body temperature. Combining these proven power sources would quickly make the lithium battery and solar cell charger obsolete. They would establish the basis for a wide array of new energy applications.

Energy from Sweat

Athletes measure their fitness and work-rate through lactate levels. Lactate is naturally present in perspiration excreted when exercising vigorously. Dr Wenzhao Jia at the University of California in San Diego (USA) strips electrons from lactate with an enzyme embedded in a temporary tattoo, generating 70 microwatt per square centimetre of skin. She did not build a biobattery – she just created a permanent supply of power for a sensor that measures the efficiency of the workout, combining physical data like heart rate with chemical data. Dr Jia delivered a proof of concept and produced a self-powered lactate sensor onto a tattoo paper. Since less fit people get tired faster, they form more lactate, and create more power.

The device is sufficiently advanced to link this tattoo to portable gadgets, adding a capacitor to store the generated current. A digital watch needs 10 microwatt, and the batteries included are the most toxic and the most easily discarded ones on the market. A space of two by three millimetres is enough to generate all the power you need and get rid of the metals forever. These biobatteries recharge quickly, never leak toxic chemicals and the risk of explosion is nil. Of course, the most powerful argument is that it relies on the use of a renewable energy source: YOU. Is this just the fantasy of scientists? The highly respected German journal *Angewandte Chemie* published a peer-reviewed article in 2014 in which Dr Jia provides details of her method. She has attracted capital and entrepreneurs to make it a reality. The creation of a new product evolves from fantasy to a vision, and can only be translated into reality through science and risk taking. The opportunity to substitute billions of tiny batteries with harmful effects by using our own sweat is too inspiring an idea to neglect.

Energy from Movement (Kinetic Energy)

Another variation of pressure is the kinetic energy generated by movement. Again, the watch industry has taken the lead on this technology. Rolex commercialised the first gravity-operated watch in 1931. It contained a small semi-circular metal device that wound the watch simply by freely moving. More recently Seiko has introduced hundreds of variations on this theme, and uses it as one of its main watch designs.

While this use of energy from movement has found a favourable market, the way in which biological systems use kinetic energy elicits our greater curiosity. Flowing blood has mass and velocity, thus it has kinetic energy. The flow of blood through our vessels would be a simple resource that could be utilised immediately. Furthermore, as the blood flows inside a vein or artery, pressure exerted against the walls of the vessel can also generate piezoelectric energy. The total energy of blood flowing within our vessels is the sum of the energies from movement and pressure. Experts might argue that such minute amounts of energy are insufficient to make a dent in the world's demand for electricity. We are reminded of the Dutch proverb, *Wie het kleine niet deert is het grote niet weerd* – if you do not appreciate the small, you are not deserving of the great. Surely advances in nanotechnology will find a way to convert these two pressures to electricity.

Even as limited funding has been made available for research into solar energy, and massive amounts of venture capital are invested in developing new types of batteries, research and development of pressure and temperature-driven electrical generation has received no support at all from governments, private investors, or venture capitalists. Investors seem uninterested in exploring ideas for renewable energy sources that do not require heavy metals and energy storage. The Max Planck and Fraunhofer Research Institutes are pioneering the field of renewable energy beyond the mainstream. There are innovators, like Alan Heeger, who discovered that thin-film polymers are highly electrically conductive and can replace batteries on just about everything; and Michael Graetzel, who is pioneering ideas to produce electricity the way a leaf achieves photosynthesis.

As an article in the Harvard Business Review of February 2008 noted, were we to cover the Golden Gate Bridge with thin-film solar cells, not only would it eliminate the necessity of anti-corrosion chemical applications, it would generate enough electricity to power much of the city's local municipal requirements. Here is another example of a multi-tiered approach that takes advantage of an economy of physics and natural temperature variations to capture electricity (revenue from renewable energy) and eliminate chemical use (and hence anti-corrosion chemical application costs). Such approaches move us closer to zero-waste models. We are now moving towards the design of integrated business models – where the combination of these innovations evolves into an ecosystem, utilising the opportunity to substitute "something" with "nothing" (no more need for anti-corrosion chemical applications), thus cutting costs while generating additional revenue (power from a local generator that is consumed within a few kilometres range). This double whammy makes thin-film solar competitive, whereas as a stand-alone technology it would be and has been discarded as too expensive.

Physicists and farmers alike easily recognise the power of pressure and temperature. Yet these forces are neglected in our modern debates about energy efficiency. It is for this reason that innovative energy sources open a vast treasure trove of entrepreneurial opportunities. These technological options permit generating small amounts of energy with limited investment for local consumption. Potential applications are limitless, and new markets are available everywhere and all the time. Even greater opportunity is open to those who bundle multiple technologies – just as natural systems do, providing a reliable energy system that consistently performs with what is locally available. At this critical juncture, instead of losing focus in a debate over oil or nuclear sources, exploring innovative energy sources is a quest that should fully engage us.

CO_2 as a Source of Energy

It is impossible to conclude a chapter on innovations in energy without discussing the potential of CO_2. While out-of-control emissions are now universally attributed to contributing to climate change, we need to consider the potential of CO_2 as a valuable input to our industrial society, helping to meet basic needs. Oxygen was originally a toxin that became a pre-condition to all life. In the same sense, if we flick our mental switch from "problem" to "opportunity," CO_2 could well become a major contributor to a sustainable society. "How?" you may well ask. One answer lies with algae.

Having lived on Earth for billions of years, algae are among the earliest photosynthetic organisms. These single-celled species were the first to develop a nucleus and to carry the memory of life known as DNA. Algae require only CO_2, water, nutrients, and sunlight to produce their own food and chemical energy through photosynthesis. Oxygen, the by-product of this photosynthesis, is abundantly released into the air and into the waters of the world's lakes, oceans, and rivers. Algae are not plants, belonging rather to the kingdom of Protista. They are tremendously efficient at capturing the power of light, and consequently are among the fastest-growing species on the planet. They grow ten times faster than sugar cane and compete with bacteria in output and proliferation. Managing algal proliferation would be like needing to mow your lawn three times a day, instead of only once every other week.

This capacity for growth renders algae an important contributor to managing climate change. Its virtues are that it gives off oxygen as it grows, it is high in oil content, and it contains high nutrient levels. The University of Minnesota Centre for Biorefining has estimated that algae produce 46,700 litres of oil per hectare per year. The Brazilian team directed by Jorge Alberto Vieira Costa from the Federal University of Rio Grande (Rio Grande do Sul, Brazil) handily cultivates spirulina at low cost, generating 18,700 litres of oil per hectare per year. By comparison, corn yields 168 litres, soybeans 448 litres, and palm trees 5,940 litres per hectare per year. This is a result that is hard to ignore. One of algae's other great virtues is that unlike corn-based ethanol, many strains can be grown in salt water on marginal land and can even sequester carbon emissions from coal-fired power stations, as well as decontaminating soil.

All oil and gas extraction processes generate brackish water, an unwanted waste product. The water is often left in retention basins that leach over time into surrounding soil, rendering the land toxic and infertile for centuries. Because warm water affects the habitat of aquatic life in rivers and oceans, coal-fired power stations also have retention basins for cooling water prior to discharge. These retention basins have been mandated by law, ostensibly to mitigate collateral damage to the environment. It takes only a little imagination to see that algae could be profitably farmed in these basins, thereby converting an unproductive waste receptacle into a system that attenuates CO_2, replenishes oxygen, and produces low-cost and renewable biofuel. Depending on the type of algae farmed, up to one-third is lipids, oils from which fuels derive. What we envision is one more simple, yet effective, way to reduce our legacy of environmental damage by returning waste to the nutrient stream. In so doing, we learn how to utilise available infrastructure for productive outputs. In a Blue Economy, we will solve our current challenges by doing more with what we have. Farming algae for food and biofuel is an admirable example. Professor Vieira Costa, with his team, even succeeded in producing polyesters from algae. It is this generation of multiple products with multiple revenues that shifts the 'business of bio' from academically interesting (but uncompetitive due to high cost), to entrepreneurially attractive and competitive – not because costs are minimised, but because so much more revenue is generated.

The National Renewable Energy Laboratory in Colorado (USA) undertook trials to document a portfolio of 300 protein, carbohydrate, and oil-rich algae that could produce biodiesel in the desert wastelands of New Mexico. In 1996 Vieira Costa adapted this research to help establish a project aimed at achieving food security at Mangueira Lake. Biodiesel was not the focus of his attention. The food security focus came from the needs of rice farmers in Southern Brazil who were struggling to compete on the world market without fertiliser subsidies. Joining Vieira Costa in his algae project was Professor Lucio Brusch da Fraga, a physicist by training, but with a special degree in quality management.

It was a remarkable partnership. Mangueira Lake is one of the most alkaline lakes in the world – a far cry from qualifying as an environmental asset. Vieira Costa and Brusch da Fraga set out to demonstrate that it is possible to farm algae everywhere, including temperate climate zones like Southern Brazil. Once they mastered the production of algae around rice paddies in Vittoria do Palmar, on the southern-tip of Brazil bordering Uruguay, they harvested the algae. It contained a high concentration of micronutrients – what in the US is called "super blue-green algae", even though these cells are in fact cyanobacteria. They distributed this nutritional food source to the local underserved population around the city of Rio Grande. The social and medical delivery services, the schools, and the media, lauded their success in alleviating hunger and malnutrition. Following this, they quickly realised that algae production in retention basins could accomplish more than only food security. An extension of the programme was explored: algae for biodiesel.

Even though Brazil only has five coal-fired power stations, compared to 3,000 in the US, they were able to run a series of industrial trials using coal-fired exhaust in combination with algae farming to produce biofuel. Building from the ground up, Vieira Costa initiated a process similar to the Brazilian development economics that earned international acclaim for producing ethanol from sugar cane. Instead of rushing into business, Professor Costa established a research institute that undertook scientific inquiry into the typical ecosystem conditions found in Southern Brazil. He recruited a group of eager students who were progressing through undergraduate, masters, and ultimately doctoral degrees. From this institute came a strong portfolio of patents.

Vieira Costa and his team went from strength to strength, working with local biodiversity, local ecosystems, and local field experience. Their projects, using Lagoa Mangueira and Laguna Morin as huge natural retention basins for algae farming, have provided experience on how to evolve from the micro-scale of a rice paddy to the industrial scale of retention basins at energy generation facilities. In essence, what we see is physics supporting biology. After extracting food, biodiesel, and esters (the latter for polymers usable for cosmetics) from the algae, the residues can be converted to ethanol. Thus, what we see is a substantial increase in productivity when conjoined with other complementary technologies.

Algae and carbon dioxide live in symbiosis. Algae grow fastest with a rich supply of CO_2 and absorb this greenhouse gas like a sponge. Scaling up the industrial processes for using CO_2 to supply the algae, requires blending more carbonic gases into water so that the algae are more productive, while maximising sunlight exposure and avoiding shade. The present technique for mixing air with water is like using a sledgehammer to crack open a nut; the effort and force is used for small results in output. Such inefficient processes help explain why the resultant products are too expensive. Worse, the producers typically settle for the core business model – in this case the biofuel – and discard everything else. It is no wonder that the present techniques are not commercially viable, even with petroleum prices on the rise.

If we assess how to best blend air into water, we would wisely look to Nature. Natural systems never use pumps or air blowers. Nature relies on the vortex. Air bubbles containing carbonic gases can be blended into water with this swirling movement and four times more air can be made available to the algae at a size that fits the algal membranes. Air bubbles that are ten times larger, and in some bioreactors even 10,000 times larger, than the pores in the algae's membranes, renders the process inefficient and uncompetitive. The oversized bubbles remain unused and end up as turbulence on the surface of the water and are then released into the atmosphere. This is highly energy inefficient. Vortex technology permits the production of micro-bubbles tailored to membrane openings. The proof that the air bubbles are small in size is that the water body acquires a milky appearance. The catalyst for the whole process is water and the energy source relies on the most dependable force on Earth: gravity. These insights allow us to design sustainable and competitive solutions.

The power of algae is that the output is not limited to lipids that can be converted to biodiesel. Once the oil is extracted, what remains is high-protein, micronutrient-rich matter, suitable for human as well as livestock consumption, as Professor Costa imagined from the outset. His students even discovered that the residual algal membranes are composed of pure esters, and can be converted to natural polyesters. Thus we return to the concept of an entire biorefinery, or, as the Brazilian team would call it, "a whole photo-biorefinery" – one that renewably produces as long as the sun shines, gravity is present and CO2 is emitted. Given the low risk that any of these three factors will cease to manifest, the odds are good.

This bundle of discoveries and innovations can help mitigate climate change, while providing energy and food, using water as the catalyst. We wonder why anyone would propose "sequestering" CO_2 by pumping it deep into the oceans or into old oil wells. Such a capital-intensive venture would lead to large revenues for the engineers, but nothing for the investors. It completely lacks economic sense, unless of course governments provide subsidies without reason. Nor would it be an asset on the sustainability ledger. "Out of sight, out of mind" is outdated thinking. It gives us overflowing landfills, recreation parks atop nuclear waste storage, and other short-sighted "protection by separation" follies that often result in irremediable loss and crippling damage. When you know that future generations will have to pay the bill, why do it?

With food and energy as the by-products of a process that transforms algae, CO_2, water, and sunlight into biofuel, what we have is an efficient symbiosis. To crown the benefits, the process generates jobs. How many jobs? The biggest CO2 emitters are power plants and cement factories. If 10,000 power plants from the US, Europe, China, and the developing world were to apply these technologies, they would on average require 100 employees per facility, in total one million jobs. This would be a marriage of the old and the new, a bridge between fossil fuel, mainly coal, and renewables. The investment required to build these facilities equals the cost of ten nuclear power stations at US$ 10 billion each. Would ten nuclear power stations generate a million jobs? Not even close! How much time would it take to put these ten new nuclear facilities on line? At least a decade for the first one!

If we take a dispassionate look at the economic and social impact of one set of solutions versus another, examining the average cost of investment, the potential jobs created, and the generation of multiple benefits for health and employment from renewable fuels and natural polymers, it is clear that a nuclear power solution loses hands-down. Nuclear power has never been utilised by any ecosystem that promotes life. Economic and business models must now change focus to enhance life. Surely enhancing life should be the starting point of any activity humanity undertakes? It is not a matter of being in favour of or against nuclear power. Even without ever considering the obvious safety concerns associated with the use of nuclear power, it is not the best option on all other counts, except perhaps if you've studied nuclear physics and are looking for a job.

It is surprising that engineers seem to ignore many potential energy sources, even though these are the real power sources for all the creatures with whom we share this planet. Discoveries as to how we can respond differently to our needs for energy never seem to reach the antennae of corporate policy makers and strategists – who believe that bigger is better, and who are risk-adverse even in times of plenty. To those industry professionals who would be quick to argue that no "alternative" technologies will ever power the grid, we offer the words of Maria, a young 10-year old student from Curitiba, Brazil, who heard engineers say that the power generated by banana peels and egg shells would never compete with that of nuclear fission or burning coal. Maria listened patiently and respectfully to the petroleum company director, then responded, "Well, in twenty-five years – when I am old – I will prove you wrong." There is nothing better for a society than when the next generation is eager and motivated to make a difference and go for what they believe is better.

13

A FRESH APPROACH TO MINING

One generation plants the trees,
another gets the shade.
– Chinese proverb

How to Restore Errors of the Past

Picture yourself at the end of a 45-minute ride from Johannesburg, the industrial capital of all of Africa. The desolate, moon-like landscape that now surrounds you could provide the perfect backdrop to the latest sci-fi movie. You are standing atop a mountain of mine tailings, rich in uranium and containing half a gram of gold per tonne. You are imagining a straight line extending four kilometres up into the air and sense the depth of the deepest mines on earth, extending four kilometres beneath your feet. While we denounce the environmental havoc, we must also marvel at the feat of engineering. Deep in the Earth's crust, the heat reaches nearly 55 °C. Imagine the expertise it took to solve the challenge of providing air and temperate conditions to 20,000 miners working as deep as 4,000 metres below the surface. Ice-making machines in the belly of the Earth are used to make the working environment tolerable. Consider again, the biggest ice-making machines in the world, powered in the hot depths of the Earth's crust, to cool the air.

The question immediately comes to mind: "Could this ever be sustainable?" Could mining companies ever conduct their operations and leave the local community better off than when they arrived? In Nature, lichens are great miners, capable of extracting specific inorganic molecules like magnesium from rocks, and sharing these with all other life in the ecosystem. Bacteria selectively separate metals through chelation; mankind is the only species that uses brute force and harsh toxins, including mercury and cyanide, to acquire desirable ores. Though we may lack the knowledge and skill to undo the errors of the past, it is within our ability to do better in the future. We may not currently be capable of transforming mining into a benign operation, yet we can at least design a strategy that begins to reduce the adverse environmental and social consequences of mining.

From atop our mountain of tailings, we are surveying one of humanity's most aggressive operations. Armed with dynamite and consuming massive amounts of water and energy, mining operations extract minute concentrations of gold from deep within the Earth. The miners who toil in the shafts endure abject and barely tolerable living and working conditions, sending their meagre earnings home to provide for their often far away families. No one knows how many will still be on the job, or even still alive, in a decade.

Mining is a risky enterprise in more ways than one. Even with the world market price for gold dropping from record levels, there is no guarantee that the extraction of this precious metal will remain profitable in the years to come, especially if all the external and remediation costs imposed on the local communities surrounding the mines, were fully recovered from the mining companies' existing revenue streams. When gold ore from deep within the South African soil reaches the surface, it sometimes comes with a natural complement of uranium. The tailings (what is left once the ore is extracted) are dumped above ground, forming a stark line across the horizon. The magnificent view of the surroundings is clouded, not by air pollution from the city nearby, but by dust released from the uranium-laced tailings. The uranium leaches into the air and the water, exposing all life forms to potentially lethal cancers. A few watchdog organisations decry this contamination and have repeatedly pressured management to find ways to abate these high levels of risk. Sadly, because shareholders prefer a steadily upward progression of capital gains, any plan or cost directed towards abatement does not even reach the Board.

Picture the richest concentrations of gold layered beneath huge water reserves amassed on a bed of dolomite. At an energy cost of *US$ 1.5 million per day*, water and air must be pumped into the shafts to provide a tolerable environment for the workers. Now, the air vented from the mine shafts releases approximately 100,000 tonnes of methane per year. As fresh shafts are explored, the volume may even double year by year for a few decades. Apart from its effect on the atmosphere, methane is highly flammable. That is why every mining tool is expensive. They are made of copper, titanium, or beryllium because these metals do not produce sparks.

Mining entails health risks and major occupational hazards. Johannesburg, affectionately shortened to Jo'burg or Jozi, and known to locals as Egoli (Place of Gold), is perhaps the only major industrial city in the world that is not located alongside a river or in a coastal zone. Rather, it is built around mining sites. The massive pumping of underground water and the diversion of a river into a 30-kilometre pipeline severed local agriculture's lifeline to water. What was once the vegetable garden for the Jo'burg megalopolis is now scarred by mine shafts, miles of tailings and sinking surfaces. The water that is available has worrying levels of pollution that will render the soil unsuitable for food production for at least a generation, if not more. Any form of farming, especially cattle ranching in and around the mines, cannot be recommended. Still, a few families try to subsist in the area, herding their animals where there should be none. Mining company executives are at pains to keep the poor, who continue to return after being sent away, off the land.

Geologists and biologists are learning more and more about the ways toxins are assimilated by water, air, and soil. Broadleaf plants accumulate toxins in their tissue. This creates health risks, particularly the irradiation and contamination of the animal life that consumes them for food. Because there is scant research and monitoring data, the statistics are unclear. Neither management nor government can obtain a full picture or a complete understanding of this complex process. As a result, anecdotal stories and brief scientific reports produced by outsiders are often based on little more than speculation.

These environmental and social realities are not the only reasons mines are under stress. While the world market price for gold has dropped from historic peaks, the cost of operation has never been as exorbitant. To make matters worse, the South African electricity grid is heavily stressed: the South African electricity public utility (ESKOM) has informed the mining industry of its inability to meet demand due to a lack of investment in capacity expansion. Thus, rising energy prices for pumping air and water are exacerbated by an uncertain electrical supply. This forces the mines to make huge investments in back-up diesel generators to secure the safety of the underground workers and provide a habitable zone by cooling the horizontal shafts to a depth of several thousand metres. Simultaneously, energy is required to move ore from 3,600 metres below, to the surface for processing. When electricity is unavailable, the mines are forced to close for one or two days per week. How do you stimulate competitiveness under these conditions? How do you take care of your workers when you are faced with such uncertainties?

A thorough inventory of mining's adverse impacts would necessarily include the rubble from ore-processing gathered in mounds on porous soil, the uranium-filled dust clouds rising from the tailings, the desertification of land from the continuous pumping of groundwater, the sink holes caused by the same process, and the accumulation of uranium in the waterways and soil. Nor should we exclude the social and health challenges posed by living conditions in mine-site hostels. After visiting these deep mines and seeing the reality of mining life first hand, it would be easy to despair at the extent of the societal and environmental degradation that is evident everywhere. Yet, to find solutions it helps to have a positive mindset, to learn creatively, and to act decisively. In South Africa, truth and reconciliation surmounted tremendous difficulties. The way forward is not about laying blame, it is about acknowledging shortcomings and designing a new business model that can simultaneously please stockholders and remediate local conditions. Advocates such as Mark Cutifani, the former CEO of Anglo Gold Ashanti and now the leader of Anglo American, are committed to pioneering a new way forward. It is not guaranteed that they will succeed.

Binding the Wound to Heal

Operating a mine should be considered an intervention into the Earth's crust comparable to a surgical intervention into a human body. Even if we consider it a necessary procedure, we must bind the wound to heal. The past two centuries of mining has left many tragic legacies, some documented and some still to surface. The advent of improved instrumentation and better understanding means that less invasive and more sustainable practices can and should be introduced.

From a core business management point of view, an economic crisis requires cost reductions at every level. Realising the difficulties associated with continuing business as usual, management must search for ways to lower expenditures. However, if we were to redefine these core business principles, if we were to turn our thinking around, we could identify applicable technologies and energy-saving solutions that would lower costs and strengthen cash flow at the same time. Innovation can generate new revenues and create social capital that will support the local communities even after the mines have been exhausted. If we can save more, generate more income, remediate more environmental damage while securing additional revenue, and create more value while investing less, everyone benefits. We can convert liabilities and provisions into investments and ensure that things which currently have no value become assets on the balance sheet. All that is required is that we think outside the box of current practice.

Paper Made from Rocks

One of the largest investments of any mine is dealing with waste: rocks and tailings. Mining engineers have learned how to create rock refuse deposits, where low pH debris is stored indefinitely. Valleys are converted into mountains – at high environmental costs. Tailings, the leftovers from crushed ore, processed and void of any precious, non-ferrous or rare earth metals, are also stored for eternity. This slurry is transported over large distances and pumped into dams where it settles and is left – for all time. A gold mine could well dump one billion tonnes of rock and tailings over its lifetime, requiring a dam of 100 metres high to hold the massive flow of waste. The permit to excavate ore always goes hand in hand with a permit to dump the leftovers, which will permanently alter the landscape.

It is time to ask the obvious question: is anyone interested in tailings or rocks? The standard answer from the mine experts is that, "if there had been a use that makes money, then we would have done this a long time ago, and everyone else would have by now applied the same solution". It is not that easy to get experts out of their comfort zones – until a crisis looms. Gold prices drop and the capital cost of rock deposits and tailing dams renders the extraction of gold and other ores non-viable. Breakthrough solutions can never be found inside the circle of ready wisdom, they must come from the outside.

China invented paper production two millennia ago, and has now, in the 21st century, re-invented paper. In 1990, Mr Shih Huei (William) Liang from Taiwan had a question: could we ever make paper without felling trees? He worked tirelessly and after 12 years of research concluded that he could blend 20% (recycled) plastics with 80% crushed stone to produce a novel paper that requires no trees and minimal water in the production process – stone paper, also known as mineral paper. The pulp and paper industry was too busy finding a response to the rapid digitisation of media, so it failed to notice the arrival of a new competitor – a paper alternative made from waste materials. While the paper industry looked the other way, the mining companies kept on piling up their waste, ignoring the revolution in the making.

While Mr Liang cracked the formula for stone paper over a decade, it took him another decade to fine-tune the machinery. Now Mr Liang offers mines the opportunity to convert all their rocks, crushed to dust particles of 3 to 5 micron, into the most sophisticated paper. The capital cost is only a fraction of the cost of a modern paper mill and the fact that no water is needed in its production makes it an ideal add-on to any primary industry. Whereas a tailing dam could absorb a billion dollars in capital, and represents a risk for all time, stone paper generates cash, eliminates the capital expenditure and reduces the risk. How long will the mines be able to argue that paper is not a part of core business? After Mr Liang inaugurated his first plant in Taiwan in 2008, and then improved operations and marketing, the first large-scale industrial production came on line in Benxi City, close to Shenyang (China) in September 2013, with two more plants opened in China shortly after. The first factory created about 1,000 jobs. Moreover, the conversion of the rolls of paper into final products like notebooks, packaging material, and labels for wine bottles, generates an additional 4,000 jobs per 100,000 tonnes of paper produced.

The world demand for paper is expected to reach 500 million tonnes by 2020. On average, South Africans consume 200 kg of paper per person per year. Approximately half of the market is water absorbent tissue that will continue to depend on fibres from trees. The other half, which is at present tree-based but coated with polymers to resist water absorption, could in one generation be based on stone paper. The one billion tonnes of rock waste around Johannesburg is only sufficient to supply the world with paper for four years! This would become the biggest job-creating machine that South Africa has seen in modern times. And this due to the mining waste that has been discarded for over two centuries!

However, the last thing that is needed is to upset the existing paper recycling system, which is one of the most successful recycling programmes ever. Mr Liang has worked out the solutions. A small amount of maximum 10% stone paper can be mixed with regular paper, since the tree-fibre based material is already laced with polymers. However, stone paper has the advantage of being recyclable indefinitely. It is a mineral that cannot be destroyed, and the polymers have a half-life of hundreds of years. Thus, a real recycling business can now be set-up, creating a resource efficiency that is unknown to SAPPI and Mondi, the South African market leaders for paper.

Reducing waste, cutting investment, and increasing revenue and jobs make this a competitive proposal. Yet, the most important advantage of this technology for the Earth, is that it has the potential to free up millions of hectares of land. The land is currently locked-in to agro-forestry, for food production or for the regeneration of biodiverse forests that regenerate top soil, as well as percolate and filter water. Who would have expected a mine to contribute to food security and biodiversity? Applying the Blue Economy logic can lead to the most astounding designs for sustainable societies by harnessing opportunities right before our eyes.

A Method for Methane Capture

As mentioned above, quite a few mines are massive producers of methane, a greenhouse gas that dramatically impacts climate change. The volume of methane from one large deep mine shaft is the energy equivalent of at least 30 megawatt electrical power. Currently, it is pumped from the mine shafts into the atmosphere because of the erroneous belief that no technology can capture it at concentrations below 0.2 percent. If this “waste” were captured, it could generate the power that the mine must otherwise buy at 18 cents or more per kilowatt-hour. Proprietary access to this naturally occurring gas in South Africa, for instance, could augment the electricity supplied by ESKOM, the highly stressed national energy supplier.

Although nearly all methane gas from mines is lost to the atmosphere, signatories to the Kyoto Protocol could be compensated with carbon credits for methane capture or even just flaring, or burning, methane at the source. If released into the atmosphere a tonne of methane will have the same global warming impact as approximately 21 tonnes of CO_2, however when a tonne of methane is flared with oxygen it creates only 2.75 tonnes of CO_2. Hence a reduction of an equivalent of 18.25 tonnes of CO_2 per tonne of methane flared, that can be awarded carbon credits. The first such carbon credits for flaring mine methane were issued to the South African Beatrix Mine owned by Gold Fields. As such, these credits could generate US$ 10 million in four years, with very little investment and significant improvement of the working conditions of those underground. The payback period on the cost of installing pipes to capture and channel the methane is less than a year. It is clear that climate change protocols need not hurt competitiveness.

Carbon credits could be a small, yet quick, addition to the bottom line that could tilt a marginally producing shaft toward profitability – while contributing to social stability in the region and additional safety investments. However, flaring methane gas for carbon credits, in a country that is facing energy blackouts, seems an anachronism that merely scratches the surface of the potential opportunity. The mines have more to offer the energy market than just carbon credits. Even at an average concentration of just 0.1%, the minimum volume of methane released per mine is three million tonnes per year. For all the shafts near Johannesburg it could be upward of six million tonnes per year for each mine, over the next 25 years. Present air purification technologies require a concentration greater than half a percent. At least a few shafts have been identified that meet this concentration level. In fact, the concentration of methane in the air from the mine is often kept below 0.5% by blending higher and lower concentrations. Creative engineers will surely go beyond current market standard to make air purification effective even for much lower concentrations of methane.

A methane concentration averaging one-tenth of a percent would make air purification on its own potentially only marginally profitable. Even though the Clean Development Mechanism (CDM) under the Kyoto Protocol exists to create additional cash flow to finance such less attractive investments, a combined programme that puts in place vortex technology, wind turbines, heat exchangers, and potable water accessibility would provide the level of revenue necessary to make the air purification strategy profitable, as discussed in greater detail below.

MEGTEC Systems AB, a Swedish supplier of air purification technology, has installed systems that efficiently abate methane concentrations as low as 0.1% without adding energy to the oxidation process. In 1983, Australia's West Cliff Collier Power Plant constructed a 1.2-megawatt power plant, and a second larger 12.5-megawatt plant in 1985, to utilise the methane gas content in the ventilation air. At the heart of the technology is a system capable of efficiently oxidising the extremely low methane content, while handling extremely large volumes of air – a combination typical of mine ventilation. It is important to note that the methane concentration is below one percent and the project only utilises one-fifth of the entire air volume from the shaft. With the production of just six megawatt of electricity, the power plant reduces methane emissions equivalent to 200,000 tonnes of CO_2 per year.

This model demonstrates exactly how Nature works with what is locally available, gathering what is useful for the task. Beneficial use can be made of even minute amounts of methane. If the giant mines outside Johannesburg were to utilise the MEGTEC or similar technology to capture the escaping methane, they could potentially operate a 90 to 180-megawatt facility. This is as much as 50% of their present energy needs. Even though these are merely estimates, the basic numbers are attractive enough to warrant follow-up. Many mines could pursue this strategy, yet none do – as management simply cannot break through their core business mindset. Surely someone will see the sense in capturing the methane in exchange for carbon credits, generation of additional revenue streams, and planetary survival. It's another great opportunity waiting to be seized.

Converting Water from Cost to Revenue

Pure, clear fissure water, devoid of bacteria and exposed to the highly positive energy emitted by gold, is drawn from cracks in the deep. Just like silver, gold has a strong antibacterial effect and has therefore been associated over time and by different cultures as a health-enhancing product. This pure water is currently used to dilute highly polluted processing water to meet wastewater quality standards. We are hard put to think of a more wasteful form of use of pure water: blending it with toxic water so that, "on average", it meets minimum safety standards! South Africa is suffering from an acute water shortage on top of an energy shortage. The projections for the shortfall between demand and supply are dramatic. While water for Johannesburg is pumped at great cost through pipelines from Lesotho, gold mines like Driefontein and Kloof siphon away 100,000 cubic metres of water every day.

Rather than diluting and polluting pure water, chelating bacteria or vortex technology could easily and inexpensively separate toxins and impurities from the processed water to meet discharge standards. Spending R10 million per day (US$ 500 million per year) to pump water out of the mines and render it undrinkable, is not in tune with the needs of a society suffering from an acute water shortage. What does make sense is shifting from the culture of cost-cutting to the mindset of generating income by responding to market demand and community needs. This equates to building social capital, and this is what the population that was oppressed by Apartheid deserves from business and policy makers alike. Not only could the water needs of the local population be met, mining companies could operate a subsidiary enterprise providing bottled drinking water.

Because the presence of uranium would be hazardous, chelation technology would be necessary to achieve the safe removal of such elements from the bottled product. In addition, mine management could easily identify those fissures not tainted by uranium and thus tap the water sources offering maximum potential revenue. The creation of a bottled water industry that at the outset sells 100,000 bottles a day is financially attractive. With just a touch of imagination, we can expand that to many other levels of profit, creating a business that provides naturally occurring high-quality drinking water for the local population, and high-end deep-earth bottled water that controls bacteria acquired from exposure to gold deposits. It could even include a minute health-benefiting gold flake. There are markets for such water.

An implementation plan based on comparable experience from around the world would hardly need feasibility studies. In less than a decade, the Fiji Water Company developed from nothing to occupy a US$ 200 million high-margin niche in the US. In Hawaii, Japanese investors pump water from 600 metres deep, bottle it, and transport 200,000 bottles per day, selling it for the yen equivalent of US$ 10 per bottle in the Land of the Rising Sun. Using select distribution channels, the Las Gaviotas

Environmental Research Centre in Colombia freely dispenses drinking water to the local population, while profiting from selling bottled water in the capital city of Bogotá. Water management at a mine site demonstrates how a cost can become an income stream. Accessing fissure water as a separate, stand-alone business would incur unrecoverable investment costs to reach the water deep in the Earth's crust. Mines have already incurred these costs to operate their core business of mining gold. By offering inexpensive and safe drinking water to the local population, mining not only turns an expense into a revenue stream, it also turns attention from pollution and sink holes to a demonstration of social responsibility, thereby creating a better local and international reputation. It seems that even the proverbial "gold mine" can do with stronger brand value!

Electrification Savings

Mines need massive amounts of electricity to pump water and air, cool the shafts, produce ice, and transport ore. Huge electricity generation stations are located at the base of each mine. It is only common sense to explore opportunities that would save electricity costs. Perhaps this is the ideal environment for implementing Jay Harman's mathematical model, inspired by the nautilus shell, to increase energy efficiency by 20-30% in ventilators and mixers, or other applications in either water or air transportation, as discussed earlier in Chapter 5. It may well also be an opportunity for Curt Hallberg's vortex technology. The ice-making machines necessary to moderate the high temperatures are placed in deep shafts and must cope with water containing vast amounts of dissolved air particles. Using Hallberg's gravity-based vortex technology to extract these air particles from the water would reliably reduce the energy costs by 10-15%. However, the latest research results indicate as much as 40% energy savings. Furthermore, when water and air must move up and down 4,000 metres, there is room to employ the forces of gravity.

The mine should generate power from the fall of water, and flywheels (that were invented during the age of Leonardo da Vinci) could recover at least 70% of all the energy spent to operate the elevators. If we consider other innovations based on Nature's adaptive technologies, we could save even more energy and reduce the risk of explosions by introducing cold light, instead of traditional light bulbs. This would save energy and reduce the risk of explosion. In the darkest shafts of the mines, light should not be based on electricity generated with coal and supplied via the grid, or via the heavy fuel used in the backup generators, when it could be based on simple chemistry.

Power from Exhaust Airflows

Just as with water, airflows are by-products of the core business of mining. These could easily generate additional revenue. Airflows created by a vacuum, exit the mine shafts at high pressure. With the release of a staggering 2,800 cubic metres of air into the atmosphere each second, we can easily imagine how a few highly efficient windmills equipped with an anti-drag device, such as that observed in whales, would capture some of the power. Pumping the fresh air needed into these deep shafts generates an exhaust air stream, and the vacuum it creates could easily keep a dozen turbines constantly turning. Compared to the price ESKOM charges for electricity from the grid, the return on investment for wind-driven turbines at both the shaft inlet and the outlet exceeds 50% of initial cost, breaking even in two years. In comparison, it would be hard to justify investment in back-up diesel generators.

Energy Generation from Temperature and Pressure Differentials

The temperature differences generated by mine operations are another vast source of energy. These temperature extremes come from ice-making, hot air exhausting, and transporting the ore from deep within the Earth. These could become useful sources of energy simply by installing appropriately placed heat exchangers. Heat exchangers are nothing new. However, this technology has not found much application in mines, except for the Mine Water Initiative undertaken in old coal mines in the Netherlands and Germany, which has been operating since 2008 as district water heating and cooling for the City of Heerlen (the Netherlands). Gone are the days when electricity in South Africa was either inexpensive or even subsidised. The need to embark on energy efficiencies is now paramount. When we consider that nanotechnology enables us to power a cell phone with a half-degree of temperature differential, imagine what could be done with the 30° C differential found in the mines! Such an energy-generating project is already technically and commercially underway in Europe with temperature differentials of only three to five degrees. More food for thought: at the depth of 4,000 metres, what method may be found to convert the piezoelectric potential into a power source?

Environmental Remediation

The persuasive logic of carbon credits, profitability, and remediation applies to all energy sources, whether from wind turbines, heat exchangers, or methane capture. It is hard to defend leaving any stone unturned when contemplating revenue generation and cost reduction, even the production of stone paper. And, yes, there are more opportunities.

Gold Fields, the corporate proprietor of one of Johannesburg's largest gold mines, owns an astounding 71,000 hectares of surrounding land. These holdings were acquired over the years from farmers who could no longer achieve reasonable productivity due to the declining availability of water. (Recall that mining operations require tremendous amounts of water, which lowers the water table of surrounding areas.) Although, to their credit Gold Fields does utilise some of this acreage to grow roses for commercial sale, much of it could be quickly converted to biodiesel production.

South Africa has a supportive policy for biodiesel that grants producers tax exemptions. Although this is to be applauded, it also raises eyebrows since it is hard to justify planting vegetation for ethanol production when this displaces crops for human and animal consumption. A country that is struggling to feed its children needs to focus its priorities accordingly. If land that should produce food were used for biodiesel, it would increase the cost of food. This particularly affects those who live on the margins of society. Since it carries a recognised risk of uranium contamination, not all the land around the mines could be used to produce food. However, it could serve perfectly well for roses and could likewise grow crops for biodiesel production.

Depending on the species selected for biofuel production, should 20,000 hectares be put into production, 100,000 to 120,000 tonnes of biofuel could be generated within two to four years. Similarly, water-guzzling invasive tree species like eucalyptus and black wattle (*Acacia auriculiformis*) could be uprooted and replaced by plants and trees that have extractable oils and that would re-establish the water table over time. To further cascade nutrients, mushrooms could be grown on the rich biomass remaining once the oils are extracted, provided there was no measurable contamination or radiation. Alternatively, or even additionally, we could capture the methane biogas escaping from the spent crops. Unemployment rates in excess of 50% of the adult population in communities around the mines could be dramatically lowered. Carbon credits alone could kick-start the initial financing for such an operation. Until recently, no one thought Africa could generate carbon credits. If the mines were to utilise this biodiesel potential, they could set the stage for a major contribution to the reduction of greenhouse gases.

Turning a mine into a competitive operation that recovers farmland, makes stone paper, renews biodiversity, produces biofuels, provides jobs for the community, creates energy efficiencies using available resources and innovative technologies, and supplies water for sale as well as for the needs of local communities, would create a business that would quickly develop greater "brand equity". This is not a costly public relations initiative aimed at generating community goodwill and trust. Rather, it is an approach that is part and parcel of the day-to-day management responsibility to increase cash flow by slashing expenses and improving revenues. From a manager's viewpoint, the social capital created in the process of cutting costs and generating additional income is just icing on the cake. Why not? If such a systems approach became part of management culture, the issues that have typically absorbed management's time are no longer a stress factor but a component of efficient resource use and income generation.

Chelating Complex Ores

Now we address the sensitive issue of uranium. Like it or not, uranium is often found in combination with gold. Thallium and copper are also standard by-products of ore processing. These are known as "complex ores." When uranium prices sank to such a low level that extraction was no longer competitive, gold mines stopped producing uranium. Revenue turned to waste and after a few decades of release into streams, uranium accumulated in the wetlands and riverbeds. According to some activists, this pollution crisis is reaching dramatic proportions and the related clean-up costs could quickly run into hundreds of millions of dollars. While the science is unclear and the costs unaccounted for, companies can discard neither the growing doubt, nor the responsibility for future and potentially significant expenditures. The instant the Board of a publicly traded company is informed of the risks, it is forced to make loss provisions. These risks must be reported to the stock exchange authorities and this immediately puts pressure on the share price. Recall that PCB and asbestos were not considered problematic in the 1960s when their usage was widespread. GE (USA) and ABB (Switzerland) recently settled 1960s-era contamination-related claims for a staggering US$ 500 million and one billion dollars respectively.

The opportunities in energy and water provision just described are realistic. If managers want to avoid the negative impact on their company's capitalisation brought on by declining share prices on the stock exchange, they need to respond proactively to a potential crisis arising from uranium pollution of the local water and soil. In such a sensitive matter, analysts typically account for the risk of a future clean-up and the subsequent media hysteria by discounting the present valuation of the shares. The shares then suffer from a strong downward trend. The time to invest in innovations that can convert problems into opportunities is well before a risk filing with the stock exchange is required.

Chelating technology has been around for a few decades. This approach to isolating precious metals and toxic compounds like uranium, thallium, and lead is well-proven. Chelating ligands bond with metal ions to render the metal inert. The leading provider of this process is the pioneering company Prime Separations, which brought together an expert team of engineers who built a career in Polaroid, the expert on thin film surface chemistry, to apply the chelating techniques observed in bacteria. The technology developed alongside other innovative means to recover metals, even those dispersed in minute amounts, like the capacity of the wood ear mushroom (*Auricularia polytricha*) to recover copper and the ability of geraniums (*Geranium spp*) to recover lead. Their efficiency is a million-fold greater than the complex ore smelters that now process these blended ores.

Managers would do well to remember that mines exhaust the available raw materials and thus cannot operate indefinitely. Gold deposits come to an end, as is predicted to occur within half a century. Prime Separations technology benefits mining operations through a continuous approach to extracting gold, uranium, thallium, and any other elements of the periodic table that can be sold in pure form. In particular the processing of uranium, from both the tailings and the surrounding wetlands, could be funded from cash reserves over the next decade or two. This would renew the land and the region for the next generation of economic activity, and avoid the fate of companies like GE and ABB, who have had to pay their pollution bill forty years after the fact.

The chelating technology learned from bacteria is not limited only to the recovering of heavy metals and chromium IV. In geographical conditions where water is very scarce, such as gold mines in Venezuela and Burkina Faso, the Prime Separations know-how could become a key factor in processing ore in a closed-loop water cycle. This technology renders obsolete the need to build pipelines, or to truck water from nearby rivers, or to spend massive sums of money on reverse osmosis facilities and the electricity to keep them running. For new mines that are found to have available thallium, the same technology could purify the metal for sale. Purified Thallium-203 is sold for US$ 1,800 per kilogram by the Los Alamos National Laboratory in the USA. This is real income, stemming from the continuous filtering of the tailings and sedimentation. This is real cost elimination. There will be no clean-up bill due in forty years. What will be there is bio-regenerated land with considerable value, located near a large urban market. Land value was the real payoff of the Las Gaviotas project. In the case of South Africa's gold mines, we can see that augmenting land value is an appreciable way to maintain shareholder value and accrue social capital.

The chelating technology has another potential benefit: it can be used by artisanal as well as large-scale mining. While large corporations abide by strict environmental rules, small-scale operations get away with the unrestricted use of mercury and cyanide. If established mining conglomerates were to make the chelation technology available to artisanal miners, they would be happy to eliminate their use of toxins. The smallest producers in the gold market could vouch for the quality of their gold, refined to world market standards and most important of all, eliminate the middlemen and the hardware salesmen selling the traditional mining equipment, in other words those who tend to take home the largest share of profit from the artisans. While the small operations can scavenge gold deposits that are uncompetitive for large operators, chelating technology could make both viable. The upside for the stock exchange quoted mining group could well be the opportunity to increase turnover by 30% – without the 30% increase in capital expenditure – while the artisans generate better revenue and the environment benefits from a better control of lethal substances. The Blue Economy model is, after all, an inclusive proposal for growth.

Mines as Biorefineries

It is an advantage that the tasks of mine management require long-term vision. There is simply no quick buck to be made when you operate a mine. The time between obtaining an exploration license, getting permission to process the ore, then selling the product, is often a decade or more. The company must be prepared to invest the funds legally required to rehabilitate the land or to provide cash for creating a future beyond the mines. In this sense, mine management is acutely aware that the future must be imagined today. Yet the availability of 160,000 hectares just 45 minutes from downtown Johannesburg has more potential to benefit the shareholders than has yet been realised.

Agriculture is not the only sector that can imagine multiple cash flows through the concept of bio-refineries that re-industrialise regions that have been labelled as uncompetitive in the race for globalisation. Mining can achieve the same benefits, merely by using what is locally available. If we imagine the reprocessing of tailings into stone paper and building materials, under a creative financial structure that returns the landscape to its original dramatic beauty, with uranium on its way to the market instead of accumulating in the topsoil and water, then the historic and cultural wealth of the region will be an asset. That asset may well-represent the investors' assessments of the ultimate value of gold mines. No one has taken the time to value these surrounding land assets. They are not even valued in the company accounts. Land holdings are considered a cost ready to be dumped to any buyer at any price. What would you pay for land that carries the risk of uranium contamination? Now what is the value of that land if it is pristine and beautiful?

Sometimes it takes an outsider to show you the extraordinary on your doorstep. This is the reason why Blue Economy teams around the world perform a scan and screen with a clear dedication to the implementation of the projects that are retained as viable. If a gold and uranium mine is converted over years into a sophisticated water extraction and energy generation system, generating more jobs than ever considered possible, combined with the public display of engineering marvels that facilitates mining at over 4,000 metres deep, it becomes a potential public attraction that is likely to pay for itself. Jo'burg is one of the most vibrant cities in Africa. Considering the cultural, natural, and industrial sites classified by UNESCO as World Heritage Sites, the gold mines, the natural environment, and its historical context certainly qualify for this international recognition.

The necessity for the mines to achieve a sustainable economic basis, combined with the national need to implement sound social and ecological policies and maintain adequate foreign exchange, have seldom been so potentially interconnected, as are the possibilities at mining sites around Johannesburg. The probability of immediate and long-term benefit is great. Some of the concepts presented are based on existing technologies; others are envisioned and need additional research. What is certain is that the same mines that have received criticism in the past, and that are still rightfully on the radar of governmental and non-governmental organisations today, have seldom been seen in as positive and proactive a light as we have looked at them in this chapter. They are interconnected systems, capable of contributing to society.

A mine that is a World Heritage Site, that provides drinking water to the poor, that serves the top of the market with gold- flaked bottled water, that generates additional revenues from stone paper and carbon credits, that slashes costs by providing a major part of its own energy needs from readily available resources, that diversifies into energy and food production providing much needed jobs, that offers a future to communities that today lack the vision or even ability to dream, is a company that will garner respect, admiration, appreciation of stock values, and public praise from the very first moment it begins to creatively deal with the burden of pollution from the past.

Financial Engineering

It does not take a financial strategist to translate these opportunities into cash flow, nor a business analyst to understand the value of lower business risk compounded with improved social capital. The Blue Economy approach is based on improvements of the profit and loss statement, a strengthening of cash flow, a reduction of capital and operational expenses, an improvement of asset values, a conversion of provisions into investments and the transformation of a culture of cost reduction into a culture of generating additional revenues and value.

Understanding the array of opportunities is not what is required. What is required is a shift in management culture. Attention now focused on only one major issue must be focused instead upon the interconnections that extend beyond the core business. It is this shift that is likely to be the biggest challenge. The gold mine will remain a gold mine but the multiple inputs and outputs that are so easily outsourced and framed into supply chain management must now be viewed in terms of additional cost reductions, substantial revenue improvements, long-term capital gains, improved market capitalisation, reduced business risk from strong cash flow, and a flexible company ready to take risks and innovate. These qualities have always characterised the market leaders who are more often than not rewarded for their foresight and vision.

Thus the way forward is based on technological benchmarks achieved elsewhere, and on progressive financial engineering applied to the real and future value of all assets. A persuasive rationale, based in solid science and economic feasibility, awaits the decision of the management and the endorsement of the stockholders. Mining companies in Russia, China, Africa, the USA, and Latin America can then demonstrate that while there is a regrettable history, there is also a future of hope and a present of good intent.

14

FINDING THE FLOWS

It is clear from da Vinci's notes that he saw the city as a kind of living organism in which people, material goods, food, water, and waste needed to move and flow with ease for the city to remain healthy.
– Fritjof Capra, *the Science of Leonardo*

The Ecosystem of the Domicile

Every living system searches for shelter, from the shell of an egg, to the nutshell, to the algal membrane. Everything alive creates subtle borders that delineate exterior and interior. Each creature finds its unique way to achieve inner stability, to control temperature and humidity, to store reserves, and to ensure health and survival.

In recent times, the design of human shelter has undergone much transformation, though perhaps not always improvement. The physical constructs of the way we live now, far exceed mere shelter. They provide the conveniences that fit our ideas of comfort and contentment. We live in an age of modernity, drifting towards home automation, where progress and comfort require the ever-greater acquisition of electronics and robotics. For most of us, the largest share of our time is passed indoors, at home, at work, at school. We spend about eight hours a day asleep. Perhaps another eight are spent at work or at school, and the remainder commuting or absorbed in household chores and activities. The design of the buildings we inhabit for two-thirds of our lives should reasonably assure health and safety. Not surprisingly, the key to a healthy environment is, once again, potential hydrogen (pH).

The ocean, with a pH of 8.2, is the cradle of life on Earth. Ecosystems and their life-creating powers thrive in an alkaline environment. Yet much of our environment, indoors as well as outdoors, has reached a high level of acidity. Our excessive use of fossil fuels and the massive volumes of carbon dioxide pumped into the atmosphere every day render the air acidic. There is no escape from this in the industrialised world or in any developed city on the globe. Those who live in rural areas or near a coastline may be less affected. If you live in a megalopolis like New York, Los Angeles, London, Paris, Sao Paolo, New Delhi, or Johannesburg, the atmospheric pH is just above four. Keep in mind that pH is measured on a logarithmic scale; that means that a pH measure of five is ten times higher than four and a pH measure of six is 100 times greater than four.

Consider the remarkable functioning of our digestive system. The food we ingest is taken into the stomach where the highly acidic environment quickly and safely reduces the grains, vegetables, meats, and other consumables to their basic components. The small intestine, where the nutritive matter is absorbed and made available to the blood for transport to the organs and tissue, is also a significant component of our immune system. It requires an alkaline pH factor to function optimally. Similarly, the air in a bedroom where sleep allows the body to repair and regenerate, should also have an alkaline pH. Starting at home, we should use our understanding of the flows of air and matter to create an environment supportive of life and health.

If you take the time to check the pH of the air in your house, you will quickly realise that the air in urban areas is acidic, and usually does not get better circulating from outside to inside. Unfortunately, it typically gets worse. Interior air quality is degraded by the off-gassing of almost everything in your home or office, even if you have the privilege of living on the beach or atop a breath-taking mountain range. The overall result is simply not good. What is the use of making sure that what you drink and eat offers a healthy balance of acid and alkaline when you breathe acids all day? What is worse is that you inhale acids all night as you sleep. As we power up our Blue Economy, the outside air we breathe will become less polluted and less acidic. In the meantime, the design and construction of our buildings can be such that their interiors naturally evolve to be more alkaline.

The Seven Flows of Building Design and Living Space

Architects, along with medical doctors, are potentially the most "connected" thinkers. Yet they too are subject to a rigid compartmentalisation of knowledge. As a consequence they conclude that acidity and alkalinity are topics for chemists. Even the most environmentally progressive architect, who has successfully designed a LEED Platinum Certified building, is likely unaware of the importance of maintaining pH levels in buildings. While physics and mathematics figure prominently in the training of architects, life sciences receive marginal attention. That is regrettable, since physical structures based on solid maths and biology are at the foundation of health and livelihood on Earth.

When an architect receives specifications for a new building, the volume and the surface area determine its size and functionality; for example, the number of bedrooms, the integration of a kitchen and dining room, the combination of a gymnasium and classrooms, a school solarium, or the pairing of open office space with a kitchenette. Some architects will consider the position of the sun, and propose a south-facing building in the northern hemisphere (and a north-facing building in the tropics and the southern hemisphere). This is straightforward and requires neither much creative insight nor detailed scientific knowledge, or even much inspiration from ecosystems.

Physical buildings cannot be viewed as merely static structures that meet functional goals and comply with local regulations. Moreover, buildings that are constructed with renewable resources and targeted energy savings are only the first step in redesign. There are seven important flows that must be brought into the design concept: air, light, water, energy, sound, matter, and occupants. Each of these flows influences the dynamic balance that provides the life-promoting conditions that allow us to survive and to thrive. Life enhancement is the driving force behind all these flows. Survival and health must always be the priority, particularly because we spend so much of our time inside. The composition and functionality of our domicile determines our health, our comfort, and how well we rest and sleep.

Air includes matter such as dust. Matter includes the food we eat and what is discarded, while water includes what we drink and what we use to wash away waste. Materials cover the flow of goods that contribute to the functionality and efficiency of our personal environment. These are all important components of our lifestyle and contributors to our comfort levels. Yet, it seems that we design our homes without considering such flows. Accumulated dust can make us ill. Biomass left to rot is a health hazard, and truly a waste. The water in our sewers transports effluent to holding tanks where it is chemically treated to attack accumulated bacteria. The rubbish generated by our packaging-obsessed consumer society bursts from innumerable landfills outside the scope of our vision or consciousness. These are all literally dead ends. Consider that a flow implies an unimpeded continuity of movement. If we were to enhance rather than obstruct our household flows we could take advantage of a wide portfolio of innovations that would contribute to comfortable and healthful living conditions, reduce costs, and save energy.

Natural systems always design for and with flow. Nothing evolves statically but rather by interaction with everything around it. Insight into this fundamental design principle will reveal connections among disparate phenomena and objectives. This in turn leads to a bundle of solutions that natural systems have adapted and modelled for millions of years. Hence our challenge becomes how to interweave a set of parameters so that we can design with these flows. In short, our challenge is to emulate ecosystems that make use of physics and locally available materials to meet basic needs and to promote greater efficiency and diversity. As we set these goals, and as architects and home designers prioritise health and comfort, it will then be possible – in fact quite easy – to achieve a better balance and more open flows.

To begin, we need to know how to design aesthetically pleasing physical spaces that maintain a proper interior pH balance and allow for interplay of the seven flows. If we successfully create a design model that encompasses all these flows, then we will experience a completely new comfort level. The structure would be in tune with its environment, and would thus achieve ideal sustainability with neither extraordinary effort nor higher expense. Such buildings would be more than green; they would reflect more than energy savings from a grass roof or from certified sustainable forestry lumber. As a first priority, these structures would contribute to health and self-sufficiency by drawing from locally available resources and energy sources. They would conform to a healthy and dynamic balance between humanity and the ecosystems on which we depend for the free supply of Commons such as water and air. Such spaces would enhance life.

The first architect to realise the importance of flow as the determining principle in the design of buildings and cities was Leonardo da Vinci. His designs demonstrate a remarkable insight into multiple flows and the need to connect with the surroundings. Moreover, da Vinci imagined the design of cities based on the flows of water, waste, and people. In the book *The Science of Leonardo* Fritjof Capra writes:

> Leonardo's special attention to how movements would flow through his buildings was not restricted to the interiors, but included the surrounding grounds as well, by means of doorways, loggias, and balconies. In fact, in most of his designs of villas and palaces, he considered the garden to be an integral part of the house. These designs reflect his continual efforts to integrate architecture and nature.

A further extension of Leonardo's organic view of building design and his special focus on their functional integrity is apparent in his pioneering contributions to urban design. When he witnessed the plague in Milan shortly after his arrival in the city in 1482, he realised that the devastating effects were largely due to Milan's appalling sanitary conditions. In typical fashion, he responded with a proposal for rebuilding the city in a way that would provide decent housing for people and shelter for animals, and would allow the streets to be cleaned regularly by drenching them.

The Thoroughly Modern Nursery

We start our observations of flows in and around buildings by focusing our attention on the spaces most occupied by infants and young children. While the young are the most sensitive and vulnerable, they are also the potential of our future. Children, like adults with weakened immune systems, are affected more subtly and more easily by the dynamics of multiple flows. This means that where flows are inadequate, or lacking, their potential to complicate health and introduce disease is greater.

Imagine a young child asleep for the greater part of the day in a room filled with formaldehyde from the glue in the particle board; with chemically laden bactericides and fungicides in the flooring and wall paint; with heavy metals from the brightly coloured clothes and toys, with bromine fire-retardants in the mattress, bedding, curtains, and carpets. The windows are triple glazed and UV protected, with heavy curtains to keep out light and a thick carpet to dampen sound while the child sleeps. Double insulation and an energy-efficient recirculation of heated or cooled air make for an airtight environment to further block noise. The disposable nappies and infant hygiene products are laden with artificial fragrances and parabenes, and coloured with chemical dyes and optical whiteners. The water is heavily chlorinated and the air conditioner filter contains chemicals to kill bacteria. The electric wires that pass over or around the bed emit electromagnetic charges that launch dust particles into the air to be inhaled. Artificial squeaks from plastic toys and the crackling of the radio waves from the baby monitor can be heard. A Wi-Fi antenna ensures that the internet works 24 hours a day, anywhere where our iPad or smart phone follows us.

Mind you, everything in this room is individually tested and approved. No single item has been proved to cause harm (except perhaps for one toy or another that contains toxins and that should not be there). The reality is that the child in this stressful environment is forced to divert too much energy to immune defence. The diversion of energy to process the stress created and accumulated, or to limit damage from the toxic surroundings, diminishes what is available to keep the immune system strong and the child exuberant and healthy. The statistical incidence of respiratory ailments and skin rashes afflicting young children is nowhere close to a comfort zone. To the contrary, we are clearly moving towards an era where more and more problems arise. While there is no one to blame, the system has flaws. The combination of all these broken flows has led to a demonstrable increase in health problems. The National Centre for Health Statistics overwhelms us with statistics that underscore this reality.

Thus, while all the material conveniences in a thoroughly modern nursery are designed to facilitate the comfort and care of the child, we can see that they in fact run counter to an environment that would optimise health and comfort. What is needed is to rethink the whole concept, choosing solutions that create a living environment that strengthens rather than stresses the immune system. What is needed are innovations that emulate the adhesive power that the gecko has, or the chemical-free one of the mussel, the formation of colour via the photo-optics used by butterflies and beetles, the pH control of seashells and seaweed. We need innovations such as food-grade chemical fire-retardants, fire sensors modelled after the jewel beetle, UV protection inspired by that of the edelweiss flower, sound control modelled on that used by the ormia fly, and hygiene products made with natural silk polymers, algae polyesters, and by using the lycopene from tomato seeds. But wait… that is not all: the bacterial control in water achieved by vortex technology, biofilm disruption via furanones, electric power generated from body heat, outside sound, or crystals under pressure – all without the need for wires or cables. Johan Gielis, the smart observer of bamboo, designed antennas using his latest superformula (also called the Gielis Formula), which permits data transmission with only a fraction of the energy requirements needed today.

Currently, allergies and respiratory ailments affect upwards of 25% of children in urban areas. An immune system that develops normally and naturally, without excessive exposure to artificial sound, chemicals, Wi-Fi, and stagnant and dust-laden air, will function to protect and maintain the health and growth of the child. We must consider how to best promote life with the solutions Nature has devised. We cannot risk the health of our children – our future.

The Flow of Air and Light

In earlier times, dwellings were constructed from natural materials, had thatched roofs and small openings or windows, without glass, for ventilation. Good airflow was the norm. More recently, ostensibly to save energy, many buildings are constructed with super insulation so that hardly allows any air in or out. The aim of saving energy is to be lauded, but eliminating airflow is not at all beneficial. The walls do not breathe, the roofs do not seep. The chemical foams used to insulate building walls and roofs are, with a few exceptions, constantly emitting acids into the air we breathe. Fire-retardants applied to buildings and their material components are another known problem. The risk of fire is considered sufficiently dangerous to mandate the use of flame-retardant chemicals even on mattresses and pillows. Of course, each of these chemicals has been approved, one at a time. Each has been tested and although some are deemed possible carcinogens, the health risk is considered worth reducing the risk of death by fire. The unfortunate combination of all these chemicals creates an overdose we should avoid. Every night, all night, we inhale a chemical cocktail, a potentially dangerous one we do not need.

When we block the natural flow of air with our building designs, we are not taking all the above-mentioned facts into consideration. We miss making the connection, and in the process we are overlooking the real dangers that exist. Were we to solve building ventilation challenges with the same methodical approach the humble termite employs, a world of connections would unfold. The flow of air, the composition of household materials, and the pH of the air and walls could all contribute, rather than complicate or obstruct. Utilising insights as to how natural systems succeed at resolving these challenges would allow us to make genuine progress in achieving real sustainability without increasing investment costs.

It is possible to have continuous airflow and save energy at the same time. Ecosystems have been evolving along those lines for millennia. At present, the best way to reduce the chemical load caused by emissions, bacterial contamination, and electrically charged dust particles would be to have more air flowing through the building. If we design the building so that all the air is refreshed at least once an hour, then exposure to suspected carcinogens in minute amounts would not pose a problem for most people. Simply opening up a modern building to allow the continuous flow of cold, hot, or humid air from the outside would increase energy use. Natural systems have reconciled both objectives: achieving airflow and saving energy with added benefits for the residents. What we stand to learn from natural systems, such as those employed by the termite, will provide multiple benefits.

One of the newer approaches to heating in buildings is radiant floor heating. Hot water circulates through pipes laid in the subfloor, providing heat with greater efficiency than can be achieved by heating the air. A new improvement – less cumbersome as well as less costly – was developed by Korean scientists Young-Suk Shu and Tae-Sung Oh. They were inspired by observations of decomposing plant matter in the soil root zone. Ants and termites transport an estimated 15% of all plant material to the second layer of topsoil. Aeration by earthworms, as well as fungi harvesting by ants and termites, assist in the further decomposition of plant matter. The heat from decomposition warms the soil around the root zone, increasing the osmosis between the roots and the leaves of the plants, thereby enhancing growth and improving the flavour of the harvested crop.

The Korean scientists developed a thin film of nanosized carbon fibres that could be placed under a wooden floor or a carpet to produce surrounding temperatures of up to 36 °C, using only a twelve-volt solar power application. This application was initially tested in Japanese and Korean greenhouses as a method for keeping plant roots warm. Having saved over 70% of the previous heating energy expenditure for greenhouse production, it is now making its entry into home heating applications.

While this innovation is just one advancement, it could be used to enhance ecologically sound carpets such as those made by Interface Global. The most advanced versions could be composed of meshed carbon fibres woven throughout a base made from either rubber or PVC. The carpet tiles electrically connect through micron size carbon fibres and could even obtain their energy from thin-film dye-sensitised solar cells attached to the windows, generating an ideal comfort level temperature for bare feet. Heating provided by direct current generated through dye solar cells that let light through, will tackle mite infestation from two angles. Firstly, the UV radiation will directly kill the mites. Secondly, the temperature in the carpet will be high enough to dry any scraps, crumbs, or morsels dropped on the floor, eliminating enough nutrient sources to keep mite proliferation under control.

Insect Insights Related to Humidity

Termites are farmers. As explained in Chapter 3, they have perfected a system that involves bringing biomass into the deeper soil to farm fungi. Precise control of temperature and humidity is imperative for success. Over millennia termites have learned that unless the temperature and the humidity are exact, fungi do not proliferate, even when offered an ideal growth medium. The temperature in termite nests is always 27 °C, and the humidity is constant at 61 percent. Everywhere they live, in every climate, termites have learned to control air circulation by building tunnels and chimneys. Whether in Dallas or Dacca, Oslo or Osaka, or in the Australian Outback, and regardless of variation in the outside temperature, termites successfully build their air-regulating infrastructure, maintaining airflow and quality merely by changing the colour, width, length, or height of their infrastructure of tunnels and chimneys.

The warm air, generated by the termites and the growth of the fungi in the ground beneath the mound, rises as exhaust from the nest up through the chimneys and creates a vacuum inside. Whether hot or cold, the incoming exterior air is channelled through tiny tunnels built into the underground nest. If the exterior air is hot and humid, it cools and sheds moisture. If it is cold and dry, it warms and absorbs moisture. This is all based on the basic laws of physics we learn in high school. Termites know exactly how tall the chimney should be, and how long and deep the underground tunnels must be, to always maintain the nest temperature and humidity regardless of outside conditions. They have acquired this ability over millions of years – without a thermostat or the need for energy and pumps.

Humans have been regulating the interior temperature of dwellings for far less time than termites, yet we think we have perfected it! Given our much shorter record of experience, we are only beginning to access the mathematical models necessary to construct buildings with a predictable and comfortable airflow that allows temperature and humidity to be effectively regulated. Lacking the tools innate to the termite, we unfortunately chose electricity, based on the combustion of fossil fuels as the driving force – neglecting the laws of physics with their wonderful fail-safe characteristics. Nearly all our inventions include mechanics, with moving parts, which in a physical world are subject to wear and tear and will sooner or later fail. The termites designed a lasting solution – without any moving parts. It is a solution we too can use, as world leading architect Mick Pearce has shown us with the Eastgate Building in Harare, discussed in Chapter 3.

A Living Filter

Flowing air in and out of a building is a great first step. We can also orchestrate flows inside the building to thoroughly purify and oxygenate the air. Remember, oxygen brings alkalinity, and exhausting the CO_2 we all breathe out removes acidity. To do this we must move beyond physics and acquire an understanding of general biology, that of plants and micro-algae in particular. It is not difficult to recreate the way in which Nature precipitates dust and charged particles into the soil in an interior environment. Over two decades ago, a small company named “Living

Filters" (Levande Filter AB) pioneered this concept for air filters, inspired by the NASA-funded research aimed at cleansing air in space ships.

Professor Lars Thofelt developed the plant system and his Living Filter systems have been installed worldwide, since 1998. These systems are designed so that air turbulence within the building channels the inside air through a collection of 150 different plants strategically located near the ceiling. The logic of this comes from rainforest ecology, where we observe that rain forests are not only a home for biodiversity and a source of oxygen but are also massive air filters. In the Amazon floating dust particles, from as far away as Africa, can be captured by the rainforest plant matter to precipitate into the soil and replenish topsoil. The collection of plants in a Living Filter is permanently lit with highly efficient LED lamps. Every 15 minutes, a mist of water is sprayed on the leaves. This forced mist percolates through the illuminated and moistened plants, cleansing the air while settling dust, and even airborne toxins. The result is noticeable: air is oxygen enriched and alkalinised.

Fungi in the Basement

When a building is closed and insulated, humidity is trapped inside. Long, humid summers cause the moisture to condense on insulation and mould to grow. Dampness in closed areas without air circulation produces the ideal conditions for fungi to invade a home or office building, especially in the basement. Fungi release spores into the air that can cause respiratory diseases. If your house is made of wood, then both building and occupants are at risk. If you have a steel frame building, then "only" your health is at risk. Expert remediation companies will treat the walls with metal oxides, freeing the building of fungus but emitting chemical gas particulates for a number of years. These are particles that you should never inhale. This is an example of the superficiality of a "one cause–one effect" way of thinking. It this not reminiscent of core business strategy where we ignore all unintended consequences?

If, on the other hand, we design the building to let air flow through the basement and allow full spectrum light (including ultraviolet radiation) to reach the interior, then we eliminate the conditions for fungus growth and in this way purify the building. Anders Nyquist uses a prisma light to bring natural full-spectrum light into basements. This not only offers free illumination during the day, it also offers a first response to the onslaught of unwanted fungi. With proper ventilation, the spores that cause respiratory problems are exhausted from the building. This is a good start, with a potential that goes beyond merely resolving a problem. A connected world can achieve multiple benefits for multiple partners. There are many opportunities here for entrepreneurs to seize.

Now we once again make the link to pH. Most materials commonly used for walls and flooring exacerbate the stifling effect of insulation and other flow barriers, creating conditions that allow mould and fungi to proliferate. The fungi growing in dark, static conditions such as basements thrive in an acidic environment. Thus, another way to control fungal growth is to change the pH of the basement to make it more alkaline. If the fungi do not find conditions conducive to their proliferation, they simply remain dormant. Wall and floor coverings could be made from sources of calcium carbonate, such as crushed seashells. If sheetrock were used, the insulation in the wall could be seaweed-based. Both seaweed and seashells are abundant, inexpensive, and highly alkaline. Used as raw material for floor coverings and wall insulation, their performance matches the functionality of the materials currently available.

A new understanding of environmental conditions such as airflow, light, and alkalinity can help us eliminate the conditions in which fungi grow – as well as lessen exposure to toxins that stress our immune systems. This is how we start weaving information together, connecting insulation to fungi, to air quality, to health, and to the design of a healthy building.

Åke Mård, founder of the innovative MRD Construction Company in Sweden, has another approach to controlling mould in basements. Pittsburgh Corning supplies him with glass foam blocks that are manufactured as structural building materials in Belgium and the Czech Republic. The inputs are air (mainly CO2) and recycled glass, and the output is a multi-functional load-bearing structure. Recycled glass enriched with carbonic gas is lightweight and has the advantage of being resistant to acids and moulds while simultaneously insulating. Vermin cannot eat their way through. This is exactly how we imagine the economy of the future: use what is available and obtain multiple benefits. These glass foam blocks replace four products in one prefabricated material. They relieve the pressure on bottle makers to produce bottles from recycled glass. Again, we see how we can emulate Nature and cascade nutrients to other partners in a system.

This innovation goes very much along the lines of the goals of Earthstone, a New Mexico (USA) business that emerged separately from the construction initiatives in Sweden. Earthstone was founded in 1993 by Andrew Ungerleider and Gay Dillingham, in response to the destructive strip mining they saw taking place in their region. Earthstone's patented technology takes glass beverage bottles out of the waste stream and puts them to work by creating abrasion products (e.g. substitutes for sandpaper), consumer cleaning products (paint remover), and horticultural products (substituting glass fibre in hydroponics). Their production design emulates natural models, cascading nutrients and energy, and over a decade of success has achieved market share. The new factory is located adjacent to the Albuquerque landfill, which is their source of waste glass, and part of their energy use (from the methane gas released from decomposing biomass in the landfill). This project is a clear example of an industrial solution that reduces the adverse impact of our excessive waste generation, putting products on the market that perform competitively, while using available resources.

The Challenge of Triple Glazing

There is more to be said about glass. Homeowners invest in double and even triple glazing to save energy. Often, it is even subsidised through government tax incentives. Though expensive, triple-glazed windowpanes are considered a sure way to save money and the environment. It is part of a sustainability strategy that requires more investment to save the money needed to pay back the investment. While we welcome the thought, we know we need to look at the whole system, and see how it gets bundled into an effective proposal. These energy-saving measures are often combined with a window covering coated with a UV-protection film intended to prevent fading of colourful carpets, wall hangings, and pictures. As we have noted, eliminating UV light is an open invitation to mites. There is no longer any natural inhibitor to their growth.

The Flow of Water

The next flow to consider is water. How do we use water in any building? The largest use of water in homes, and definitely in schools and office buildings, is for washing and waste removal. We block the flow of air and light in modern buildings but exaggerate the flow of water through multiple tubes and pipes, some for cold, some for hot, others for grey water and yet more for black water. Oddly, the first thing we do with digestive waste is mix it with potable water. Our body's method of acquiring nutrients involves a complex system of stomach, kidneys, liver, bladder, and intestines. The human body has one input pipe with a valve to direct water and solids to the stomach and air to the lungs. There are two output channels, one for liquids and another for solids and gases. It works quite efficiently.

Pure drinking water, a necessity for life, is unfortunately not a commodity available to all. When we use it to wash away waste matter, we are not seeing the connections! Water is the most precious substance on Earth. In many places, drinking water is expensive, more expensive than even petroleum at US$ 100 a barrel. When we have the luxury of easy access to clean drinking water, why do we render it unusable by blending it with human digestive waste? As if that were not enough, we add harsh chemicals and chlorinated paper.

You may not consider urine is a remarkable liquid, yet it is rich in potassium, one of the core nutrients that give our heart the ability to regulate blood flow. Our body cannot accumulate potassium because it is a toxin in our blood stream. Thus it is discharged as rapidly as it accumulates from consuming a healthy diet. Urine should not be wasted but should be returned to the nutrient cycle. In the era of the Roman Empire, it was the emperor himself who had the unique privilege of collecting urine from the citizens' dwellings to be used as a cleansing agent.

Faeces are a different matter. Few animal species deliberately drop faeces in water, except perhaps birds, such as the flamingo, whose droppings stimulate the growth of algae on which prawns thrive, and on which the birds in turn depend for nutrients. There are good reasons why our digestive system separates faeces from urine. The combined odour of faeces and urine is unpleasant. In current custom, urine and faeces, along with voluminous quantities of drinkable water, are flushed away and pumped to water treatment systems. Here the organic matter is devoured by bacteria stimulated by massive amounts of air pumped into the water at great cost. If faeces and urine were collected separately, as excreted, there would be little or no odour, provided there was sufficient airflow to quickly dry the faeces.

That is how the dry separation toilet that was designed, operated, and fine-tuned by Dr Matts Wolgast, a Swedish scientist from Uppsala University, operates. Alternatively, a simple vortex set up to take advantage of the power of gravity could quickly separate solids from liquids. Water cleansing systems such as those evolved by clams would also contribute, as would purifying water using the methods devised by pistol prawns. This technology for end-of-pipe solutions, for some reason, goes unused in modern buildings. Were we to eliminate the need to use water to transport digestive waste to central water treatment plants where *E. coli* and *Vibrio cholerae* thrive, then we would eliminate not only the risks linked to these potential sources of disease, but also the voluminous, industrial-scale quantities of harsh chemicals required to control these harmful bacteria. Although bactericides reduce the risk of disease, they render the wastewater totally useless for any form of consumption unless it is subjected to a lengthy and costly recovery process.

At the Laggarberg School in Sweden, designed by Anders Nyquist, the on-site operation that processes all toilet waste operates with the logic of an ecosystem. Although flushing toilets are the legal requirement, once liquids and solids are flushed they are immediately separated using a simple vortex. Waste heat is used to dry the solid matter. This destroys all pathogens, parasites, and any excreted antibiotics and hormones before they can have a detrimental impact on humans and their environment. Children at Laggarberg who spend their school years in this learning environment, innately comprehend, the common logic of sustainably managed waste systems from being exposed to it daily.

We think of water as the liquid that flows through pipes from somewhere where it is in abundance to wherever we need it. Cities have established efficient water distribution networks. Imagine the thousands of miles of pipes that bring water from the Colorado River to Los Angeles. Imagine the huge investment New York is making to install septic tanks upstate to preserve its watershed.

Now consider what happens to rainwater. It is collected in the sewerage pipes buried beneath city roads and simply drained away! Although water is increasingly costly, the State of Colorado even used to prohibit its urban residents from capturing rainwater How was that possible? How can allowing rainwater to flow into the sewerage system be permitted, in order to dilute the organic load? It is time to think of water as our most precious resource. Prior to birth, we are more than 98% water. Our adult bodies are more than 80% water. Our daily consumption of water fuels our survival. We treat water the way we do because we do not see the flows – where it comes from and where it goes. Let us broaden our thinking and ask the simple question, "Where on Earth is the largest quantity of untapped drinking water to be found?" It is in the air.

The first and foremost solution to meeting our needs for water is to capture rainfall. In every building and on every street there are water catchment areas that could channel water towards its most immediate use, without the need for pumps or chemical treatments, since gravity can do the job. Whether a skyscraper in New York or a farm in Colombia, rainfall capture would supply the building occupants' water needs.

Capturing moisture from the air is not seriously considered as a mainstream solution. Yet we would gain fresh insight into rich opportunities to tap water from the air by visiting the driest ecosystems and learning how the local plants and animals survive. The head-stander beetle (*Onymacris unguicularis*) of the Namib Desert of southern Africa is a 'fog basking beetle' as it catches water from the air using its shell. The shell has a series of ridges all over the shell that attract water, and a surface that repels water. This combines to make the water drop, once it becomes too big to be contained by the ridges, run off for capture by the beetle. The Main's frog (*Cyclorana maini*) from Australia can absorb 30% of its body weight in water and encapsulate it in a cocoon. Another Australian native, the Thorny Dragon (*Moloch horridus*) is a lizard that accumulates moisture through osmosis into an internal reservoir. The *Welwitschia mirabilis*, a desert plant, has similar abilities to the head-stander beetle in condensing water from the air as discussed earlier. The Cactus Thorn sucks water out of the air as do pine trees and the *Guadua angustifolia*, an Andean highland bamboo species. The Garoé laurel tree (*Ocotea foetens*) that grows on the ridge of the summit of El Hierro Island in the Canary Islands, produces such streams of water from the clouds that it sometimes looks like a waterfall.

If you have ever observed an air conditioner, you know that it drips water all the time. In a similar fashion, a cooling tower on top of a large office building condenses water vapour that accumulates as sweat along the surface of the tower. To get an idea of how much water is suspended in the atmosphere, consider that if the air expelled every day from the top of a large building were to first flow along an industrial sized 'fog basking beetle' shell, it could funnel as much as 100 cubic metres of water per minute from the roof to the floors below. Interestingly, when we study the flow of air from cooling towers we are discovering the opportunity to let water flow from the top of the building downward, reducing energy costs. Using the force of gravity and thus avoiding having to pump water also saves energy. Since water "on top" requires no pumps, we save capital costs. Here is a proposal with considerable appeal in an economic crisis: invest less, get more.

Leonardo da Vinci studied water extensively. He was fascinated with water, the flows of rivers, eddies, spiralling vortices, and other patterns of turbulence. He identified two principal forces operating in flowing water: gravity and internal friction or viscosity. At the centre of Leonardo's investigations of turbulence was the water vortex, or whirlpool. Utilising the vortex was creatively approached in the 20th century by Viktor Schauberger, an Austrian scientist and forester. As noted before, a vortex has the capacity to purify water. The relationship to building design is an easy step. Capture water from the cooling towers to flush toilets, wash windows or mop floors, pump it through a vortex-generating pipe, oxygenate and purify it through the internal pressure, and each floor down it can be used again, then delivered clean to the basement. This is an efficient use of water that truly makes a difference.

When the water then flows through a vortex, separating solids from liquids, water from the tenth floor could be reused for toilet flushing nine times, all the way down to the first floor. Since flushing toilets are one of the largest water guzzlers in office buildings, a vortex system would save both water and energy. If the surface of the building is covered with material inspired by the physics of the self-cleaning lotus flower or the ability of the abalone to maintain a clean and shining interior shell, then neither water nor chemicals are needed to clean it, saving yet more water. Costly window-cleaning machines could be eliminated from the operational expenses of the building. Are these solutions a reality or a dream? It is up to us. Many applications have already been proven – plants and insects prove they work. For instance, the water repellent substance on the legs of water striders is so effective that no moisture ever sticks to them, enabling these insects to walk on water.

These ingenious solutions have been fine-tuned over millions of years of survival in the desert or on water bodies, and by the pragmatic application of physical laws that work all the time, without exception. Compared to Nature's solutions, our complex systems of pumping water from the mountains through dams, or converting salt water to potable water with the massive energy expenditure required by reverse osmosis, begin to look like archaic, inferior technologies.

The combined flow of air and water offers a vast range of opportunities that can be appreciated by understanding the laws of physics and chemistry. Though easy to comprehend, these laws are seldom adapted as solutions. Take the example of a chequered surface with hydrophobic and hydrophilic textures. The massive clouds of air that dissipate from cooling towers could instead flow over a sheet of squares. Some squares are hydrophobic; they repel water while others, that are hydrophilic attract water. Tiny bubbles of water are ejected from the hydrophobic surfaces before they have time to evaporate. These bubbles collect on the hydrophilic surfaces, forming droplets and flowing downward by gravity alone to fill tanks on the top of a building. This supply may not be enough to satisfy every need. Nonetheless, the idea helps us contemplate vast water resources we have never before considered. If the cooling towers were to expel their saturated air in a swirl, thereby generating a vortex, it could even "press" the water out of the air without any chequered surfaces. El Hierro is the place to pioneer this system.

Once we perfect the design of these innovations, we can combine them with the latest insights into utilising a vortex in water pipes for water purification. By redesigning the production and consumption models, and taking the time and effort to rethink the entire system, we have a chance to achieve a solution that could save us from massive worldwide water shortages. These innovations, once applied, can cut costs immediately and relieve the stress on scarce water resources that characterise every megalopolis in the world.

The entire coastal zone of California has suffered from water shortages for decades. If there were access to water from the moist air that is always present because of the temperature inversion between the cold ocean currents and the hot inland deserts, the largest economic benefit would be increased land value. Recall the case of Las Gaviotas, a desolate area once considered worthless and now a regenerated rainforest valued at 3,000 times its original cost. An increase in property value based on the inclusion of a Commons, such as abundant water resources, would be a welcome reversal to the current trend of property devaluation and speculation. Good land that meets basic needs, starting with pure drinking water, holds good value.

The Heat Island Effect

In the sweltering summer heat of New York or Boston, Brisbane or Dubai, air conditioners are on full blast. Hot outside air is pushed through these cooling systems and water-saturated heated clouds surround the buildings. The air conditioners produce cool air inside. The warm and humid air exhausts to the outside, rendering the exterior air in the immediate vicinity – including that available for the air conditioning intake system – likewise warm and humid. Thus the energy required for cooling hot, moist air increases. With little wind, the area becomes a heat island. In the summer, when such a heat island effect is at its peak, the warm conditions needed for the spread of *Legionella spp.* (the bacteria responsible for Legionnaire's disease) will be at a peak. Rising temperatures cause bacterially proliferated biofilm to thicken, and consequently the health risks increase. When you enter a building through revolving doors meant to avoid heating or cooling loss, there is no decompression, thus no movement of air. The more people gathered in these airtight buildings, the more heat is captured inside. Anders Nyquist's design of a sporting hall at the Laggarberg School in Sweden uses an ingenious approach. When heat is emitted by excited spectators during a lively school sports event, the hot air rises and naturally occurring airflows bring in the cooler outside air. His design demonstrates that as more people enter the hall, greater airflow occurs, keeping the inside air refreshed and comfortable. That is a systemic design that works!

Building designs create sets of unanticipated problems. The solutions serve multiple purposes while producing cost and energy savings and reducing the risks to human health. Healthier buildings that save energy with lower capital and operating costs are the bottom line of this bundling of innovations provided by solutions from natural systems.

The Flow of Sound

Prior to birth, a human fetus is composed primarily of water. The sounds that resonate through the amniotic fluid affect the unborn infant. In fact, some paediatricians have suggested that pregnant women listen to classical music, or to the chanting of Gregorian or Tibetan monks, because they consider that these sounds enhance an infant's mental development.

Sound is energy in a waveform; waves produce pressure, and sound waves have different levels or frequencies. Alexander Lauterwasser's work in the field of cymatics demonstrated that a flow of sound suffusing a body of water achieves a constant and therefore predictable shape. Lauterwasser placed a drop of water on a metal plate and applied a sound source. He observed that as sound waves caused the water to vibrate, the water moved. Different waves at different pressures generated different complex patterns of movement. A specific frequency always produced a particular movement and shape of the water at a fixed surface tension. A minimal change in frequency caused alterations in the complex but rhythmic movements.

Each of us knows from experience that pleasant sounds are soothing, and unpleasant sounds can range from mildly annoying to positively unbearable. We can imagine the serenity of living near a babbling brook or within hearing distance of ocean waves at the seashore. Living or working next to a freeway or a railroad line requires a structure that minimises noise.

Since even inanimate objects such as buildings produce noise, exploring innovative ideas that channel the flow of undesirable sounds in our daily environments might help us find ways to reduce the effect such sounds have on us. Scientists study how the streamlined shape of bottlenose dolphins and whales allows these mammals to convert the pressure from water and wind vortices into efficient power. Perhaps we might similarly capture the energy potential of sound and convert it by using minute piezoelectric transformers, gaining sufficient electrical energy to power small battery-driven devices such as mobile phones. Instead of just blocking noise from freeway traffic, we could devise ways to capture and convert it to energy. Thus solutions to noise amelioration could also achieve energy savings.

The Flow of Energy

The cost of energy delivered to a building depends on two factors: demand and supply. The cases described in this chapter, and throughout the book, demonstrate that a dramatic reduction in energy use can be accomplished by using solutions that require less and provide more. In fact, utilising only the innovations described could potentially reduce the need for electricity in any building, from a gymnasium to a child's room, by 75-80 percent. To this we may add the wonders of the cold light produced by squid and fungi, the self-cleaning demonstrated by lotus flowers, and heat conservation accomplished by tuna. Technologies provided by the sandfish lizard could give us friction reduction, which is an energy saver, because our incapacity to reduce or overcome friction requires additional energy. As noted earlier, all these ways and means to reduce energy consumption are possible and do not compromise our health. While this is good, there are even better possibilities ...

If we turn our focus to supply, as we have already noted, a building has tremendous potential to generate its own electricity. While the pressure from sound and noise will not be enough to power everything in a modern building with electronics, security systems, computer networks, lifts, and air conditioning, we might once again emulate natural systems, welcoming the contributions of all, even the smallest numbers and the tiniest volumes.

The largest source of energy must be the most readily available power generator – the source that subjects the whole building to structural compression and requires the tensile strength that dominates the design. Throughout this book we have referred to the great power of gravity. Why not use it in building design?

As we mentioned previously, a redesign of the building structure could set the foundations of each floor on crystals like quartz, silk, or even sugar cane. Based on nanoscale crystals and a ten-storey building, it has been guesstimated that the total power from gravity-induced piezoelectricity could reach 6,000 kWh. That is not bad. If the quartz crystals were precisely located on each floor, typically under each one of the columns, it would be possible to have electricity available throughout the building with a limited need for cabling. That further reduces the need for copper and mining. It would take only one generation to have these building techniques approved and implemented in new structures. If the science can be demonstrated, then the conservative and risk-adverse construction industry will shift for the better, and buildings will require less investment and achieve lower operational costs. If bamboo was incorporated with reinforced concrete in the structure, the building would not only be energy efficient, it would in fact sequester carbon dioxide, since the carbon absorbed by the bamboo would offset the emissions from the cement. Now we are talking!

A second large potential energy source that is not yet harnessed is to use local gusts of wind. Each large building impacts the local climate, generating turbulence. This turbulence could even be enhanced through planned exterior colour choices, the way a zebra does, not just reflecting the sun but ensuring that the light and dark skin variations provide surface cooling and generate local airflows. It does not make much sense to place windmills in the centre of town, since these would make too much noise and not catch sufficient wind. However, it would be possible to place there a series of mini- and micro-windmills that would constantly generate energy, each equipped with the smart surface that Nature provided to the edges of whale flippers for the purpose of reducing drag and increasing lift.

Each person in a building emits the energy equivalent of 60 watts of electricity per hour and thus should be considered a source of energy. The technology from the Fraunhofer Institute, discussed in Chapter 12, is capable of capturing energy from even just half a degree of temperature difference between the body and the sensor. Once it is commercially available, this innovation will allow us to move building design another step closer to sustainability. The more people inside, the less additional energy needed. A building with a thousand people inside for eight to ten hours per day would generate an estimated 60 kWh during working hours. If this is efficiently transformed, it could power every computer in the building. It works currently at laboratory scale. It could soon work in large-scale office buildings, and generate significant quantities of additional local energy for local consumption. The very low distribution costs will convince forward-thinking architects to include sound, pressure, temperature, and micro-flows of wind into their designs for optimal energy generation and application. All the scientific confirmation is in place. What is needed now is an entrepreneurial effort to bring a portfolio of these innovations into an integrated design.

The Flows of People and Matter

Movement flows of people and products have been studied in considerable detail by systems engineers and city planners and designers. We strive for efficiency and optimal flow in airport and shopping queues, in delivery and removal of goods consumed, in transport of product and people, and in consumption of goods and services, entertainment and education. When we link these flows to the other flows we have discussed, we might realise that we could indeed design a building capable of generating nutrients. A bathroom, generally moist and warm, could provide an ideal breeding ground for mushrooms. The starch in our food waste could be converted into bioplastics using only a fungus. Rooftops could become gardens, not only producing local fruits and vegetables but also reducing the building's surface temperature and energy consumption. Buildings designed to recycle nutrients and augment food security could yield unintended benefits, by providing an energising and relaxing environment where food crops could flourish, and healthful exercise could take place. This would be a building worthy of the genius of Friedensreich Hundertwasser, the brilliant Viennese architect.

The Centre for Ecoliteracy in Berkeley, California, and Slow Food in Torino, Italy, have both been active in creating school gardens in urban environments. Now we have the opportunity to surpass this accomplishment and create a self-sustaining environment. Brasilia, the capital of Brazil with two million inhabitants, meets 90% of its fruit and vegetable needs within the city boundaries – thanks to the visionary urban design by Lucio Costa, and the buildings' architecture by the world famous architect, Oscar Niemeyer. If access and allocation were designed into the flow of the buildings and the surrounding space, with comfort and sustenance as priorities, then water and nutrients can be abundantly available for our needs. Waste generated from consumption is kept locally available and is contributed to the nutrient stream that simply, yet remarkably, returns to us as nutrients for sustenance. It is an elegant cascade that cycles and recycles, benefiting and utilising all materials. It is a whole systems model perfected by Nature and available to meet the needs of all.

Schools as Sustainability Classrooms

Schools are an ideal testing ground for learning how to work with flows. Between the first and the final year of school, children spend an estimated 20,000 hours in classrooms. This is a staggering amount of time, which many feel is not spent well. Considering the tremendous investment of time and energy that goes into schooling, how is it possible that saving money determines how schools and classrooms are designed? Shouldn't the overarching principles be establishing a healthful environment for optimal learning and participation? How much is that worth? We have only scratched the surface of these issues. Nonetheless, there are many ready and available options for designing school buildings that are optimally healthy, less costly to maintain, and which utilise the dozens of scientific insights described herein. What is required though, is that we shift our thinking in order to change the way we live.

Conditions for good health should not be subject to calculations of financial profit or cost cutting. School buildings are an ideal place to implement principles of health and sustainability and to showcase them in the public domain where they may contribute to the public good. Imagine a school building where over a hundred core concepts in physics, biology, and chemistry are visibly and functionally integrated into the building and the operation of the school. Imagine the connections students would make by seeing these sciences on display every day. The children and their teachers would have the opportunity to become familiar with the innovations and to learn the science behind the way they function through daily appreciation and exposure. The school itself becomes a living science laboratory. Living what you learn makes acquiring knowledge effortless. Such a school structure would steer society towards sustainability. The obvious differences between the new and old technologies would inspire many youngsters to become tomorrow's innovators and entrepreneurs. This is the springboard from which imagination becomes reality.

In such a building, simple and pragmatic combinations of meteorology with the basic principles of airflow maintain constant interior temperature and humidity even as the exterior pressure and temperature change. Highly efficient LED lights shine day and night on a hundred varieties of plants automatically sprinkled every fifteen minutes with rainwater collected from the roof. The levels of dust particles and air pollutants entering the building or generated inside are kept low by this misting, decreasing the risk of respiratory diseases. The lights are coated not with mercury but with keratin, inspired by the beetle that creates a white colour layer without chemicals. Chelating bacteria assist in recycling cast-off metals. The inner walls are composed of crushed seashells and filled with dried seaweed, providing a practical and efficient, highly alkaline, anti-fungal, moisture-absorbing sound barrier. Natural airflows in the building pass over these materials, keeping the humidity stable and the pH alkaline. The windows allow only a very limited passage of UV rays to control mites in the chemical-free carpeting. The carpet tiles electrically connect through the micron sized carbon fibres that obtain their energy from thin-film dye-sensitised solar cells attached to the windows, keeping the floors at an ideal temperature for warmth and dry enough for mite control.

And now the new standard for internet arrives: Li-Fi to complement Wi-Fi. Light-based internet applies the laws of physics: the speed of light is faster than the speed of sound. LED lights flicker up to ten million times per second, and data is added in between each photon permitting to download 23 videos in just a single second. This will be the gamers' paradise. Now the LED at home will eliminate a lot of wires, while the street LED lighting will offer the internet backbone that links up with an optical wire often connecting every home. Suat Topsu, inventor of the integrated light-based transmission of data, and Professor at the University of Versailles (France), founded Oledcomm based on the tremendous advantage of light over sound. He, like all of us, knew that lighting is seen long before thunder is heard, and yet the internet standard is based on a transmission through sound radio waves. It is obvious for everyone that we can do better, much better indeed. The power lies in that the savings in no longer having wires, added to the energy using LED, finances the introduction of this novel way of communicating – one that is at least 100 times faster than the best available today. The true application of the best of physics, offers us a competitive force that may even threaten the world of internet. And by the way, it is impossible to hack Li-Fi, since it is too fast.

Rather than only the mastering of any one technology, we should implement detailed and definitive design plans based on portfolios of innovations and technologies introduced here. This would naturally require insight into a system integrated with the local environment where all we need and use is available cheaper and healthier, and where we can act faster and at bigger scale. It is here where the difference lies between the regenerative and adaptive capacity of an ecosystem and the genius of a single species. Ecosystems simply cannot be reduced to a set of rules. The whole is more than the sum of the individual components.

Housing for All

It is impossible to close this chapter without reflecting on the pioneering design work of the late Linda Garland, who was based for decades in Bali, Indonesia, and Simon Velez who operates around the world from his base in Bogotá, Colombia. They have done remarkable work with bamboo in designing and constructing affordable, renewable, and attractive housing that could be the most sustainable of all types of housing. From the perspective of its composition, the relative strength of bamboo defies logic. Its marvellous adaptation is to use tensile and compression strengths to perfect advantage. Even though bamboo is a grass and not a tree, its fibres outperform any other cellulose source when put to the task of building or papermaking. Since we should not speak in absolute terms, we also recognise hemp and flax; however, bamboo is the master for technical functionality. It can demonstrably replace both concrete and steel. With over 2,000 species in the Americas alone, bamboo has qualities that make it capable of effortlessly, ecologically, and inexpensively meeting our growing needs for construction materials. At the end of the 20th century, bamboo was still the preferred building material for more than a billion people around the world, especially in the tropics. Sven Mouton, a Belgian architect who graduated from the Jesuit University of Rio de Janeiro, under the watchful eyes of Professor Khosrow Ghavami, calculated that bamboo embodies sixty times less energy (and CO_2) than steel, offering flexibility and elegance steel cannot pretend to have.

After the Kyoto Protocol was signed in 1997, Masatsugu Taniguchi, director of Taiheiyo, Japan's largest cement manufacturer, searched for a way to achieve a low carbon footprint using cement. The materials for reinforced concrete are mined and manufactured at high pressure and temperature and leave the face of the Earth scarred for centuries. Taiheiyo succeeded by utilising bamboo fibres. Simply pressing bamboo with cement, weight for weight (50/50), or 75/25 by volume, without any additives or chemicals, they created a cement board with a neutral carbon footprint. The bamboo itself is farmed and sustainably harvested on 2,000 hectares of land next to a factory on the outskirts of Jakarta.

Innovative architects Renzo Piano and Shigeru Ban were inspired to create architectural wonders based on the beauty and performance of bamboo. Maestro Simon Velez, the grand bamboo architect of our time, demonstrated that bamboo could comply with the most stringent construction engineering rules of modern society – German building codes. Velez designed the ZERI Pavilion, erected in Manizales, Colombia, which was at the time probably the largest bamboo structure in the world (later the most popular pavilion at the 2000 World Expo in Hanover, Germany). Two severe earthquakes since its construction have merely shifted a few tiles on the roof.

The king of all bamboos is the *Guadua angustifolia*. When the Spaniards conquered the highlands of Colombia, Peru, and Ecuador, they had to wade through dense bamboo jungles. The life force of bamboo was widely and wildly described by the Spanish colonisers, whose letters home told how the native Andean cultures used bamboo defensively in combat, as it would pierce quickly through the body, seemingly without force. These colonisers also quickly learned that their European wood and stone construction techniques did not long survive in the earthquake-prone zones of the southern Americas. They found out, the hard way, that, "buildings must dance to the rhythms of the Earth," as Simon Velez characterises the behaviour of bamboo. That is exactly what bamboo does: it "dances", as will soon be explained.

As this 25-metre tall "grass" was cleared to make space for coffee and cattle farming in the southern Americas, it became the preferred local building material. Two hundred years later, these buildings from colonial times still stand, having survived everything the shaking Earth delivered. This Latin American experience is confirmed in Asia. At 3,000 years and counting, the world's oldest bamboo building still stands as an open pavilion in Manchuria.

Bamboo does not resist an earthquake but rather moves with it. Neither does a bamboo structure require bracing through cross-links to withstand the chaotic upward and sideward pressures. Curiously, bamboo is hollow. It is flexible enough to stand as long as the building has an inward inclination. The mere reduction of the vertical angle to 85° provides such stability that the tiles on the roof don't even move. It is a pity that the domination of CAD/CAM in the architectural design and construction fields since the late 20th century has demanded 90° angles for all construction, resulting in death and destruction every time the Earth trembles.

Achieving affordable and beautiful housing for all in the tropics is a goal that can be met with the use of bamboo. A 92 m2 plot of land in the Andean highlands would be sufficient to grow enough bamboo for a house. Planted with the giant *Guadua angustifolia* bamboo, some 60 bamboo poles would be harvestable after three years. This is enough building material to construct a two-storey, 60 m^3 house with a magnificent balcony as well as a staircase in the back that allows airflow. Each subsequent year's bamboo harvest would provide enough poles to construct an additional modest home.

Simon Velez's housing design includes a large staircase in the rear, which acts like the chimneys of a termite mound to facilitate airflow; a heavy roof structure to stabilise the building; and a wide balcony for comfortable ambiance. There are no 90° angles. This prevents a sudden collapse in the case of an earthquake, making it an extremely safe design. Instead of trying to build a building that does not move, the bamboo, and the method of joinery used, allows movement along with that of the Earth during an earthquake. The air in the house is remarkably fresh, with light entering freely. The massive overhanging roof protects the structural bamboo from any deterioration due to ultraviolet light or rain. Rainwater flows around the house, hardly touching the bamboo's surface, collecting in cisterns for drinking water. Although there is wind play, not even a hurricane could lift the house.

The bamboo not used in house construction, considered by many a waste product, can be used to produce charcoal. Charcoal production releases noxious gases. Antonio Giraldo from Armenia (Colombia), has developed a method of curing bamboo in its own charcoal gases, much like the traditional curing systems used in Japan. The flow of the gases is channelled to a huge chamber. Under slight pressure, bamboo poles just over nine metres long are cured with the fumes from their own charcoal. Instead of using toxic chemistry to preserve the bamboo against termites and fungi, it is cured by its own chemistry. The negative flow of contaminants is converted into a positive flow that not only preserves the bamboo but also replaces the pollutants that pose health risks. The way the building materials are made and prepared for use is once again inspired by natural systems, a cascading of nutrients and energy. This same method was used at the Picuris Pueblo in New Mexico, with small-diameter wood that was slated to be burned, now converted to window and door frames, (discussed in Chapter 4).

Lucio Ventania, a well-known Brazilian bamboo artisan, explains that, "as long as structural bamboo is protected from direct sun and never stands in its own water, it will stand, forever." Hence, the logical design features a large overhang that protects the load-bearing poles from water and sun, the two most destructive atmospheric forces. The experience gained at Manizales and Hanover with subsequent designs gave rise to numerous social housing initiatives. While Simon Velez provided the first designs for a two-storey, low cost house with a balcony (to symbolise middle-class aspirations) for only US$ 12,000, the Jesuit-supported Hogares de Cristo en Guayaquil of Ecuador pushed the logic to extremes and established pre-fabricated, simple social housing units for as little as US$ 950.

This business model surprises: a poor family arrives with US$ 50 cash, applies for US$ 900 credit, which is approved quickly provided they have access to a piece of land, and 24 hours later their house is standing tall. The new home owners pay a monthly mortgage payment of less than US$ 20, lifting people off the streets and having a roof over their heads at low cost. Hogares de Cristo's production system cranks out 42 prefabricated houses a day for an annual turnover of about US$ 12 million, and this requires a sustainable supply of bamboo from an estimated 2,000 hectares of land. Who provides the land?

More Magic from Mines

AngloGold Ashanti, the third largest gold mining company in the world, with a market capitalisation in excess of $6 billion, searched to secure water supply for its mines in the Andean Highlands. It learned from Dr Luis Miguel Álvarez Mejía, a vanguard botanist at the University of Caldas, in Manizales (Colombia) that eliminating exotic species from the mine's land concession, and replanting native vegetation, dominated by bamboo (*Guadua angustifolia*), drops the surface temperature by some 10 °C, which increases rainfall and guarantees a supply of water – indefinitely. Once planted, bamboo proliferates for seventy years until it flowers and dies. Since bamboo is a grass, it can be harvested and without any need for replanting, it will grow again. The regeneration of the forest in the Vichada, by the Las Gaviotas Environmental Research Centre, is now complemented in size and impact by the recovery of the Andean Highlands with its original bamboo forest.

Pure and abundant water is only a first and obvious benefit, for the mine and the local communities that have faced severe potable water stresses. The local bean farmers harvest bamboo to make 3-4 metre posts, and deliver the rest to the valley to produce housing, which requires poles of another 5-6 metres. Then there is still at least 15 metres left that can be pulped to produce water absorbent paper. Kimberly Clark, the maker of Kleenex tissues and owner of the Scott brand has decided to replace eucalyptus and pine-based pulp with locally supplied bamboo. The business cluster around the mine now evolves into a second income and job generating cycle after a first one emerged turning rocks and tailings into paper products and cash. Both cycles around mining dramatically increase resource efficiency, while generating multiple benefits for society and the environment. Who could have imagined these hidden benefits from a mining operation – even before the mine is operational?

Bamboo remains undiscovered by those who live outside its tropical growing range. Not a single species of bamboo grows naturally in the northwestern United States or in Sweden, where the largest forestry research institutes are located. Thus, the focus of the worldwide forestry industry, even in tropical locales, is on species such as eucalyptus and pine, which grow in temperate climates and have nowhere near the renewable potential of bamboo. As awareness of bamboo's sustainable growth habit and building material qualities becomes more widespread, it will serve as an inspiration for innovative architectural projects around the world.

Since the Brazilians and Colombians spearheaded this integrated approach to using bamboo, it has led to a transformation of the labour market. Ever since the ZERI Pavilion at the World Expo in Hanover in the year 2000 demonstrated that bamboo has the flexibility and the tensile and compression strength to qualify for a German building permit, 250 new companies and 7,000 jobs have been created. Now, if this is considered a success, then look at Vietnam where an estimated 200,000 jobs have been created since bamboo turned into a key component of Vietnam's emerging economy. South Korea also embraced the bamboo wave after it realised that next to its prowess in electronics and mobile phone systems, it can also develop this massive new industry, based on traditional raw materials that can be harvested renewably, while turning tradition and culture into an engine of the local economy.

All Flows Considered

An appreciation of how the flow of air, light, water, energy, sound, people, and matter affect our physical space brings a new understanding of how to design structures that interweave and utilise these flows. It gives us some very practical insights into how to build and furnish homes, offices, and schools to achieve true functionality, cost-savings, and aesthetics. A better understanding of all the material, water and energy flows at a mine, gives us very practical insights into how to operate this in a community, and how transformative this can be for our model of society.

Pioneering entrepreneurs have shown us that sustainable buildings need not be more expensive. Practical applications from the world of science, well researched and well documented, are opening up new possibilities that can finally steer us towards sustainability. Architects dedicated to green building design have the ability to turn possibilities into actualities. Public demand and common sense will help authorities revise building codes and approve industry standards that allow integration of innovations based on solid science and smart business. When we embrace these innovations as a society, we will be supporting the health of our families, our domiciles, our workplaces, and our environment. We will be creating the industries of the future inspired by the ingenuity of Nature. We too can function as an ecosystem, generating what we need from what is available, finding resource in waste, welcoming the contributions of all, and taking part in a cascade of abundance.

Epilogue

You only reach maturity in life once you have gone beyond your dreams

When I met Paolo Lugari for the first time in 1984, and he shared his vision of the massive regeneration of the tropical rainforest in the Orinoco Basin of Colombia, I listened to this remarkable man. He had just completed the largest solar water heating project in the world for the Banco Central Hipotecario, a social housing financing institution in Colombia. Paolo had just completed the installation of 70,000 water heaters, designed and built by the teams of Las Gaviotas. Paolo wished to dedicate time and resources to the regrowing of the "skin of the Earth".

I was amazed that, apart from myself, there was no one else prepared to join Paolo and ensure that this fantasy would become a reality. Today, Las Gaviotas has regenerated the rainforest, is self-sufficient in water, and is independent in fuel, in an area where we were told there was nothing – and now there is full employment. I have returned to this region more than twenty times, and was inspired that even the chairman of JP Morgan could get excited about the prospects of financing the expansion of this initiative.

It was in 2004 that I first learned about stone paper – an amazing sheet to write on, print on and use as packaging – that required no water, no cellulose and could be recycled indefinitely. When the first booklet lay in my hands, I realised that a new era of paper had arrived. What I also found astounding was that so few people believed that William Liang would ever succeed in taking this idea to reality. When I visited the 18,000 tonnes per year facility in Tainan it was clear that this was going to scale. By 2018, production will have increased to one million tonnes, and thanks to the touch of a genius, the rock and polymer mix is now enhanced with small air bubbles – stone paper now weighs the same as cellulose paper.

It was 2014, when the Industrial Technology Research Institute of Taiwan showcased their broadband internet over LED lamps, that I was once again impressed. Would it really be possible to move from radio waves and satellites to the fastest transmission ever imagined in the Universe? When I sat down with Suat Topsu, the inventor of visual light communications (popularly called LiFi), I realised the profound changes that were about to materialise in the industry that we thought was the revolution itself. Now this revolution was being revolutionised!

Nearly a quarter of a century ago, I decided to sell all my businesses and properties and focus on the design of a new business model – one that is capable of responding to the basic needs of all, with what we have. We backed more than 200 innovations and played differing roles in the transformation of an idea into a vision, with clarity that it has the potential to change the world. Nothing more – nothing less. Sometimes I was nothing more than a fly on the wall, eavesdropping on the marvels that emerged in the minds of these innovators; sometimes I was the catalyst, triggering a few changes and shifts, that catapulted concepts to new heights; sometimes I was instrumental in getting the first contract, or securing the right endorsement; and a few times I rolled up my sleeves and got directly involved, always with ethics at the core.

Wherever I go, I see opportunities and since the first time I drafted an inventory of everything that I considered possible, I got hooked on the idea that while everything around us seem to be crumbling, and all statistics before us are discouraging, we clearly have the future in our hands – provided we are ready to look reality in the eye, refuse to judge between the good and the bad, and focus on one clear goal: to always do better. When I review the work of Catia Bastioli, who takes green chemistry from the world of the bioeconomy and transforms this into a strategy for sustainable territorial development, then it is clear that we only need a few great minds who will not accept "No" for an answer when it comes to turning the world around, for the better.

Now that I look back and realise that more than five billion dollars had been invested in just over two hundred projects, it hits me between the eyes that we have only just begun. Whatever we have achieved so far is not even a drop in the ocean. We need to achieve so much more. However, with the unfolding waves and the underlying currents that shape the world today, it is clear that there are multiple forces moving in the right direction, ensuring that we are transforming our lives, our communities, our societies, our Earth … for the better, for all time.

This edition of *The Blue Economy 3.0*, prepared for publication in Australia, is intended to inspire all, by showing that there is never an end to a start. It is only the beginning.

It has only just begun…

The 50 Books on Sustainability that have Shaped the Author's Thinking

When Carlo Petrini, the founder of the Slow Food Movement suggested that we establish *The Aurelio Peccei Library* to inspire future generations, a dozen books immediately came to mind. My own thinking has been profoundly influenced by Aurelio Peccei, the Italian top executive who created the Club of Rome with a few friends. This Club went on to shock the world in the early 70s questioning growth in an epochal book entitled *Limits to Growth.* I had the immense privilege to also meet some of the great minds that had influenced the thinking behind this book – his friends who had driven and shaped his vision, from the disasters that he saw looming on the horizon and the solutions that were desperately needed, to the vision and the philosophy that offered the framework – one that is long-term, interconnected and multi-disciplinary.

This list does not attempt to be exhaustive. It is rather intended to set a trend: the future is complex and there are many – so many – possible publications to read. In 2009, Cambridge University also compiled a list, one I beg to differ from, as far as its tone and content. The heart, soul and practice of sustainability was not predominantly shaped in English, by British authors. The emerging philosophy, science and practice of sustainability is a process, one that touches a wide range of cultures and religions, regions and ecosystems. The Anglo-Saxon framework limits our access and inspiration to a universal Anglo-Saxon view. We need a view that drives us to think beyond the status quo, and inspires us to imagine a much better society.

We set out to find a select number of books that would offer philosophy rather than prescriptive concepts. We prefer frameworks of thought, rather than "How to" menus. We give priority to context, instead of just text, however important or eloquent the analysis may be. Reading these books will lead one to finding the space in which to imagine another world, even another way of life, and then to harnessing the energy to continue reflecting on it, and from there to embracing action. This may sound somewhat ambitious – but why would we settle for anything less?

It is thanks to the work of Aurelio Peccei that the international think-tank, The Club of Rome, has been able to offer remarkable insights. It is achieved by way of the concept of a "Report to the Club of Rome". This concept connected a vast network of pioneering thinkers, many of whom were motivated to crystallise their thoughts into *Reports to the Club of Rome – Limits to Growth and No Limits to Learning*. These dialogues and exchanges inspired others, like Erich Jantsch and Mario Calderon, and they then wrote books that have shaped cutting-edge thinking.

The books listed here may not be the most popular or the best sellers. They are, however, the ones that shaped the framework for a deep ecology, a broad philosophy and a firm theory to develop, and continue to evolve for years to come. The list includes books that offer information on ancient wisdom (Confucius), the origins of humankind (Lasse Berg) and early emotional pleas to protect the environment (Rachel Carson). It even contains some esoteric reflections, such as on animal communication. With this list, we hope to provide a framework for the present – by building on the foundations laid in the past, and by pushing for new boundaries in the future.

A review of this list will certainly raise some eyebrows, and rightfully so. Since we opted for an approach based on deep ecology, we felt obliged to include seminal work on ethics (*The Night*), the use of power (*Les Mémoires d'Hadrien*). Seminal works on learning and teaching (written by Paulo Freire), on a deeper understanding of life that is so dependent on water (written by Viktor Schauberger), and the emerging forms of life in ecosystems where symbiosis complements evolution (written by Lynn Margulis), are also included. It is however key to offer exposure to action on the ground. We do so by including books on Africa (written by Wangari Maathai), Latin America (written by Marina Silva and Jaime Lerner), Europe (written by Karl Ludwig Schweisfurth) and Australia (written by Bill Mollison).

A few of these authors are remembered for writing only one book, others have been prolific writers. We have opted for listing original work, which provides fresh first insights, accompanied by the initial statements. We wish to expose the reader to a wealth of insights and encourage further reading beyond just the first statement. This is a process of discovery, one we hope the reader embarks on, and once immersed in it, continues on his or her journey of discovery.

Papa Francisco (Argentina)	Laudatio Sí
Yann Arthus Bertrand (France)	The World Seen from the Air
Lasse Berg (Sweden)	Dawn over the Kalahari
Fritjof Capra (Austria)	The Tao of Physics
Rachel Carson (USA)	Silent Spring
Mario Calderon Riveras (Colombia)	Las Gaviotas
Masaru Emoto (Japan)	The Hidden Message in Water
Don Hélder Câmara (Brazil)	Revolution through Peace
Confucius (China)	The Analects
Janine Benyus (USA)	Biomimicry

Cheikh Khaled Bentounes (Algeria)	Thérapie de l'âme
Gro Harlem Brundtland (Norway)	Changing Course
Erich Jantsch (Austria)	The Self-Organising Universe
Paulo Freire (Brazil)	Pedagogy of the Oppressed
Buckminster Fuller (USA)	Synergetics: Explorations in the Geometry of Thinking
Eduardo Galeano (Uruguay)	Open Veins of Latin America
Maurice Guernier (France)	Le Tiers Monde Trois Quarts du Monde
Satish Kumar (India)	No Destination: The long walk of a gentle hero
Jaime Lerner (Brazil)	Urban Acupuncture
José Lutzenberger (Brazil)	Wege aus der Ernährungskrise
Wangari Maathai (Kenya)	The Greenbelt Movement
Elisabeth Mann-Borgese	The Law of the Sea
Lynn Margulis (USA)	Symbiosis
Humberto Maturana and Ximena Dávila	The Tree of Life

Manfred Max-Neef (Chile)	Human Scale Development
Donella Meadows, Dennis Meadows,	Limits to Growth
Mircia Militza, J. Botkin, Mahdi Elmandjara	No Limits to Learning
Bill Mollison (Australia)	Permaculture One: A Perennial Agriculture for Human Settlements
Edgar Morin (France)	La connaissance de la connaissance
Arne Naes (Norway)	Deep Ecology
Ben Okri (Nigeria)	Astonishing the Gods
Andrew Parker (UK)	In the Blink of the Eye
Aurelio Peccei (Italia)	The Human Quality
Carlo Petrini (Italy)	Slow Food
Tharuk Powdyel (Bhutan)	The Green School
Thomas Rau, MD (Switzerland)	Biological Medicine
Johan Rockström (Sweden)	Planetary Boundaries
Rupert Sheldrake (UK)	The Science Delusion

Vandana Shiva (India)	Monocultures of the Mind
Viktor Schauberger (Austria)	Living Energies: An Exposition of Concepts Related to by Callum Coates the Theories of Viktor Schauberger
E.F. Schumacher (Germany)	Small is Beautiful
Karl Ludwig Schweisfurth (Germany)	Der Metzger der kein Fleisch mehr isst …
Stan Shih (Taiwan)	Wangdao
Marina Silva (Brazil)	Women Changing the World
Jan Tinbergen (Dutch)	Reshaping the International Order
Marguerite Yourcenar (Belgium)	Les Mémoires d'Hadrien
Elie Wiesel (USA)	The Night
Francisco Varela (Chile)	Ethical Know-How
EO Wilson (USA)	The Life of Ants

DVD: The Great Dance *by the Foster Brothers*

The Hundreds of Fables that Turn The Blue Economy into a Reality for Children

The fables are available on <www.TheFableShop>

In order to reach younger generations, every insight into sciences, every design of a new business model, every challenge that needs to be met, every ethical question posed, every breakthrough achieved, and every person to be celebrated in our quest to promote a Blue Economy (as described in *The Blue Economy 3.0)*, is transformed into a fable for children.

By August 2017, some 265 fables have been written, and 144 have been published. Digital, audio, and print copies (also print on demand) are available in multiple languages. Please see the website for what would be of interest to you. The entire set of 365 fables is expected to be completed and available by 2022. The information contained in the set of fables will form an encyclopaedia containing information on science, emotions, arts and connected thinking, and will inspire young and old to take action to promote sustainable life on Earth.

The Desert Witch
Getting water in the desert

Orange Soap
Making soap from citrus peel

Forest Drinking Water
Planting trees to get water

The Mountain Goat
Clean water in the mountain

Walking on Water
Water surface tension

Red Rice
Grow spirulina in ice paddies

Don't Eat Me Alive
Ethics of boiling live animals

The Smart Mushroom
Growing food on waste

Shiitake Loves Caffeine
Using coffee waste for food

Grandma's Bison Garden
Cascade fungi to animal feed

Where is Home?
Surprises in biodiversity

Grow a House
Plant bamboo to build homes

Why don't they like me?
Discovering the unknown

Don't Leave me Behind
The drama of pets left behind

Scratch my Back
Symbiosis of finch & tortoise

The Hippo Beauty Parlour
Natural cosmetics

Noses and Ears to See
Use of radar & echolocation

Animal Medicine
Animals use natural medicine

The King of Hearts
Natural electricity generation

Tree Candy
Producing healthy sugar

Males Only
The technique of fish farming

The Zebra Aircon
How to use black and white

Going Against the Current
Use force to go against it

The 5 Kingdoms of Nature
The five families of life

The Magic Hat
Beer, bread, and sausage

How to Take it Apart?
Engineer for disassembly

Green Hair and Four Eyes
The unknowns of genetics

Colombian Mushrooms
Exporting manure is absurd

The Ant Farmer
The first farmers on earth

The Strongest Tree
The ethics of respect

Who is the Most Beautiful?
Beauty is in the eye of…

The Bear and the Fox
Do goals justify means?

Please Play with Me
The cost of overfishing

Talking Water
Physical structure of water

Fishing without Nets
Using air bubbles to fish

Dressed up in Algae
Algae extract as fibre

Drink it – Wear it
Coffee to control odour

Fuel from the Tree
Turpentine as fuel

Farmers of the Sea
How Hawai'i fed itself

Can Plants Sing?
Plants express emotions

Paper from Stone
Convert rock waste to paper

Solar on Both Sides
Use top and bottom of PV

Light my Fire
Making of cold light

Math for Beginners
Non-linear math

Metals without Moulds
3-D printing

Strong as Silk
Natural fibre for health

Maggot Spit
Maggots healing ulcers

Stinging Nettles
Nettles as fibre for cloth

Crystal Palace
Recycled glass for housing

Colour without Paint
Optical effects of light

High and Cool
How a giraffe keeps cool

Water in the Coconut
Water moves against gravity?

Metals without Mining
The bacteria chelation

Gold Everywhere
Recycling electronic waste

Farming in the City
Using rooftops to farm

Jobs & Beauty from Straw
Why burn it if you can use it?

Cakes with Wind
How wind power can bake

A Throne for All
The use of the dry toilet

A Tooth Fairy
Elephants have rights too

Rabbit Fuel
Converting CO to ethanol

The Magic of Chilli
The power of hot food

Shoes from Silk
Cocoons are fungi free

The Kelp Dance
Growing faster than bamboo

Shooting with Air
Air pressure as power

Rare on Earth
Rare metals everywhere

A Soup of Bacteria
Blocking bacteria talking

Fluttering Flags
Making power from flutter

How Smart are You?
Eating live animals

Crabs for Dinner
Integrated farming in Fiji

Building a Cathedral
Tortoises reflect on life

African Farms
Turning citrus competitive

Forgive to Forget

Mosquito Bites

Hand in Hand
About Nelson Mandela

Crazy Crickets
Protein from Insects

Thank you for the Music
Enriching life with art

Slow Food
Produce quality and more

Spinning Like a Spider
Big spider webs are art

Masters and Grandmasters
Teachers learn from students

Clouds in the Sky
Explain formation of clouds

Fleas and Lice
What are these good for?

Cutting Wood while Growing Forests
Energy without Depleting

Mine Water
Converting heat into power

Generous Grass
How bamboo makes water

The Earth's Skin
The need for rich top soil

Learning to Teach
Ecological school building

Coral Care
Regenerate sea forests

The Incredible Fly
Reduce overfishing with flies

Dragons Everywhere
Animals called dragons?

Grand Geraniums
The biodiversity of Fynbos

Everyone is Welcome
Male and female chicks

Honey Math
The geometry of beehives

Roots and Shoots
Dental care and mutation

Edelweiss in the Sun
Protection against UV

The Solar Blue Dragon
Sea slug on solar power

Making Money on Money
How money is made

Ticks for Life
The role of ticks in nature

Bees at Home
Sharing limited space

Plastics in my Tummy
Plastic pollution in the sea

I am Bored
Why bored pigs bite tails

Mite Farm
Carpets and house mites

Sailing with the Sun
No nets, use sun power

Tea for Tigers
Tea farmed next to park

From Poo to Tree
How to make black earth

Keep on Turning & Turning
Why rivers meander

Chew Your Soup
How digestion works

My Special Dad
Exceptions make a rule

Watchdog or Thief?
All about cheating

The Goddess of Tropics
The beauty of heliconias

The Dress-Up Party
Trusting who you don't know

Dancing Fairies
Teaching lessons with pain

Facing the Same Direction
Go along with the crowd

Freeze or Squeeze
Surviving freezing weather

Perfume for Rats
How to control pests

Seeing in a World without Sight
The language of braille

The Black Goat
Overgrazing causes desert

Healthy Horses
How to get strong bones

Which Languages do you Speak?
The power of being multilingual

Oil from Trees
Some trees produce diesel

Goats love Apples
How to make ice-cream

The Happy Robot
Slime moulds

Turn off the Lights
Night light pollution

I like to Move it
How bees talk to each other

Fast Relief
Killing pain with sugars

Where did all the Lambs Go?
Feeding babies cow's milk

Who is the Sweetest?
The monk fruit from China

Ready to take Risk?
What it takes to change

Are you Prepared?
Connected thinking

THANK YOU

This version of *The Blue Economy 3.0* would never have been possible without an incredible team. A very special thanks to the Australian Research Support Team: Oliver Pyke, Daniel Conley, Ieva Daenke, Harry Carpenter, Andrew Hojem, Christopher Guzik, Joshua Wood, and Craig Theron, from the University of Adelaide and Curtin University. Thanks also to the hosts of the 2016 Australian Blue Economy Tour, the University of Adelaide, University of Melbourne, The Water Corporation (Western Australia), Curtin University, Townsville City Council, and Suncorp – and in particular an incredible support crew on the tour: Charlie Hargroves, Daniel Conley, and Wendy Lindsay. We reached out to thousands of people and planted seeds of perennials. The harvest will be great.

A word of special appreciation goes to Willemien van der Walt for the final editing. Thanks are also due to the design and production team for the book layout and cover. Gratitude to the ZERI Teams from around the world, who have continued to provide hands-on support over decades to make this adventure so exciting. I would like to thank all, including Carlos Bernal (Colombia), Lucio Brusch (Brazil), Eduardo Ferreira (Spain), Charles van der Haegen (Belgium), Ivanka Milenkovic (Serbia), Yusuke Saraya (Japan), and Li Kangming (China). Of course, none of this would have been possible without the professionalism and the loving care of Katherina Bach, my dear wife, and the patience of all my children: Chido, Carl-Olaf, Laurenz-Frederik, Philipp-Emmanuel, Louis-Hadrian and Francesco-Aurelio.

www.ingramcontent.com/pod-product-compliance
Lightning Source LLC
Chambersburg PA
CBHW020733180526
45163CB00001B/219

* 9 7 8 1 5 2 4 5 2 1 0 6 6 *